FREEDOM
PASS
LONDON

MAKE TH~~E~~ ~~MOST~~ OF
YOUR TRAVEL PASS
25 SPECIAL DAYS OUT

MIKE PENTELOW
&
PETER ARKELL

EDITION 1
Bradt Travel Guides Ltd, UK

1

ALONG THE WATERFRONT

Waterside walks along canals, rivers and lakes have the advantage of being flat, easy to follow and almost always scenic. Why not find a quiet spot and stop for a picnic? And there's usually the chance for a spot of fishing, fruit picking or birdwatching for those so inclined.

1 A short stroll through the Broad Colney Nature Reserve featured in **walk 21** offers good year-round wildlife-spotting and, if the season is right, the chance to pick

2

3

4

5

apples, sloes and blackberries. **2** Beak to beak: riverside walks are the perfect opportunity to get up close to local wildlife. **3** A lone fisherman casts his line into the Thames at Laleham Park, **walk 14**. **4** One of the great pleasures of a canal-side walk is admiring the beautifully painted canal boats you encounter along the way, such as here on the Grand Union Canal, **walks 4 & 8**. **5** This sculpture marks the point where the River Colne flows into the Thames near Staines Bridge, **walk 14**. **6** Feeding the birds on Aldenham Reservoir, **walk 16**.

6

We're **40**...
how did that happen?

How did it all happen? George (my then husband) and I wrote the first Bradt guide – about hiking in Peru and Bolivia – on an Amazon river barge, and typed it up on a borrowed typewriter. We had no money for the next two books so George went to work for a printer and was paid in books rather than money.

Forty years on, Bradt publishes over 200 titles that sell all over the world. I still suffer from Imposter Syndrome – how did it all happen? I hadn't even worked in an office before! Well, I've been extraordinarily lucky with the people around me. George provided the belief to get us started (and the mother to run our US office). Then, in 1977, I recruited a helper, Janet Mears, who is still working for us. She and the many dedicated staff who followed have been the foundations on which the company is built. But the bricks and mortar have been our authors and readers. Without them there would be no Bradt Travel Guides. Thank you all for making it happen.

Hilary Bradt

AUTHOR

Mike Pentelow was editor of *Landworker* (the newspaper of rural workers) for ten years and is currently editor of *Fitzrovia News* (London's oldest community newspaper, to which he has contributed for 40 years), giving him a feel for both town and country.

An author and journalist for 50 years, his previous books are *Characters of Fitzrovia*, *Norfolk Red* and *A Pub Crawl Through History*. He is a keen rambler having walked the entire length of the River Thames and many other waterways. A real ale enthusiast, Mike also enjoys a game of darts and pool.

Mike is a member of The Ramblers, the Woodland Trust, the Campaign for Real Ale, the Inn Sign Society, Camden History Society, Socialist History Society, St Marylebone Society, Society of Authors, National Union of Journalists and the Mecca Bingo Club. He has lived in London for over 43 years.

PHOTOGRAPHER

Peter Arkell has been a photographer since 1970, covering news, social issues, the environment and sport. He co-wrote *Unfinished Business, The Miners' Strike for Jobs, 1984–5* and took the photographs for *A Pub Crawl Through History*, about commoners who have had pubs named after them. A keen rambler (with Mike and others) he has walked the Thames Path, the South West Coastal Path, the Isle of Wight Coastal Path and Peddars Way/Norfolk Coast Path. He has lived in London for 45 years and currently produces photo features and writes reviews for *A World to Win*.

First published September 2014
Bradt Travel Guides Ltd
IDC House, The Vale, Chalfont St Peter, Bucks SL9 9RZ, England
www.bradtguides.com

Project Manager: Anna Moores
Editor: Tim Locke

ISBN: 978 1 84162 565 2 (print)
e-ISBN: 978 1 78477 102 7 (e-pub)
e-ISBN: 978 1 78477 202 4 (mobi)

British Library Cataloguing in Publication Data
A catalogue record for this book is available from the British Library

Cover illustration Neil Gower (www.neilgower.com)
Maps David McCutcheon FBCart.S & Leanne Kelman
Internal Design Pepi Bluck, Perfect Picture

Typeset from the author's disc by Pepi Bluck, Perfect Picture
Production managed by Jellyfish Print Solutions; printed in India
Digital conversion by the Firsty Group

FEEDBACK REQUEST & UPDATES WEBSITE

At Bradt Travel Guides we're aware that guidebooks start to go out of date on the
day they're published – and that you, our readers, are out there in the field doing
research of your own. So why not write and tell us about your experiences? Contact
us on ☎ 01753 893444 or ✉ info@bradtguides.com. We will forward emails to
the author who may post updates on the Bradt website at ⌨ www.bradtupdates.
com/freedompass. Alternatively you can add a review of the book to ⌨ www.
bradtguides.com or Amazon.

ACKNOWLEDGEMENTS

We would like to thank Robbie Griffiths and Francis Beckett for their technical support and encouragement.

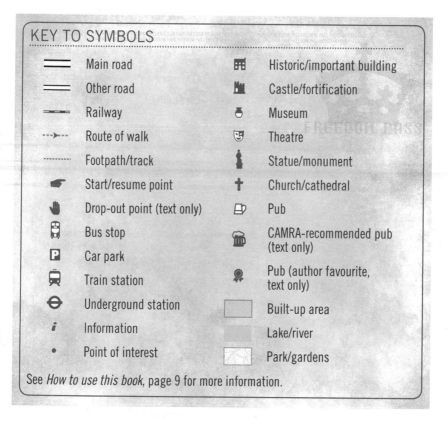

KEY TO SYMBOLS

═══	Main road		⊞	Historic/important building
═══	Other road		▥	Castle/fortification
═╾═	Railway		⬯	Museum
--►--	Route of walk		☺	Theatre
········	Footpath/track		▮	Statue/monument
☛	Start/resume point		†	Church/cathedral
✋	Drop-out point (text only)		☐	Pub
🚏	Bus stop		🍺	CAMRA-recommended pub (text only)
🅿	Car park			
🚆	Train station		⚜	Pub (author favourite, text only)
⊖	Underground station		☐	Built-up area
i	Information			Lake/river
•	Point of interest		◹	Park/gardens

See *How to use this book*, page 9 for more information.

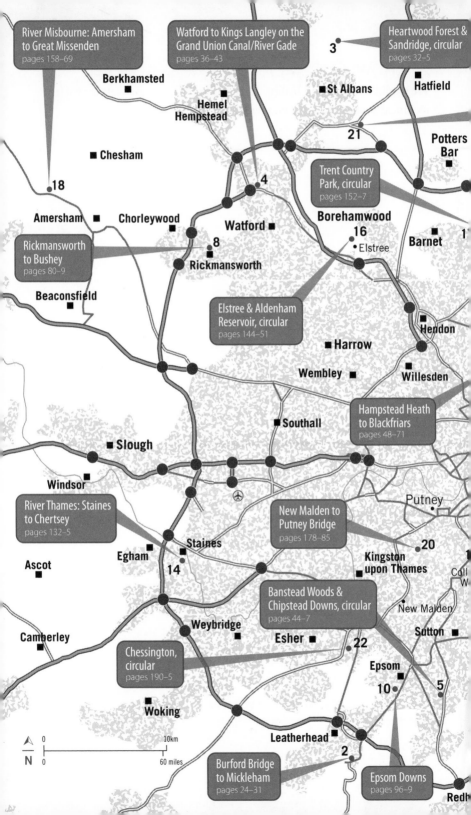

River Misbourne: Amersham to Great Missenden
pages 158–69

Watford to Kings Langley on the Grand Union Canal/River Gade
pages 36–43

Heartwood Forest & Sandridge, circular
pages 32–5

3

Berkhamsted

■ St Albans

Hatfield

Hemel
Hempstead

21

Potters
Bar

■ Chesham

18

Trent Country Park, circular
pages 152–7

4

Borehamwood

16

Barnet

1

Amersham ■

Chorleywood

Watford ■

8

• Elstree

Rickmansworth to Bushey
pages 80–9

Rickmansworth

Hendon

Beaconsfield

Elstree & Aldenham Reservoir, circular
pages 144–51

■ Harrow

Wembley ■

■ Willesden

■ Southall

Hampstead Heath to Blackfriars
pages 48–71

■ Slough

Windsor ■

Putney

River Thames: Staines to Chertsey
pages 132–5

New Malden to Putney Bridge
pages 178–85

20

Egham

Staines

Kingston
upon Thames

Ascot ■

14

Coll
W

New Malden

Sutton ■

Camberley ■

Banstead Woods & Chipstead Downs, circular
pages 44–7

22

Epsom

10 •

5

Chessington, circular
pages 190–5

Weybridge

Esher ■

Woking ■

Leatherhead

2

Burford Bridge to Mickleham
pages 24–31

Epsom Downs
pages 96–9

Redh

N
0   10km
0   60 miles

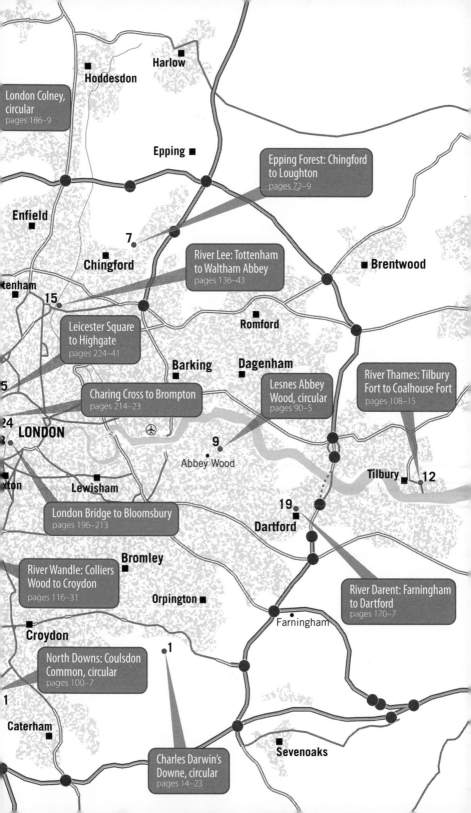

Harlow

Hoddesdon

London Colney,
circular
pages 186–9

Epping

Epping Forest: Chingford
to Loughton
pages 72–9

Enfield

7

Chingford

Brentwood

River Lee: Tottenham
to Waltham Abbey
pages 136–43

...tenham

15

Leicester Square
to Highgate
pages 224–41

Romford

5

Barking

Dagenham

24

LONDON

Charing Cross to Brompton
pages 214–23

Lesnes Abbey
Wood, circular
pages 90–5

River Thames: Tilbury
Fort to Coalhouse Fort
pages 108–15

9

Abbey Wood

...xton

Lewisham

Tilbury

12

London Bridge to Bloomsbury
pages 196–213

19

Dartford

Bromley

River Wandle: Colliers
Wood to Croydon
pages 116–31

Orpington

River Darent: Farningham
to Dartford
pages 170–7

Farningham

Croydon

1

North Downs: Coulsdon
Common, circular
pages 100–7

1

Caterham

Sevenoaks

Charles Darwin's
Downe, circular
pages 14–23

CONTENTS

1   A NATURAL SELECTION AT DOWNE   14
Charles Darwin's Downe, circular

2   ON THE BOX   24
Burford Bridge to Mickleham

3   THE FOREST'S HEART   32
Heartwood Forest & Sandridge, circular

4   A GRAND CANAL & A GREAT ROAD   36
Watford to Kings Langley on the Grand Union Canal/River Gade

5   BLUEBELL BLITZ   44
Banstead Woods & Chipstead Downs, circular

6   FLEET OF FOOT   48
Hampstead Heath to Blackfriars

7   EPIC FOREST FIGHT   72
Epping Forest: Chingford to Loughton

8   THE CANAL, THE OLD RAILWAY & THE QUAKER   80
Rickmansworth to Bushey

9   HOLLY, IVY, CHESTNUTS & SHARKS' TEETH   90
Lesnes Abbey Wood, circular

10   A RACING CERTAINTY   96
Epsom Downs

11   HAPPY VALLEY   100
North Downs: Coulsdon Common, circular

12   TILBURY'S SEAL OF APPROVAL   108
River Thames: Tilbury Fort to Coalhouse Fort

13   WANDERING ALONG THE WANDLE   116
River Wandle: Colliers Wood to Croydon

14 PICNICKERS' PARADISE 132
River Thames: Staines to Chertsey

15 DRAGONFLIES & GUNPOWDER 136
River Lee: Tottenham to Waltham Abbey

16 DEATH IN THE CHURCHYARD, LIFE BY THE LAKE 144
Elstree & Aldenham Reservoir, circular

17 A DRAGON & QUEEN GUINEVERE'S GHOST 152
Trent Country Park, circular

18 MIDSOMER MURDERS TRAIL 158
River Misbourne: Amersham to Great Missenden

19 FROM DICKENS TO THE ROLLING STONES 170
River Darent: Farningham to Dartford

20 BROOKSIDE & THE BIG GREEN SPACE 178
New Malden to Putney Bridge

21 COLNE RIVERSIDE RAMBLE 186
London Colney, circular

22 ANIMAL WORLD 190
Chessington, circular

23 LITERARY LONDON 196
London Bridge to Bloomsbury

24 FEISTY FEMALES PUB CRAWL 214
Charing Cross to Brompton

25 KARL'S TRAIL, ON YOUR MARX 224
Leicester Square to Highgate

INDEX 242

INTRODUCTION

The Freedom Pass is truly a treasure for Greater London's senior citizens. It is a passport to the countryside for city dwellers; and to London's rich cultural heritage for those living in the outer suburbs. This is the first book to aim to help both sets make the fullest use of their free travel, by detailing 25 days out, involving walks of between 2½ and ten miles.

Walks in the greenest countryside in this book extend from Box Hill near Dorking in the south, Heartwood Forest near St Albans in the north, East Tilbury and Farningham in the east, and Great Missenden and Chertsey in the west. Those in central London take in a wide variety of museums and historical sites on themes such as literary figures. And some go through both town and country on rivers and canals.

We've peppered the text with historical nuggets about great people and dodgy characters, as we pass places associated with them. Charles Darwin, for example, ate an owl, while his contemporary Karl Marx prescribed himself opium, arsenic and creosote to treat his carbuncles. On a less salubrious note, we tell the stories of the last two women to be hanged in this country for separate murders in the same street a year apart, and of the 'Witch Queen of Kentish Town' whose three husbands all met grisly ends. We also visit historic buildings and churches, containing art treasures and relics of history going back over a thousand years, and seek out the graves of many notables.

One of the glories of London is the way town meets countryside, not just in the surprisingly rural terrain of the Green Belt, but in the villagey corners of suburbs, and along urban rivers and the city's commons, parks and patches of woodlands. Some of the most prized wildlife spots are designated as nature reserves, and we point out some of the species you might glimpse on the grasslands, in the woods and in and around the water – and give a few tips for food foragers. And for gardeners (or those wishing to get up the noses of tiresome neighbours) there are two places to get free

HOW TO USE THIS BOOK

Each route begins with a **summary**, giving length and approximate walking time (excluding stops), which map to take, a list of places to pause for refreshment (*Taking a break*), and details of how to get to the starting point by public transport.

Some **walks** are circular, others go point to point, with return by public transport: 🚌 bus, 🚃 train and ⊖ tube.

We have included **grid references** ❄ for the start and end points of each walk.

We have given very detailed **route directions** within the main text, to get you round the intricacies of the countryside and the urban landscape, and giving you plenty of information confirming you're in the right place. Please bear in mind that things inevitably go out of date: signposts change, path junctions appear and disappear. If you find any directions that don't work as well as they should, please let us know (see page 2 for details). The icon ☛ indicates where the walk directions start or resume.

Each point of interest gets its own number (**1**, **2**, etc), which is also shown on the route map. Our maps show you how it links together; but you'll very probably want a detailed OS or street map for all the other stuff (see Maps, below). Under the icon ☺ we give an idea of opening times, but as these change so much it is always worth checking before you go, using the websites or phone numbers we include.

For those who only want to do part of the route, we have indicated drop-out points with the symbol ✋, telling you how to get to stations or bus stops and thus bring the walk to an early conclusion. Many pubs are listed for those wishing to break up a long walk or to relax after a short one. These include some recommended by the Campaign for Real Ale (indicated with the symbol 🍺) and range from historic coaching inns to modern gastro pubs. Those with dartboards and pool tables are identified for those who enjoy pub games. We also give the postcodes of all the pubs for those with satnavs and a particularly urgent thirst. The icon 🏅 indicates our favourite pubs.

Where there is an entrance fee for places of interest *en route*, we have included the following symbols to give you an idea of cost: **£** <£5; **££** £5–£10; **£££** £10+. Where there is a senior citizen's discount, we have indicated it thus: 🪙.

horse manure. Out of consideration for fellow passengers it is not advisable to carry it on public transport, of course.

USEFUL PUBLICATIONS
Maps
Some street maps are useful as a framework to identify where you are if you go off course at any time in the countryside. There are two which cover most of our area:

AA Street by Street Visitors Guide & Atlas to London (Automobile Association). This is a handy softback pocket edition which is easier to carry on walks, but does not cover Aldenham, Amersham, Box Hill, Epsom, Loughton, St Albans, Staines, Tilbury, Rickmansworth or Watford.

Master Atlas of Greater London (Geographers' A-Z Map Company). An A4 hardback which covers the area of all walks except Amersham, Box Hill and Tilbury. It is bulky to carry around but useful to photocopy relevant maps before walking.

Books
Many of the walks quite often cross over the Capital Ring and the London Loop. So the following two books may again be useful for reorientating yourself if you are a bit off course, or offer you a diversion to nearer your home:

The Capital Ring, Recreational Path Guide, by Colin Saunders (Aurum).
The London Loop, Recreational Path Guide, by David Sharp (Aurum).
Similarly, some of the walks go along the Thames, the Grand Union Canal, and the River Lee Navigation. So the following will be useful for more detail:

The Thames Path, National Trail Guide, by David Sharp (Aurum).
The Grand Union Canal Walk, London to Birmingham, by Clive Holmes (Cicerone).
The Lea Valley Walk, from its source to the Thames, by Leigh Hatts (Cicerone).

Fruit and nut cases will find plenty to pick on many of the walks, as mentioned. For help in identifying them and how to prepare them for eating or drinking, the following will be useful:

Food for Free, by Richard Mabey (Collins 2007).
Foraging: Discover Free Food from Fields, Streets, Gardens and the Coast, by Paul Chambers (Pen & Sword, 2012).
Edible Wild Plants and Herbs: A Compendium of Recipes and Remedies, by Pamela Marshall (Grub Street, 2010).
The River Cottage Hedgerow Handbook, by John Wright (Bloomsbury, 2010).
Fungi Identification Swatch Book (Woodland Trust, 2010).
For the less squeamish there is a fascinating booklet called:
Why Not Eat Insects?, by Vincent M Holt (Pryor Publications, 2007).
It tells you how to prepare grasshoppers, make sauce from woodlice, soup from slugs, and many other equally appetising dishes.

Finally, we have identified all the CAMRA real ale recommended pubs *en route* (🍺), but for those willing to stray slightly off course for a decent pint, the recognised annual bible is:

CAMRA's Good Beer Guide, edited by Roger Protz (CAMRA Books).

LADIES WHO BUS

In March 2009, the 'Ladies Who Bus', Linda, Mary and Jo, decided to travel every London bus route from end to end. Visit their blog to follow their adventures: http://londonbusesonebusatatime.blogspot.co.uk/.

For the author and photographer of this book, the Freedom Pass is a means to access an interesting walk in or around London – perhaps by train (leaving after 09.30, of course) to a rural starting point, or a combination of bus and tube to the source of a 'lost river' or pilgrimage route in a part of London new to them...

For us, 'The Ladies Who Bus', the point of our five-year project was the journey itself, using our Freedom Passes to ride the full length of every one of London's bus routes. For each journey the aim was to discover where exactly such places as Brimsdown or Yiewsley might be, and to see what we might pass in the way of neighbourhood shops, communities and any particular sites of interest. In this way we criss-crossed London; sometimes accessing the more suburban routes took longer than the eventual trips but all was possible due to the wonderful Freedom Pass.

Of course the Freedom Pass was really launched to ensure London's more vulnerable residents could continue to keep up with friends and family and other aspects of their lives. It was certainly clear from our own excursions that the pass is well used by many to access healthcare, community facilities, places of worship and markets (you see more trolleys and vegetables on buses than you do on the underground). Access for buggies or wheelchairs and innumerable travellers with sticks is better by bus with the drivers always on the alert for the potentially frail who might tumble. The journey may be less smooth (depending on the age of the vehicle and the traffic calming), but for the bulk of Freedom Pass users it is probably safer and friendlier. On several of the really infrequent services (twice an hour or even fewer) we enjoyed the way the passengers knew and asked after each other and the driver.

While the authors of this guide travelled to walk, we frequently walked to travel. Although there are many bus 'hubs' in London where all you need to do is find another bus stop or stand to continue your journey, you can make life more interesting. On an early outing, a pleasant diversion through Richmond

The Ladies Who Bus, from left: Linda, Jo and Mary.

Park linked a journey from Russell Square to one end of the Roehanpton Estate by way of East Acton (routes 7 and 72) to a different way back to South Kensington (430).

One Christmas we managed to start in Mitcham with a 270 to Putney Bridge for a walk along the Thames Path to Chiswick to catch the 272 and finish in Shepherd's Bush. We were not always so successful – trying to find a scenic route across Hounslow Heath between the H25 and H26 with too wide a choice of paths and too few signposts we found ourselves passing under the same railway bridge and checking out the same graffiti three times before giving up. And not all the walks are scenic – the railway line and back of the market in Walthamstow may be an acquired taste…

But 'walking to travel' is still an approach we would recommend – the bus journeys themselves can be a novel revelation.

1	DISTANCE 5 MILES DIFFICULTY EASY–MODERATE TIME 2–2½HRS	CHARLES DARWIN'S DOWNE, CIRCULAR

A NATURAL SELECTION AT DOWNE

A REMARKABLY RURAL KENTISH LANDSCAPE MUCH WALKED BY THE GREAT VICTORIAN EVOLUTIONARY THINKER.

On this ramble you're in very good company. The great Charles Darwin (1809–82) lived here for 40 years, at Down House, and though often unwell frequently made it a rule to walk three times a day. It was here that he wrote his world-changing thesis *On the Origin of Species by Means of Natural Selection*, the sensational publication which in 1859 provoked mass book-burning by Creationists and changed the view of how life on this planet evolved. Indeed this walk within the London Borough of Bromley is a 'natural selection' for those keen to find out more about the man, to view the hallowed study where

DISTANCE/DIFFICULTY Just over 5 miles. Easy on the flat with two steep climbs of 400 strides each.

DROP-OUT POINT After 3 miles

TIME 2–2½hrs

MAP OS Explorer map 147

START Downe Church ✵ TQ432616

TAKING A BREAK Blacksmith's Arms, Cudham; Christmas Tree Farm & Tea Garden, George & Dragon, Queen's Head, Richmal Crompton

GETTING THERE 🚆 To Bromley South station from London Victoria (16–26mins; 8–10 an hour, including Sun)

DIRECTIONS TO START Turn right out of the station to Bus Stop Y for 🚌 146 to Downe Church (20mins; 1 an hour, including Sun)

he carried out his research, and to wander the grounds of his house.

The route through woodlands and rolling farmland also takes in his church (where there is a memorial to him), and a woodland which he used as a 'living laboratory' to observe wildlife development. Elsewhere on the walk, you'll find the 300-year-old tavern in which music hall star 'Little Titch' was born and a church that is over a thousand years old, and have the chance to feed the animals at a farm,

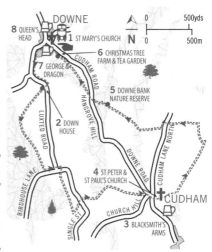

and to come back with armfuls of blackberries. For gardeners, free horse manure is available from Greatfield Farm in Single Street (a few yards off the route).

1 DOWNE CHURCH

Downe Church (St Mary's), next to the bus stop, is where Charles Darwin was an active member of the congregation for 40 years. A memorial sundial is dedicated to him on the outside of the church tower and you'll find a flat granite tomb to his memory between the main gate to the churchyard and the front door of the church. The building itself dates from 1291.

Despite his active support for this church he was attacked from its pulpit during the height of the controversy over his theory of evolution, seen by many to contradict the church's view of creation. This so upset a fellow member of the congregation, his friend and fellow naturalist Sir John Lubbock (who became the first Lord Avebury), that he stopped attending services here.

Darwin was a long-standing friend of the parish priest, Rev. John Brodie Innes. During the evolution controversy Innes defended Darwin to bishops, declaring: 'I never saw a word in his writings which was an attack on religion. He follows his own course as a naturalist and leaves Moses to take care of himself.'

Although his faith later dwindled, Darwin remained an active parishioner, supervised the finances of the church and its school, ran its Coal and Clothing Fund for the needy, and started its Friendly Club for those in financial hardship (and was its treasurer for over 30 years). His wife Emma is buried near the fence bordering High Elms Road. She also helped the local poor and needy, by giving them bread and homemade gin cordial which was 'a heady concoction of wine laced with laudanum, sugar, peppermint and bitters.'

Four of their children, Mary Eleanor (who died in 1842 after just two weeks), Charles Waring (1856–58), Elizabeth (1847–1926) and Henrietta (1843–1927), are buried in the same grave near the main door to the church. And his faithful butler for 36 years, Joseph Parslow, is buried with his wife Eliza in the northern part of the churchyard.

☛ Come out of the church, cross diagonally to Luxted Road, and follow it for a few minutes to:

2 DOWN HOUSE

Downe Village BR6 7JT ☎ 01689 859119 🖱 www.english-heritage.org.uk
🕐 opening hours vary – check website for the latest details **££** 🍵

Down House was Darwin's home for the last 40 years of his life. In its extensive garden Darwin conducted experiments with worms, insects and plants. He even devised a system of giving IQ tests to some of the million worms in the garden which involved them pulling down triangles of paper.

Down House: Darwin's home for the last 40 years of his life.

He thought through a lot of his ideas while walking. The sandwalk in his garden he nicknamed his 'Thinking Path' for that very reason. To measure how far he had walked he kicked a flintstone to one side after each circuit, although his children sometimes mischievously removed them or added to them to mess up his calculations. On one of these strolls he was so struck by one particular notion that he stopped dead in his tracks, frozen in thought. He was so still in fact that two young squirrels ran up his back. The discovery that gave him the greatest pleasure was that the local cowslips were in two kinds and so not self pollinating.

He became a pigeon fancier to observe the effects of selective breeding (joining one club which met in a gin palace). But when it came to human selective breeding, as espoused by those of his followers who supported eugenics, he distanced himself. He believed the instinct to care for the weak and helpless was to humanity's evolutionary advantage, and that nobody should be prevented from reproducing.

In the house you can see the billiard room, which he had converted from a dining room. When he wanted a game he summoned the aforementioned butler, Joseph Parslow, with a bell pull.

A 250-year-old mulberry tree, which was quite old when Darwin was here, grows in the garden. Also surviving from his time is the weed garden, where he tested his ideas, and a laboratory where he observed honey bees.

☛ To continue the walk, go past the greenhouses in the back garden, and out through a kissing gate into a field. Bear left (in the direction of a yellow arrow) through the field, over a stile into woods. At a crossing of paths, take the left one (signposted to 'Birdhouse Lane'). Continue along the woodland path (with a golf course on the right) and pick up signs for 'Cudham Circular Walk'.

When the track reaches a lane, turn left (into Birdhouse Lane) then right at the road junction, then right at Luxted Farm into a track (signed 'Cudham Circular Walk'). Climb over a stile to follow a path between a hedge and a fence (signed 'Cudham Circular Walk' and 'Berry Green Circular Walk').

Continue by the side of a field, and over a stile at the far side. Then immediately turn left over another stile almost hidden between a holly bush and a telegraph pole. This takes you between house garden fences on to a road (Single Street, where the free manure is available at Greatfield Farm, a short distance to the right), which you cross and go straight ahead between a fence and a hedge into a Woodland Trust woodland. Follow the track ahead around the woods and then through them, eventually going down steps. Emerge via a kissing gate into a strikingly beautiful valley.

Go straight ahead, along a path down a field in the valley and up again (a climb which continues for 400 strides and gets steeper as you ascend). Go through a kissing gate at the other side, up a woodland path on to a lane. Turn left (Church Hill), then immediately right at a junction, and up to another crossroads. Turn right at this crossroads (Cudham Lane South) and after about two or three minutes you will come to the junction with New Barn Lane where on the left is:

3 BLACKSMITH'S ARMS

Cudham Lane South, Cudham TN14 7QB

Little Titch, the music hall star, was born Harry Relph in the pub on 21 July 1867 (as confirmed by the blue plaque on the pub). He was the 16th child of Richard Relph who ran the pub from 1865 to 1878 and his height – only four feet six inches – made him a star for nearly 50 years, from the age of 12 until a few months before his death in the 1920s. Music hall posters have pride of place in the bar along with his celebrated boots, known at the time as 'slapshoes': these he wore for his most popular act, his comic 'Big Boot Dance' which involved dancing in boots that stuck out 28 inches from his toes (of which he had six on each foot).

His stage name came from an ironic reference to the obese 'Tichborne' claimant (a famous legal case) which he abbreviated to 'Titch' – hence the adjective 'titchy'. Originally a farmhouse built in 1628, the building became an inn in 1730, and now has an extensive beer garden and serves hot food as well as real ales (including Sharp's Doom Bar, Adnams and Hogs Back).

If you wish to end the walk here you can get the R5 or R10 bus to Orpington railway station (no Sunday service). The R10 on the same side takes 40 minutes, and the R5 on the other side 20 minutes, to the station. Take whichever comes first, as it's the same bus doing a circular route, alternating direction (and its route number) every hour (no service on Sun). There is no designated stop so you have to hail it to stop; it is wise to sit outside the pub to make sure you don't miss it.

The 10-metre girth of this yew tree at St Peter and St Paul's Church indicates this tree is over 1,000 years old.

☛ If you are sober enough to continue the walk, turn right, retrace your steps (about 350) to the crossroads, then turn right into Church Approach, at the top of which is:

4 ST PETER & ST PAUL'S CHURCH

Church Approach, Cudham TN14 7QF

Two yew trees in the churchyard here have girths of over 30 feet, which indicates they are over a thousand years old. The church itself has been renewed over the centuries but dates back as far back as that too: a street signpost refers to it as 11th century but the earliest records date back to AD953. The oldest of its ten bells in the tower was cast in 1490.

☛ Go out through the other side of the churchyard and turn left, round the edge of playing fields. This is a good place to have a picnic on one of the benches under the shade of copper beech trees.

Continue out of the playing field through a kissing gate on the left, over the lane and through another kissing gate and through a paddock. Go through another kissing gate into a field, then through a woodland path to a lane. Turn left into the lane and, after about 100 steps, turn right into a field (signposted 'Downe 1¼m'). Go through the field to another, to a hedge where you turn left and follow it on your left as directed by a yellow arrow sign. Cross over a stile (signposted 'Cudham Circular Short Walk') to a short grass track up to a lane. Turn left and then, after about 100 steps, turn right at another signpost (also 'Downe 1¼m') into a short track into a lane, then into a track ahead through woodland.

Where the path splits, take the right fork between posts (with 'No Horse Riding' and 'Cudham Circular Short Walk' signs). Follow the path downhill then up again. There now follows a steep climb of about 400 strides. Near the top on the left is:

5 DOWNE BANK

This is where Darwin studied the local flora and fauna – a living laboratory in which Darwin developed his theory of evolution and natural selection. In particular he studied the special relationship between orchids and their insect pollinators, which is why he called it Orchis Bank (although it was officially Rough Pell). Nine species of wild orchid still grow here along with bryonies, primroses, cowslips and other plants.

Downe Bank forms part of Hangrove Wood where Darwin observed what he described as 'the quiet but dreadful war going on in the peaceful and smiling fields'. You can explore it by turning left off the path which you have been following, and along the 'permissive footpath' which soon turns right uphill (just before a gate), then right at the top and back to the main path. Several unusual plants such as stinking hellebore, squinancywort and adder's tongue fern thrive in this area. In the spring it is smothered with primroses and cowslips, and in the summer with orchids. Butterflies abound (including a few of the rare white-letter hairstreak). Rare and endangered species here include dormice, slow worms and roman snails.

☛ After returning to the main footpath continue up the steps to the top of the hill, then turn right into a track (signposted 'Downe ⅓m'). This takes you into a

COURAGEOUS TASTINGS

Some of Darwin's research was distinctly brave. He ate the caterpillars of the sphinx moth and found them 'very palatable' according to the book *Why Not Eat Insects?* (see *Useful publications*, page 11). He also consumed an owl, as president of the Glutton Club at Cambridge University, opining afterwards the taste was 'indescribable'.

lane (Cudham Road) where you turn right, and after just 20 yards take the path (on the left between a fence and a hedge parallel with the road) in the same direction along the side of a horse field. When the path rejoins the lane, follow it a few yards and on the left is:

6 CHRISTMAS TREE FARM & TEA GARDEN

Cudham Rd, Downe BR6 7LF ☎ 01689 861603 🖱 www.xmastreefarm.co.uk
🕒 Nov–Feb daily 10.00–16.00, Mar–Oct 10.00–17.30 £

At this 'children's petting farm' you can feed (for a small charge) various extremely friendly farm animals including pigs, donkeys, cows, sheep, alpacas, rabbits, ducks, chickens, geese and goats. It has an adjoining tea garden.

☞ To finish the main walk turn left out of the farm and continue along Cudham Road about 200 yards to a choice of two pubs, either side of the bus stop where you started, for the return journey:

7 GEORGE & DRAGON

🍺 26 High St, Downe BR6 7UT

A real log fire blazes in this beamed 15th-century coaching inn. It is family friendly (with a play area and garden), has a dartboard and serves hot meals and real ale (including Harveys Sussex Best Bitter, Fuller's London Pride and Timothy Taylor Landlord).

8 QUEEN'S HEAD

🍺 25 High Street, Downe BR6 7US

This 16th-century pub has three fireplaces, plus hot and cold food and real ale (including Sharp's Doom Bar, Harveys and Adnams).

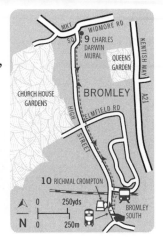

☞ After refreshing yourself get the 146 bus back to Bromley South station. When you get off at the station walk up the High Street in the same direction as the bus for about five minutes until it forks and becomes Market Square. Take the right fork where you will find a:

The Darwin mural on the side of a house in Bromley.

9 CHARLES DARWIN MURAL

A huge mural depicts Darwin under a tree in his garden at Down House with the various branches representing evolution. It was painted by Kentish artist Bruce Willows.

☞ Retrace your steps down the High Street to Bromley South station, opposite which is the:

10 RICHMAL CROMPTON

23 Westmoreland Pl, Bromley BR1 1DS

This Wetherspoon pub is named after the author of the popular *Just William* books, describing the adventures of the eponymous child rebel against adult authority. Crompton (1890–1969) taught at Bromley High School just north of this pub from 1917 until contracting polio in 1923. For a while she continued working, cycling to the school with her stiff leg sticking out at a dangerous angle, but eventually had to give up the job. It was a blessing in disguise as she turned to writing for a living. In the 1960s she broke both her legs. When the doctor tried to set the stiff leg at the usual angle she insisted he set it at the odd angle to which she had become accustomed. Among her prized possessions were newspaper cuttings of William being banned from libraries. She said of William: 'The boy of eleven is at the stage of the savage – loyal to his tribe, ruthless to his foes, governed by mysterious taboos, an enemy of civilisation and all its meaningless conventions.'

ON THE BOX

SCALING THE HEIGHTS TO BOX HILL, A NORTH DOWNS LANDMARK ABOVE THE RIVER MOLE.

One of the best-known features of the North Downs, Box Hill is a Sunday afternoon favourite with Londoners escaping from the city. The only snag is that on the best summer days everyone seems to be escaping at the same time, and the car parks are brimming to capacity. But for walkers, it's a satisfying summit to reach, and you soon lose the crowds. Box Hill takes its name from box trees, which are among the numerous tree species in the locality, in addition to yew, beech, pine, sallow, willow, oak and hazel.

This has for long been civilised countryside, with opulent houses looking out over the Surrey hills and towards the distant South Downs. On this route through downland

DISTANCE/DIFFICULTY 5 miles. Moderate; includes a steep climb.

DROP-OUT POINT After 3 miles

TIME 2½hrs

MAP OS Explorer map 146

START Burford Bridge ❋ TQ171518

FINISH Running Horses bus stop, Mickleham ❋ TQ171534

TAKING A BREAK National Trust shop, top of Box Hill, Burford Bridge Hotel, Stepping Stones, Running Horses

GETTING THERE 🚆 To Chessington South (34mins; every 30mins, daily) or Surbiton from London Waterloo (23–28mins; 8 an hour, daily)

DIRECTIONS TO START 🚌 465 to Burford Bridge (2 an hour, 1 an hour on Sun). From Chessington South turn right out of the station, right at the junction to Bus Stop D on the right (28 mins). From Surbiton turn left at end of the station approach road into Victoria Road to Bus Stop NP on the left (40 mins).

cloaked with woods, a river valley, rolling farmland and a park, you encounter the former residences of the pioneer of birth control, the inventor of television and a very eccentric major, among others, as well as the resting place of an early aviator.

You may well spot deer among ancient trees and butterflies (including rarities such as the silver spotted skipper) as well as orchids on the grassy downland slopes. Bats find sanctuary in the Old Fort (which was built in the 1890s when a French invasion was feared).

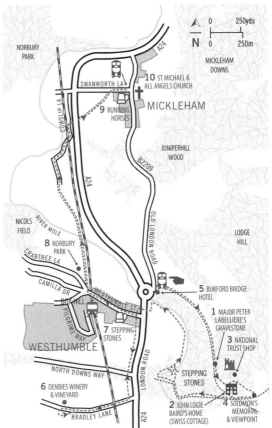

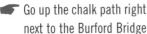 Go up the chalk path right next to the Burford Bridge bus stop, between woods and open fields up Box Hill. At the top of the fields bear right to a footpath through more woods. (The Old Fort involves a detour to the left but cannot be entered by visitors.) As you get near the summit this takes you to:

1 MAJOR PETER LABELLIERE'S GRAVESTONE

The eccentric Dorking resident buried here in 1800 at the age of 75 was placed head downwards because he believed 'as the world is turned upside down on judgment day only he would be the correct way up'. After correctly predicting the precise date of his death, he asked for the youngest son and daughter of his landlady to dance on his coffin as he wanted it to be an occasion of rejoicing rather than sorrow. The girl just sat on it while the boy danced with abandon. A major of the marines, Labelliere was very generous to the poor, often giving away his own coat or shoes to those who needed them more. The grave marks the spot of his favourite view – until he lost an eye after falling into the dense undergrowth there.

☞ Continue up the path to the top and then turn left. On the right is:

2 JOHN LOGIE BAIRD'S HOUSE (SWISS COTTAGE)

The inventor of television (1888–1946) lived here from 1929 to 1932. His experiments had something of a knack of backfiring, having been evicted from a previous residence for causing an explosion in one of his scientific investigations, and on another occasion managing to cut off most of Glasgow's power supply. In 1924 he produced his first television transmitter from a tea chest, a hat box and a darning needle. By 1928 he had demonstrated colour television for the first time, but many years before it was introduced into living rooms. While living here he had to organise events to televise himself (such as boxing matches between his staff) because of a lack of interest by the BBC. In 1932 he became the first person in Britain to demonstrate 'ultra short wave' television transmission.

☞ To the left is:

3 NATIONAL TRUST SHOP

You can get local maps and information about the area here and take a break in the adjoining refreshment bar or picnic area.

☞ To the right is:

4 SOLOMON'S MEMORIAL & VIEWPOINT

Stone seats here make a tempting stop to munch your sandwich 634 feet above sea level with a wide-ranging view encompassing 25 miles in all directions, including Devil's Dyke and Chanctonbury Ring on the South Downs in Sussex.

☞ Take the footpath in front of the viewpoint, to the right downhill. At the first fork bear left, continuing downhill through yew trees on an earthen path with wooden steps.

The stepping stones over the River Mole which winds round Box Hill.

Ignore a small path to the left and stick to the main path, which bends to the right. Just after this bend you will get a great view of the River Mole down to the left.

At the next fork you can **either** go left and cross the river by stepping stones **or** go right and cross the river by a wooden footbridge a few yards away.

On the other side of the river turn right and follow the bank for a short distance until you reach the A24 road by Burford Bridge. Here you can stop for refreshments, end the walk, or continue.

To stop off, turn right and cross the bridge to:

5 BURFORD BRIDGE HOTEL
Box Hill RH5 6BX

Two distinguished guests to have stayed at this 16th-century inn were Horatio Nelson and John Keats, when it was called the Fox & Hounds. It has oak beams and a beer garden.

✋ Opposite the hotel, there is a bus stop where the 465 bus goes back to Chessington South and Surbiton railway stations.

👉 To continue the walk, go through the subway under the A24 (signposted 'Thames Down Link'), and then left (signposted 'North Downs Way'). Follow the A24 for ten minutes or so until on the right you reach:

Bunches of grapes just before the harvesting at Denbies Winery, below Boxhill.

6 DENBIES WINERY & VINEYARD

London Rd, Dorking RH5 6AA ☎ 01306 876616 📱 www.denbies.co.uk

Southeast England is liberally dotted with vineyards, mostly producing on a very small scale. Denbies is no giant by French or Australian standards, but is the UK's largest single estate vineyard, covering 265 acres and producing 400,000 bottles a year. Its reputation has spiralled and it has picked up a good number of awards in recent years. You can take tours of the indoor winery throughout the year, and the vineyards from March to November.

Its visitor centre also hosts the Surrey Performing Arts Library which includes the Vaughan Williams exhibition, honouring one of the country's greatest composers, who lived for many years at Leith Hill House, a few miles away. There is also a farm shop where you can buy the different wines and their own beers also produced here.

☛ Retrace your steps along the A24 until you come to Westhumble Street on the left and turn into it. A short distance on the left is the:

7 STEPPING STONES

Westhumble St, Westhumble RH5 6BS

Food is the main theme here, but you can pop in just for a beer or glass of wine, and it's dog friendly.

☛ Continue along Westhumble Street a few minutes to Box Hill and Westhumble railway station (it is just outside the Freedom Pass zone). Cross the bridge over the railway track and immediately go down the footpath to the right, alongside the rail track through:

8 NORBURY PARK

A working landscape with three farms and a working sawmill, Norbury Park is designated a Site of Special Scientific Interest for its wide range of plants and animals. These include all three British woodpeckers, deer, badgers, foxes and several butterfly species.

Marie Stopes (1880–1958), the pioneer of birth control, lived in a manor in these grounds for the last 20 years of her life, after separating from her second husband, Humphrey Roe, whom she had married after her first husband, Reginald Gates, who was impotent, had died.

☛ As you follow the path through the park you rejoin and cross the River Mole over a wooden footbridge (near a railway bridge). Continue ahead through a kissing gate into an arable field, bearing left away from the rail track, through another kissing gate into a lane alongside a farm with pigs and other animals. Keep to the main lane, which turns right, then left, after which you will see the River Mole again (about 50 feet below on the left). Continue under a railway bridge and then (just before the lane bends right) take a small signed 'Public Footpath' on the right, up to the main road. Cross over it and go through a gate on the other side (signposted 'Public Footpath, Mickleham ¼ mile'). This takes you through more woods and a meadow (sheep grazing on the right and football pitches on the left). When you come to a track (with a pony paddock on the right) turn first left, then right into Swanworth Lane. At the end you come to the main road and on the right is the:

9 RUNNING HORSES

🏵 Old London Rd, Mickleham RH5 6DU

A 16th-century traditional country inn with timbered beams and a real log fire, the Running Horses used to be a coaching house which stabled horses who were exercising on nearby gallops for the Derby. A picture of the 1828 Derby, which was a dead heat, is on the pub sign. The two horses were Cadland (4–1) and The Colonel (7–2 fav.). In those days they did not share the prize money so a run-off between the two took place with Cadland winning by just a neck.

Real ales include Fuller's London Pride, Brakspears and Ringwood; it has been a main entry in the *Good Pub Guide* for some years and has won their Surrey Dining Pub of the Year.

☛ Opposite the pub is:

10 ST MICHAEL & ALL ANGELS CHURCH
Old London Rd, Mickleham RH5 6EB

Of Saxon foundation, the church has some notable connections. One is buried in the churchyard: Graham Gilmour (1885–1912), an early aviator who died after his plane crashed, which is depicted on his gravestone. He asked there be 'no moaning or mourning at his funeral, and that everyone should be merry and bright'. Hundreds of villagers gathered at this unusual funeral when 'the little corner of the churchyard blazed with every conceivable hue – glorious red tulips, pink carnations, yellow daffodils, violets and crimson roses'.

Married in the church in 1793 were Fanny Burney (1752–1840), the novelist known for her wit and satirical caricatures, and General Alexandre d'Arblay, the royalist who had fled the French Revolution. They moved to France in 1802, but when the general refused to fight against England he was interned until 1812, when the couple returned to England.

☛ Outside the pub you can get the 465 bus back to the railway stations.

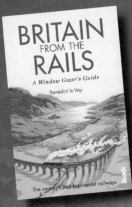

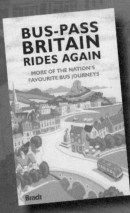

THE FOREST'S HEART

A FEEL-GOOD TALE OF TREES TRANSFORMING A LANDSCAPE INTO A WILDLIFE HAVEN NEAR ST ALBANS.

Definitely a walk deserving binoculars as well as a camera, this shows you the fruits of an ambitious plan started in 2008 to turn bare land into England's largest new native woodland of 600,000 trees. Since then volunteers, particularly children, have already helped the Woodland Trust plant saplings in 170 acres of new land around the existing ancient woodlands every October.

DISTANCE/DIFFICULTY Short walk: 2½ miles; long walk: 5 miles. Easy.

DROP-OUT POINT Throughout: the walk is never far from a road well served by buses.

TIME Short walk: 1 hour; long walk: 2hrs

MAP OS Explorer map 182

START St Leonard's Church, Sandridge ❋TL171106. Maps showing footpaths and areas of public access in the forest are available from pubs and shops in the village, or can be downloaded from www.woodlandtrust.org.uk/heartwood.

TAKING A BREAK Wicked Lady, Green Man, Queen's Head

GETTING THERE Tube/rail then bus. ⊖ To High Barnet, exit left, then left down Barnet Hill to Bus Stop W on the other side and get the 84 bus for a 50-minute journey (3 an hour, 1 on Sun) to St Peter St, St Albans. 🚃 By London Overground from Euston (45mins; 3 an hour) to Watford Junction station (note: Freedom Pass valid for this but not for faster mainline trains). Next to the station go to Bus Stop 5 and get 🚌 321 (39mins; 4 an hour, 1 on Sun) to St Peter St, St Albans.

DIRECTIONS TO START At St Peter St, St Albans, go to Bus Stop 13, and get 🚌 304 or 620 to St Leonard's Church, Sandridge (11mins; 4–5 an hour, 1 on Sun).

Wildlife is further being encouraged by the creation of new hedges to provide habitats; these supplement the long-established ones of hazel, field maple, blackthorn and hawthorn. Thousands of young saplings of ash, oak and hornbeam have been planted on areas of rough grassland, where cherry trees, wild raspberries

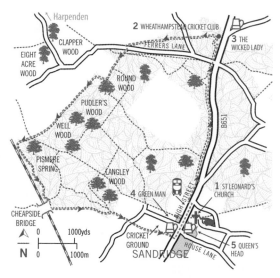

and poppies flourish. Around the new plantations are three blocks of ancient woodland that display superb examples of oak and hornbeam, and in spring there are impressive carpets of bluebells and wood anemones. It is in these areas that you may see buzzards circling above the woods hunting for food. The meadow by Well Wood is where to look for red kites (easily identified by their forked tails), yellow hammers, linnets and buzzards.

1 ST LEONARD'S CHURCH

Church End, Sandridge AL4 9DL

The kernel of the building was consecrated in 1119, but part of the arch is thought to date back to AD946. It is named after the patron saint of prisoners and pregnant women. The vicars and curates, recorded back to the time of the Black Death in 1349, include John Ball (1338–81), a leader of the Peasants' Revolt of 1381, who was born and lived in nearby St Albans. In one of his rousing sermons during the revolt he declared: 'When Adam delved and Eve span, who was then the gentleman? From the beginning all men by nature were created alike, and our bondage or servitude came in by the unjust oppression of naughty men. For if God would have had any bondmen from the beginning, he would have appointed who should be bond and who free. And therefore I exhort you to consider that now the time is come, appointed to us by God, in which we may, if ye will, cast off the yoke of bondage and recover liberty.' Found guilty of high treason after the revolt was crushed he was hanged, drawn and quartered.

☞ Turn right out of the church along the main road, past the next bus stop at Langley Grove, to a footpath (signposted to Nomansland Common), left into a field where you turn right, and follow the path by the hedge and the road. This is where a lot of the tree planting is taking place. Follow this path all the way to Ferrers Lane, and follow the path over it bearing left, which takes you to:

2 WHEATHAMPSTEAD CRICKET CLUB
Nomansland, Wheathampstead AL4 8EL

One of the oldest cricket clubs in Hertfordshire (established in 1824) with a pitch conveniently situated between the forest and a pub. They have five adult teams and several youth teams, and welcome passers-by stopping to watch.

☞ Continue right round Wheathampstead Cricket Club's pitch, back to the road, past a sign 'Wheathampstead, Pre Roman Riverside Village' to:

3 THE WICKED LADY
Nomansland (corner with Dyke Lane), Wheathampstead AL4 8EL

A modern gastro pub with a beer garden, open log fires, opposite the village cricket pitch, with a stop for the 304 and 620 buses to St Albans.

☞ Return to the cricket pitch, walking round it to the right, past a bench marking the Queen's Golden Jubilee of 2002, and straight ahead through a path, to a cottage on the end of a cul-de-sac. Follow the cul-de-sac to the other end, and then over a road (Down Green Lane) and straight ahead into a path through the woods (Nomansland Common). Follow this path right to the end of the woods, where you rejoin Ferrers Lane. Cross over it and into another path through the woods on the other side.

When you come to an open green area, follow the bridleway ahead to Round Wood. At Round Wood it bends right then left. Here you will be greeted by a panoramic view of the countryside to the right. Follow the bridleway past Pudler's Wood, Well Wood and a smaller wood called Pismire Spring, all on your left. When the bridleway reaches a railway track, follow it to the left. Recently planted saplings are on your left as you follow the railway track on your right.

Volunteers at Heartwood Forest help to extend this ancient woodland (see page 32).

When you reach a railway bridge (Cheapside Bridge) go through the gap in the hedge and turn left into the footpath which is part of the Hertfordshire Way, signposted with white arrows on a green background. Here are more newly planted trees and you eventually go past Langley Wood on your left. Just near the end of Langley Wood the path bears left towards it, then there is immediately a kissing gate on the right which you go through continuing along the Hertfordshire Way. Follow it over a lane and ahead past a cricket ground on the right, through a car park, to Sandridge Village Hall in the High Street. Turn left and after a short distance is:

4 THE GREEN MAN
🍺 31 High St, Sandridge AL4 9DD

As well as a dartboard with some unusually good pub darts, this pub has a beer garden, a wide range of real ales (including Black Sheep and Greene King), several ciders (including Rum Cask Scrumpy) and hot food.

👉 Continue up the High Street, past the Village Store (which stocks tasty Cornish pasties) back to St Leonard's Church and the bus stop back, on the corner of Church End. Right next to the bus stop is a great place to wait for the bus. This is the:

5 QUEEN'S HEAD
🏅 7 Church End, Sandridge AL4 9DL

A traditional timbered pub with a real fire, real ale (including Sharp's Doom Bar, Fuller's London Pride and Young's bitter), a dartboard and a beer garden.

A GRAND CANAL & A GREAT ROAD

WATFORD'S WATERWAY WANDER, WITH A CURIOUS ROYAL CONNECTION.

'Danger Crocodiles', improbably announces a sign to deter swimmers by a lock-keeper's cottage on this fascinating river/canal walk close to the M25 which takes in a king's burial place as well as a *Star Wars* film location – and even a replica Loch Ness monster. You might spot (as we did) anglers cooking their own freshly caught fish over a campfire; chubb and pike can be caught on the waterway. The meal could feature locally picked blackberries to follow. The River Gade is part of the Grand Union Canal for much of the walk.

The walk passes right under the M25: that might seem off-putting, but once you get used to the background noise the motorway's monumental presence is actually a striking feature of the route, in a landscape that's usually a rapidly

---

DISTANCE/DIFFICULTY 5½ miles. Easy.

DROP-OUT POINTS After 4 miles

TIME 2–2½hrs

MAP OS Explorer maps 172 and 182

START Watford tube station ✳ TQ095966

FINISH Saracen's Head, Kings Langley ✳ TL072026

TAKING A BREAK King's Head, Harry's Bar, Rose & Crown, Saracen's Head

GETTING THERE ⊖ To Watford station (Metropolitan Line; 45mins from Baker Street, frequent service)

DIRECTIONS TO START Turn right out of the station

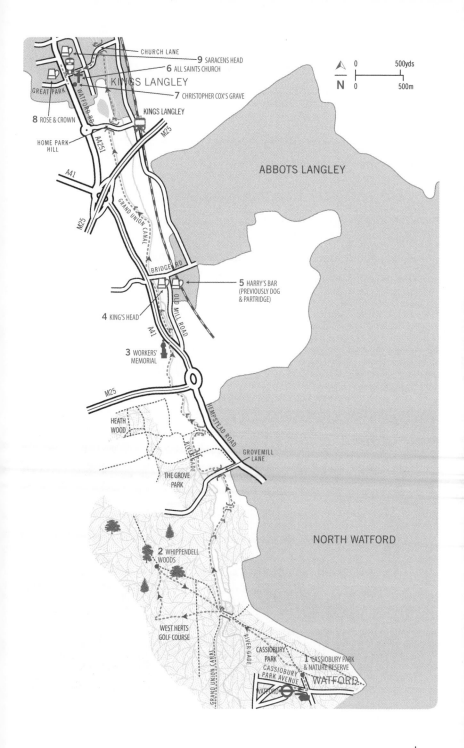

encountered blur for motorists. We observed foxes on the snowy hillside and narrow-boat dwellers warming by a log fire in the icy conditions, all near the motorway, and on the water you should spot ducks, moorhens and swans; in the woods you might glimpse deer.

☞ After turning right into Cassiobury Park Avenue, take the first left into Shepherds Road, which takes you into:

1 CASSIOBURY PARK & NATURE RESERVE

Watford's major open space has the usual playing fields you might expect, but also includes a much-valued woodland nature reserve of alder, willow, lime and oak trees. It is a rich habitat for all sorts of species: 46 types of birds, including red kites and kingfishers, muntjac deer, butterflies, over 300 species of moths, five species of bats, great crested newts and dragonflies.

☞ Inside the park go ahead past the tennis courts, and turn left round them and follow the path as it bends right diagonally through the park, to a crossing of paths where you turn left. This takes you through a tree-lined avenue down past

Navigating Ironbridge Lock on the Grand Union Canal.

a playground on the left. Then you cross the 1920s Rustic Bridge over the River Gade with willow trees and water cress on its bank, and then another (labelled as Bridge 167) over the Grand Union Canal by a lock (Ironbridge Lock).

Ahead is Public Footpath 31 which takes you through West Herts Golf Club to:

2 WHIPPENDELL WOODS

This long-established woodland (dating back to 1672) of oak, beech, silver birch, ash, hazel, holly, hawthorn and wild cherry has an unlikely connection between professional football and Hollywood. Many scenes from the *Star Wars* films were shot here, along with television episodes of *Silent Witness* and *Holby City*. Watford football players were also made by the legendary manager Graham Taylor (later the England boss) to run through the woods as part of their training regime. Spectacular expanses of bluebells appear in late spring, usually around late April and early May.

☞ After wandering around the woods, return to the canal and turn left along its towpath (signposted 'Hemel Hempstead 9 miles'). After about eight minutes you reach the lock-keeper's cottage by Cassiobury Locks with that unforgettable warning notice: 'Danger Crocodiles. No Swimming'. Just past the locks cross a wooden bridge to the other side of the canal and follow the towpath there. Then go under Bridge 165 and Bridge 164 (Grove Bridge), which has a plaque stating it was unveiled on 16 September 1987 to commemorate the restoration of the bridge by British Rail, British Waterways Board and the Railway Heritage Trust. At the next bridge (No. 163) cross the canal to the other side (signposted 'Public Footpath 50a') and continue along the towpath (also signposted 'The Grove Trails'). This takes you past some meadows and under the M25 exit road to Watford.

Just before the next bridge, which takes the A41 over the canal, there is on the left a:

3 WORKERS' MEMORIAL

The stone commemorates the deaths of two workers who were killed when constructing the nearby Gade Valley Trunk Sewer in 1970. They were G Christopher on 1 January and Charles Curran on 7 June.

☞ Continue under the bridge, past the Hunton Bridge Locks to Hunton Bridge itself (Bridge 162), with a sign directing you to the Dog and Partridge on the other side of the canal. Here is an opportunity to have a drink and/or to drop out. To do either do not scramble up the steep muddy bank before the bridge, but go under it to the steps up to the road on the other side. Cross over the canal and on the right is the:

4 KING'S HEAD

Bridge Road, Hunton Bridge WD4 8RE

A traditional pub with timber beams that serves a good Sunday roast dinner and real ales such as Abbot.

☞ For another pub, continue along Bridge Road to the next corner (Old Mill Road), turn right and on the left is:

5 HARRY'S BAR

Old Mill Rd, Hunton Bridge WD4 8RB

A Fuller's pub with very cheap real ales such as Fuller's London Pride, a pool table and a dartboard. It also serves hot food all day and has outside seating. Children and dogs are allowed (fresh water and dog chews available for the latter free). It changed its name from the Dog & Partridge to Harry's Bar in 2013 and has many framed pictures of famous people called Harry.

☟ If you are feeling tired return to the corner with Bridge Road and turn right to find a stop for the 501 bus for the eight-minute journey to Watford Junction station (2–4 buses an hour, except Sundays 1 an hour).

☞ Otherwise return to the canal and continue along the towpath, past North Grove Lock, and under the M25 (Bridge 160), then under Bridge 159, past another Lock (Home Park, No. 70), follow two yellow arrows ('Grand Union Canal Walk to Birmingham' and 'Grand Union Canal Circular Walk, Kings Langley–Hemel'). As you continue there is a lake on the left, with a large model of the Loch Ness Monster, and then some allotments.

When you reach Bridge 158, take the road off it to the left (Water Lane). This soon becomes Church Lane which you follow ahead, until you come on the left to:

Monster of the deep near Kings Langley.

6 ALL SAINTS CHURCH

Church Lane, Kings Langley WD4 8JT

A medieval church with parts dating back to the 13th century, All Saints has several royal connections. Richard II (1367–1400) was buried here without state on 6 March 1400, then dug up 13 years later and reinterred in Westminster. He came to the throne at the age of ten and was only 14 when he had to deal with the Peasants' Revolt of 1381. He did this by promising their leaders (Wat Tyler, Jack Straw and John Ball) that he would grant the peasants freedom from serfdom, then betrayed them and had them executed. He got his comeuppance when falling out with the lords and being forced to abdicate in September 1399 in return for a promise that his life would be spared. This promise was worth as much as the one he had made to the peasants and, after a spell in the Tower of London, he was transferred to Pontefract Castle where he died in February 1400 after probably being starved to death (or, according to Shakespeare, more directly murdered).

Edmund de Langley (1341–1402), the first Duke of York and brother of the Black Prince, has a tomb in the church's Langley

Chapel (the Plantagenet Royal Palace used to stand at the top of nearby Langley Hill), while Queen Victoria's life is commemorated on a stained-glass window in the church.

☞ Continue up Church Lane, then turn left into Watford Road, and a short distance on the left is the main entrance to the churchyard, just inside which is a war memorial. Just to the left of the memorial is:

7 CHRISTOPHER COX'S GRAVE

A local farm worker (1889–1959), Cox received the Victoria Cross for exceptional bravery in World War I. While serving as a stretcher bearer during the Battle of the Somme in July 1916, he was shot in the leg but was soon back on the front after the bullet was removed. During several days near Achiet-le-Grand in March 1917, he carried around 20 wounded men from where they fell back to the dressing stations under a horrendous barrage of sustained machine-gun and artillery fire, and dressed a further 40 to 60 as they lay wounded in shell holes. Six weeks later he was wounded twice in the foot during the Battle of Arras and was invalided out of the army. He was offered a commission and a house but refused both out of respect for his fallen comrades. He returned to Kings Langley and showed bravery again as a member of the Home Guard during World War II, entering the bombed-out Griffin pub to rescue the publican who was found dead. (This pub was in Water Lane and used to stable horses that towed the canal barges in earlier days.) Cox worked for 32 years as a maintenance labourer at the nearby Ovaltine factory, until falling off its roof in 1954, which meant he spent the last five years of his life in and out of hospital. His grave is inscribed: 'In loving memory of a devoted husband and father, Christopher A Cox VC, Beds & Herts Regiment, 1914–18, died 28 April, 1959. Until we meet.' A memorial to him was also unveiled outside Achiet-le-Grand in 2007.

The grave of war hero Christopher Cox in Kings Langley.

☞ Return to the junction of Watford Road and Church Lane where there is a choice of pubs. On the junction on the left is the:

8 ROSE & CROWN
High St, Kings Langley WD4 9HT

A modern food pub that sells gourmet burgers and other home-cooked food, as well as guest real ales.

☞ A little further on the right is the:

9 SARACEN'S HEAD
🏅 47 High Street, Kings Langley WD4 9HU

A 16th-century coaching inn with real ales and a real log fire which is one of the best pubs we have visited. A friendly and cosy timber beamed pub, it serves food (including a Sunday roast) and a range of real ales such as Fuller's London Pride, Sharp's Doom Bar and Adnams.

☞ Between the two pubs, on the same side as the Saracen's Head, is the Langley Hill bus stop where you can get the 501 bus for a 13-minute journey to Watford Junction station (2–4 buses an hour, except Sundays 1 an hour). At Watford Junction you can use your Freedom Pass on the London Overground for the 45-minute journey to Euston (3 an hour) or the faster main-line trains for a small supplement.

SEND US YOUR SNAPS!

We'd love to follow your adventures using our *Freedom Pass London* guide – why not send us your photos and stories via Twitter (@BradtGuides) and Instagram (@bradtguides) using the hashtag #freedompass. Or you can email your photos to 📧 info@bradtguides.com with the subject line 'Freedom Pass pics' and we'll tweet and instagram our favourites.

BLUEBELL BLITZ

A SURPRISING WILDLIFE-RICH WOODLAND ABUTTING CHALK
DOWNLAND ON THE FRINGES OF THE SURREY COUNTRYSIDE.

We saw deer, pheasants and a fox on this stroll through ancient woodland and a pleasantly open patch of chalk downland that makes a memorable escape from London's southern fringes. Time it if you can to coincide with the carpets of bluebells in Banstead Woods, usually at their peak in late April. It is part of a nature reserve next to Chipstead Downs Site of Special Scientific Interest, and depending on when you are here you might encounter red rhododendrons, forget-me-nots or cowslips.

Trees in Banstead Woods include sessile oaks (which are rare in Surrey), goat willow, sweet chestnut, ash, yew, birch, hazel and maple. There are some very rare arable weeds such as ground pine, cut-leaved germander and mat-grass fescue.

The downland grass is grazed by goats and sheep to keep down invasive scrub and to encourage wild flowers, and is a habitat for a wide range of insects, including grizzled skipper, brown argus and chalk hill blue butterflies.

DISTANCE/DIFFICULTY 2–3 miles. Easy.

TIME 1hr

MAP OS Explorer map 146

START Chipstead railway station ✵ TQ278582

TAKING A BREAK Ramblers Rest

GETTING THERE 🚌 To Chipstead railway station, from London Victoria (40 minutes, change East Croydon), London Bridge (37–44mins, direct or change Norwood Junction) and East Croydon (20mins; 3 an hour, 2 an hour Sun)

DIRECTIONS TO START Take exit from Platform 1 of the station

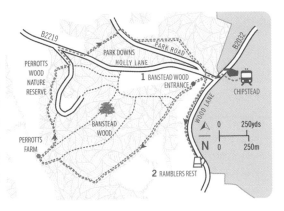

Walk down Chipstead Station Parade, turn left at the bottom (into Outwood Lane). Then take first right (into Lower Park Road), and a few yards round the corner to a car park on the left. Go uphill through the car park to the northeastern corner of:

1 BANSTEAD WOODS

The Domesday Book of 1086 recorded these woodlands as belonging to the Lord of the Manor. The villagers had no rights, just an obligation to cut wood for the lord. In the 13th century it was fenced off as a deer park and hunting lodge for royalty, then in 1881 the land was bought by Francis Baring (founder of Baring's Bank) who built a mansion in the middle. This mansion was turned into an emergency military hospital in 1939, and the woods housed a prisoner-of-war camp. From 1946 until 1998 it housed the Queen Elizabeth Hospital for Children, and since then was made a public open space (about three-quarters of a mile square) by the local authority.

A deer stalks through Banstead Woods.

☛ Several footpaths are signposted from the top of the car park, including one to Perrotts Farm (1½ miles) and the Banstead Woods Nature Trail.

We chose to skirt the perimeter of the woods in a clockwise direction, starting in the northeast corner and ending in the northwest corner. The latter was near Perrotts Wood Nature Reserve, in Elizabeth Drive (a private gated road in the woods) where the old hospital was, but is now private housing, off Holly Lane.

Turn right into Holly Lane, walk a few yards to 'Permissive Ride' and 'Public Footpath' signs on the left which you follow to Park Downs. After turning right and going through the downs you reach Park Road. Cross over the road into the woods opposite, then turn right following the line of the road. This will take you back to the car park where you started.

Turn left, then first right into Outwood Lane. You can walk on a grass track parallel to the road. After about 10 minutes you come to:

2 RAMBLERS REST

Outwood Lane, Coulsdon CR5 3NP

An old farmhouse, this is now an excellent traditional pub which serves hot food (🕙12.00–18.00 daily) as well as real ale (including

View of Banstead Woods from the Ramblers Rest pub. The wood sits on a plateau above the surrounding countryside.

TWO BANSTEAD CHARACTERS

Henry 'Dog' Smith (1546–1625). A rich eccentric, he was a City of London Alderman who dressed as a tramp and walked round the area with his dog. According to how he was treated by the locals in this guise he would give large sums of money for the relief of the poor. Banstead still benefits from this.

Matthew Buckle (1718–84). This naval hero was the model for the *Hornblower* novels. He joined the navy at the age of 13 and rose to become a vice admiral. He lived in Nork House (the building is no longer there) in Nork Park, which was part of the estate owned by his family.

Sharp's Doom Bar, Broadside and guest beers), wine and cocktails. In good weather this can be enjoyed in the large beer garden. Dogs and children are welcome.

☛ Retrace your steps along Outward Lane and right into Chipstead Station Parade back to the station.

UPDATES WEBSITE

Why not post your comments and recommendations, and read the latest feedback and updates from other readers online at 🖰 www.bradtupdates.com/freedompass?

FLEET OF FOOT

FROM NORTH LONDON'S HIGH GROUND TO THE HEART OF THE CAPITAL, WITH AN EXPLORATION OF ONE OF THE CITY'S LESSER-KNOWN RIVERS.

Not many people notice the River Fleet as it makes its way through north London to the Thames as it is underground most of the way, yet it was once London's second largest navigable river. Londoners didn't treat it very kindly and it became so heavily polluted that it was turned into a sewer in 1766.

Following its route from Hampstead Heath to Blackfriars Bridge, however, has something for everyone: beyond the countrified heights of Hampstead Heath you pass the houses of some of the famous artists, writers and politicians of NW3 and NW1, look over central London from Primrose Hill, and wander through an unexpected nature reserve in the inner city. Beyond the Gothic spikiness of St Pancras Station the mood changes as you head

---

DISTANCE/DIFFICULTY 9 miles. Easy.

DROP-OUT POINT Numerous potential drop-out points.

TIME 4½hrs

MAP Any A–Z

START Hampstead tube station ✳ TQ264858

FINISH Blackfriars tube station ✳ TQ317809

TAKING A BREAK The Flask, Magdala, The Roebuck, The Engineer, The Constitution, British Museum café, The Ship, Seven Stars, Ye Olde Cheshire Cheese, The Black Friar

GETTING THERE ⊖ (Northern Line, Edgware Branch) to Hampstead station

DIRECTIONS TO START Turn left out of the station

---

through Bloomsbury, past the British Museum, stopping off maybe for a drink at one of the few London pubs to survive the Great Fire of 1666, and entering Lincoln's Inn Fields, with its two remarkable museums (both free to enter), the Sir John Soane Museum and the Hunterian Museum within the Royal College of Surgeons (not for the faint of stomach). Among the seedier aspects is the very street where both of the last two women to be hanged in Britain committed their murders.

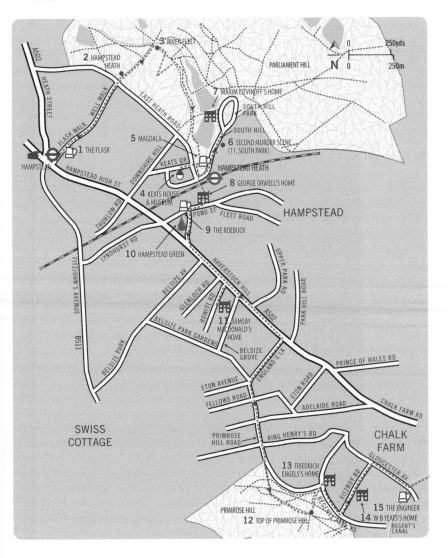

☞ Take the first left into Flask Walk (which gets its name from flasks used to collect water from the nearby well which was fed by the River Fleet). Here on the right is:

1 THE FLASK

14 Flask Walk (corner of Back Lane), Hampstead NW3 1HE

A great Victorian pub with two bars and a real fire, it was built in 1874 on the site of the Thatched House, where water from local springs had been sold by the flask. Hot food every day and Young's beer are served.

☞ Follow Flask Walk ahead (past the Wells and Campden Baths and Wash Houses of 1888) to the end and go straight ahead past the Wells Tavern (on the right on the corner of Christ Church Hill) into Well Walk (which both get their name from the Fleet-fed well). At the end of Well Walk cross over East Heath Road and go straight ahead into:

2 HAMPSTEAD HEATH

Like Epping Forest (the next walk) there was a struggle in the 19th century to prevent this common land from being built over by their respective Lords of the Manor. The villain of the piece in Hampstead was Sir Thomas Marylon-Wilson who tried to put through parliamentary bills to enclose it, and felled a lot of trees to make way for a sand-extraction business. The local people fought the enclosure bill, forming the Heath Protection Committee, which successfully defeated the bill to prevent further building. The sand pits are now lovely hollows that adorn the landscape and these 800 acres of rural land (the highest in London) are now safe for people to enjoy. They can swim in its ponds and observe the natural wildlife which includes kingfishers, muntjac deer, foxes, parakeets, bats, rabbits, squirrels, frogs and jackdaws.

☞ Follow the main track ahead, and keep following it downhill to the very bottom to a stream going under the track. This is the:

3 RIVER FLEET

The somewhat beleaguered river has its main source underground nearby to the left, with another in Highgate Ponds. 'Fleet' comes from an Anglo-Saxon word meaning tidal inlet capable of floating boats, and in its better days had five bridges and a harbour. Things gradually turned sour, though, and by the 13th century it had become so polluted that it was known as 'the stinking river' and contributed to the spread of the plague in 1665.

☛ Turn right and follow the path by the stream. When the path forks you can bear right and go to the top of the hill, which is the highest point on Parliament Hill. From here you have a great view down to the Thames where the River Fleet ends up. After that go back down to the left and rejoin the path along the River Fleet (obscured by bushes). This will take you to the first three ponds in a row on the left with a 'Hampstead Mixed Bathing Pool' noticeboard. These are all headwaters fed by the River Fleet. Follow the edge of them and when you come to the end of the last pond, you will see where the river goes off underground through a grill (as the path departs from the pond, look to the right bank and you will see it about 30 yards away). The river from here on was covered up and turned into a sewer, as mentioned, in 1766.

Follow the path to a stretch of green parallel to South End Road. Just before the end there is a path to the right which takes you a few yards to the road, where directly opposite is Keats Grove. Go up it and a short distance on the left is:

4 KEATS'S HOUSE & MUSEUM

10 Keats Grove, Hampstead NW3 2RR ☎ 020 7431 2062 ✆ www.londonshh. org/houses/keats-house-museum ◷ Apr–Oct Tue–Sun, 12.00–17.00; Nov– Mar 12.00–16.00 **££** 🛞

This is where the poet John Keats (1795–1821) lived from 1818 to 1820, and is the setting which inspired some of Keats's most memorable poetry. Here he wrote *Ode to a Nightingale*, and fell in love with Fanny Brawne, the girl next door. It was from this house that he travelled to Rome, where he died of tuberculosis aged just 25. The son of an ostler, he was attacked by critics as a member of the 'low born Cockney school of poetry' (see *Literary London* walk, pages 197–8). He was an anti-militarist, like his friend Shelley. When Keats contracted tuberculosis Shelley invited him to Italy in the hope the climate would benefit him, but he died *en route*.

☛ Return to South End Road and turn right, going downhill, then, just before Hampstead Heath rail and London Overground station, turn left into South Hill Park. A short distance on the left is the:

5 MAGDALA

2a South Hill Park, Hampstead NW3 2SP

This pub is where Ruth Ellis (1927–55), the last woman to be hanged in this country, shot her unfaithful lover, David Blakely, on 10 April (Easter Day) 1955. The pub was called the Madalan then; she shot him outside it after he had persuaded her to leave another man for him and then deserted her for another woman. Seen by many as a crime of passion, there was huge public opposition to her execution but she refused to appeal against the sentence. The bullet holes are still in the pub wall and marked with a plaque. The pub landlord had just cashed a cheque for Blakely and was rather miffed when it was returned by the bank marked 'payee deceased' (nowadays he surely would have delightedly framed it in the pub).

☛ A bit further up the road on the right is:

6 NO. 11 SOUTH HILL PARK

Hampstead NW3 2ST

By a strange coincidence this is where the penultimate woman to be hanged killed her victim – a few yards away from the scene where Ruth Ellis killed hers, and less than a year earlier. Styllou Christofi, a Cypriot woman born in 1900, was hanged in 1954 for killing her German daughter-in-law Hella, here where they both lived. She battered her skull, strangled her and then set fire to her body in the garden just before midnight on the night of 28 July. While awaiting trial in Holloway prison, she was declared insane by a doctor. She refused to plead insanity, however, yet made the seemingly insane claim that the death had been an accident. Back in 1925, Mrs Christofi had been tried in Cyprus for the murder of her own mother-in-law by ramming a burning torch down her throat, but had been acquitted.

☛ Continue up the road until it forks both ways. Confusingly the houses on the left are still South Hill Park, while those on the right are South Hill Park Gardens. Take the left fork and a little way up on the left is:

7 NO. 86 SOUTH HILL PARK

Hampstead NW3 2SN

Maxim Litvinoff (1876–1951), a Russian Bolshevik refugee, lived here from 1907 until the revolution of 1917. First jailed in Russia in 1901 he escaped after 18 months and fled to Switzerland. He joined the Bolsheviks in 1903 and returned to Russia to take part in the 1905 revolution. When the government started arresting Bolsheviks after suppressing the revolution he again fled the country. In 1907 he came to London for the fifth congress of the party, sharing accommodation with Josef Stalin. Later the same year he settled in London where he met and married Ivy Lowe. After the 1917 revolution he was appointed by Vladimir Lenin to return to London as the Soviet government's representative. In 1918 he was arrested by the British government and exchanged for a British spy imprisoned in Russia. He then became a roving ambassador for the Soviet Union and in 1930 was appointed by Stalin as People's Commissar for Foreign Affairs. Because he was a Jew he was replaced by Molotov in 1939 to facilitate the short-lived non-aggression pact with Hitler's Nazi Germany. After Germany invaded the Soviet Union, Stalin appointed Litvinoff Deputy Commissar of Foreign Affairs.

☛ Go back to Hampstead Heath station, cross over South End Road, turn left and continue to the corner of Pond Street where is:

8 GEORGE ORWELL'S HOME

1 South End Road, Hampstead NW3 2PT

The author (1903–50) lived and worked here from 1934 to 1935, when it was called Booklover's Corner. Just above head height is a plaque to him; the small bust of him which used to accompany it has been stolen. This is where he wrote the 1936 novel *Keep the Aspidistra Flying*. During World War II he worked for the Ministry of Information at Senate House, Malet Street, Bloomsbury (also on the walk) which he used as a model for the Ministry of Truth in his 1949 novel *Nineteen Eighty-Four*.

☞ Turn right into Pond Street, going uphill, with the Royal Free Hospital on the left. Just past it on the right is:

9 THE ROEBUCK
15 Pond St, Hampstead NW3 2PN
A comfortable pub with a real fire and a garden, serves hot food every day and Young's real ales.

☞ Opposite the pub is a footway off Pond Street. This footway has no name sign at this end, but is in fact Hampstead Green. This takes you up to (on the right):

10 HAMPSTEAD GREEN
The green area is protected to encourage wild flowers, such as daffodils, cowslips, primroses and bluebells. The juice of the latter, an information board tells us, used to be turned into starch by Elizabethans to 'stiffen their ruffles', and later gum for bookbinding. In addition to the oak, sycamore and poplar trees, logs are stacked to encourage woodlice, spiders and beetles. Special boxes are also provided to shelter birds.

Next to the green is the Gothic building of St Stephen's Church, which once became derelict but has now been restored to stage theatrical productions.

☞ At the top of Hampstead Green, turn left into Haverstock Hill, and then right into Howitt Road (opposite Belsize Park tube station). A few doors on the left is a plaque to:

11 RAMSAY MACDONALD'S HOME
9 Howitt Rd, Belsize Park NW3 4LT
James Ramsay MacDonald (1866–1937), the first Labour prime minister, lived here from 1916 to 1925. The illegitimate son of a ploughman, he lived in the deepest poverty when first moving to London. From 1923 to 1924 he was prime minister for the first time (but without an overall majority) and again from 1929 to 1931 (again without a majority). Then from 1931 to 1935 he led the National Coalition government which tarnished his reputation for betraying the socialist cause. He also lived in Lincoln's Inn Fields (see page 67).

Enjoying the view of London from the top of Primrose Hill.

☞ Continue down Haverstock Hill until reaching Englands Lane on the right and turn into it. There is an interesting mixture of shops including an old-fashioned butcher, and the Chamomile café at number 45 on the right just before the end. Then turn left into Primrose Hill Road. Just past St Mary-the-Virgin and St Paul's School on the right, turn right into the green area of Primrose Hill itself. Take the path to the left and go uphill, over a crossing of paths ahead, and left at another crossing of paths a few yards further on, to:

12 THE TOP OF PRIMROSE HILL

From here you get a great view of London to the Thames in the distance. A landscape illustration and sundial style diagram both show you the landmarks in the distance, including Guy's Hospital which is close to the end of the walk at Blackfriars. Turn left from the top, going downhill to the corner where Primrose Hill Road goes into Regents Park Road.

☞ Turn left into Regents Park Road and a few yards on the other side opposite the Queens pub is:

13 FRIEDRICH ENGELS'S HOME

122 Regents Park Rd, NW1 8XL

Engels (1820–95) lived here from 1870 to 1894 where he was often visited by his comrade and collaborator, Karl Marx. They jointly wrote *The Communist Manifesto* in 1848. Engels on his own wrote the book *Conditions of the Working Class in England* in 1844 and donated the royalties to Marx. Another classic of Engels was *Origin of the Family, Private Property and the State* in 1884. After the death of Marx in 1883, Engels edited and translated Marx's writings, thus producing the second and third volumes of *Das Kapital* in 1885 and 1894.

☛ Go back along Regents Park Road, past the junction with Primrose Hill Road, until you almost reach a zebra crossing and turn left into Fitzroy Road. Four doors past Fitzroy Yard on the right is:

14 THE HOME OF W B YEATS, SYLVIA PLATH & TED HUGHES

23 Fitzroy Rd, NW1 8TP

W B Yeats (1865–1939), the Irish poet and playwright, lived here from 1867 to 1872. When returning to London as a youth interested in mysticism, he joined the Hermetic Order of the Golden Dawn, which held magic rituals and believed sex was a source of power. A strong Irish nationalist, he became a senator of the Irish Free State from 1922 to 1928, and received the Nobel Prize for Literature in 1923.

Sylvia Plath (1932–63), the poet and novelist, committed suicide by gassing herself on the top floor here, where she had lived since 1962, and almost inadvertently gassed her neighbour downstairs at the same time. In 2009 her son hanged himself. Like the house's previous occupant, W B Yeats, she and her husband, the poet and writer Ted Hughes (1930–98), had an interest in the occult and evoking spirits. She thought that the fact Yeats had lived here was a good omen…

☛ Continue along Fitzroy Road to the end, then turn right into Gloucester Avenue where on the right, on the corner of Princess Road, is:

15 THE ENGINEER

65 Gloucester Av, Primrose Hill NW1 8JH

A cosy pub with a restaurant serving hot food every day and a garden. As well as real ales (such as Sharp's Doom Bar and Saddle Back) it serves cocktails and wine.

☛ Directly opposite the pub on the Gloucester Avenue side are steps running down to the Regent's Canal. When you reach the canal turn left (signposted 'Camden Lock' and 'Kings Cross 1½ miles') and follow the towpath on the left bank. Almost immediately go under a railway bridge (Bridge No. 18). A bit further along, opposite Pirate Castle, go under Bridge 20a (Oval Road), past the huge Camden Lock Market, and over a footbridge across the canal and continue along the right bank. You will soon reach Bridge 24 (Chalk Farm Road).

✋ Turn right into Chalk Farm Road and follow it into Camden High Street (where Camden Town tube station is a short distance on the left).

☛ To continue the walk, cross the bridge over the canal to the other side and continue along the towpath on the left bank. This takes you past more stalls of Camden Lock Market and then under Bridge 25 (Kentish Town Road), Bridge 26a (Camden Street), Bridge 27 (Camden Road), Bridge 28 (Royal College Street) and Bridge 29 (St Pancras Way). Here is:

The Regent's Canal is part of the Grand Union Canal, pictured here at Camden Lock.

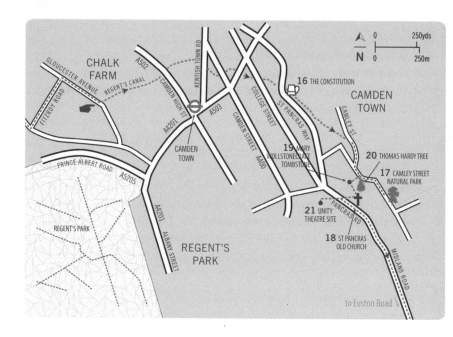

16 THE CONSTITUTION

42 St Pancras Way, Camden NW1 0QT

The beer garden overlooks the canal and has barbecues in the summer. A traditional pub with real ale and hot food it also has live music in the evenings.

☞ Continue along the canal to Bridge 31 (Camley Street). Come off the canal here into Camley Street and turn right. Continue past Granary Street on the right and just after the road bends under a railway bridge, on the left is St Pancras Cruising Club, and next door to it is:

17 CAMLEY STREET NATURAL PARK

12 Camley St, Kings Cross NW1 0PW ☎ 020 7833 2311 🖰 www.wildlifetrusts.org
🕐 daily till 17.00 or dusk if earlier

Created from an old coal yard in 1984, this is now a quiet refuge from the city and surrounding railway tracks. It features key wildlife habitats including grassland, woodland and wetland, and has an amazing range of wildlife such as the Daubenton's bat, reed bunting, holly blue butterfly, snake's head fritillary, reed warblers, kingfishers, geese, mallards and rare earthstar fungi. Pond dipping and education classes are available for children, along with trainee schemes in conservation skills and numerous family events throughout the year.

☛ After visiting this, retrace your steps under the railway bridge and turn left after a few yards through a gateway into St Pancras Gardens and:

18 ST PANCRAS OLD CHURCH

Pancras Rd, NW1 1UL

One of the earliest Christian churches in Europe it dates back to AD314, but was ruined in the 13th century, rebuilt in the 14th century, and half abandoned in the mid 19th century. During the Civil War it was taken over by Oliver Cromwell's troops as a barracks and stables.

The River Fleet behind the church is shown in an 1827 picture on the railings in front of the church. *The Tale of Two Cities* by Charles Dickens, published in 1859, has body-snatcher Jerry Cruncher stealing corpses from the churchyard. The Beatles were photographed in and around the churchyard (including next to the tomb of Sir John Soane, see page 66) on 28 July 1968. The pictures were eventually used in 1973 on the sleeves of two compilation albums – *1962–1966* (Red Album) and *1967–1970* (Blue Album).

☛ About 20 yards ahead as you enter the churchyard from Camley Street you will see a four-sided tombstone about four feet tall which is:

19 MARY WOLLSTONECRAFT'S & WILLIAM GODWIN'S TOMBSTONE

Mary Wollstonecraft (1759–97), the feminist author of *A Vindication of the Rights of Women*, and her anarchist husband William Godwin (1756–1836), who wrote *Political Justice*, were both married and buried in St Pancras Old Church. Godwin lived in nearby Chalton Street and, when he married Mary in 1796, they moved also nearby to 29 The Polygon (on the corner of Chalton Street, Werrington Street and Polygon Road), which is now occupied by a block of council flats called Oakshott Court. A plaque to Mary is on the Werrington Street corner of the square. Mary's daughter, also called Mary (1797–1851), married poet Percy Bysshe Shelley (1792–1822) and plighted her troth to him over her mother's grave here. William's second wife, yet another Mary, was also buried here.

☞ Also in the churchyard to the left of this tombstone (between the church and the rail track) is the:

20 THOMAS HARDY TREE

Thomas Hardy (1840–1928), the novelist, worked for the Midland Railway Line, which built the railway track over part of St Pancras Old Church's graveyard in the 1860s. He was responsible for removing the bodies and dismantling the tombstones, so spent many hours in the churchyard. Some headstones were placed around an ash tree, known as the Hardy Tree, which has since grown in and around the stones.

Between Mary Wollstonecraft's tomb and the Hardy Tree is the tomb of Sir John Soane (whose astonishing museum is later in the walk). It is said to have been the inspiration for Giles Gilbert Scott's K2 telephone box (the type still seen on our streets, and now protected by listed building status).

☞ Come out of the front of the church and turn right into Pancras Road, and a few yards on the left is Goldington Crescent. Follow this to the second turning on the left which is Chalton Street, and on the left is:

Thomas Hardy's Tree in St Pancras Old Church's graveyard is surrounded by tombstones.

21 UNITY THEATRE SITE

Unity Mews, 150 Chalton St (just off Goldington Crescent), Somers Town NW1 1NP

A plaque proclaims: 'Unity Theatre run by the people for the people, 1936–75'. Unity Theatre began as a theatre club to avoid the censorship of the Lord Chamberlain in order to put on left-wing plays as part of the Workers' Theatre Movement. It started in a hall in nearby Britannia Street on 5 January 1936 but moved to this site the following year. Although an amateur group, it attracted many professional actors

appearing free, including Paul Robeson who turned down several West End roles to do so in 1938. Many famous playwrights used it to stage the premieres of their plays, such as Sean O'Casey, Jean-Paul Sartre, Maxim Gorky and Bertolt Brecht. Music hall shows were also staged. It burned down on 8 November 1975. A DVD, *The Story of Unity Theatre*, presented by one of its actors, Harry Landis, is available at 🖱 www.unitytheatre.org.uk.

👉 Retrace your steps to St Pancras Gardens and Old Church and continue down Pancras Road, ahead into Midland Road past St Pancras station on the left, and the British Library on the right, to Euston Road. Turn right, then first left into Mabledon Place, right at Mable's Tavern into Flaxman Terrace, right into Dukes Road and immediately left into Woburn Walk, through to Upper Woburn Place.

So far the walk has roughly followed the course of the River Fleet. From here the underground river actually goes east to Kings Cross Road, then south via Farringdon Road and Farringdon Street to Ludgate Circus. This walk, however, takes a more picturesque and historic route to Ludgate Circus (based on one recommended by The Ramblers).

Turn left into Upper Woburn Place and a few yards on the left is:

22 CHARLES DICKENS'S HOME

Tavistock House (now BMA House), Tavistock Square, Bloomsbury WC1H 9JP

A plaque confirms that Charles Dickens lived here from 1851 to 1860. During this time he wrote *Bleak House* and other novels. A lover of

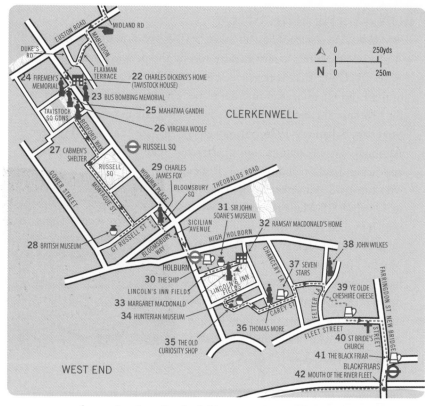

amateur dramatics, he also had his own private theatre here where he put on productions with his friends such as fellow novelist Wilkie Collins and artists George Cruikshank, who illustrated *Oliver Twist* and *Sketches by Boz*, and Augustus Egg. Egg shared digs with Richard Dadd, the artist who killed his own father in 1843, on which Dickens based his novel *Martin Chuzzlewitt*, serialised from 1843 to 1844.

☛ A bit further along on the same building is another plaque:

23 MEMORIAL TO THE BUS BOMBING OF 7 JULY 2005

It reads: 'In memory of those who were killed in the bomb attack on a route 30 bus near this spot on 7 July 2005.' The 13 victims are listed and it adds: 'London will not forget them and all those who suffered that day.' Four suicide bombers struck on the morning rush hour that day killing 52 people and injuring over 770 others. One of the bombs was on the tube between King's Cross and Russell Square which led to the diversion of the 30 bus to here.

☞ Directly opposite on the corner of Endsleigh Place is another plaque:

24 MEMORIAL TO FIREMEN KILLED ON DUTY DURING THE BLITZ

The plaque reads: 'In memory of auxiliary Firemen Stanley Harold Randolph and Harry Richard Skinner who died from injuries received as a result of enemy action near this site on the night of 16th–17th April 1941, while serving under Station 73 Euston.'

☞ Go a few yards up Endsleigh Place and turn left into Tavistock Square Gardens. In the centre is:

25 MAHATMA GANDHI'S STATUE

Mohandas Gandhi (1869–1948) became known as Mahatma (meaning 'great soul') after his campaign of civil disobedience and passive resistance finally won independence for India. He studied at nearby University College London in 1888. The statue was sculpted by Fredda Brilliant and unveiled by the prime minister, Harold Wilson, in May 1968. The site was chosen by Vengali Krishnan Krishna Menon (1897–1974), a St Pancras borough councillor and a close friend of Nehru.

☞ In the far right corner of the gardens is:

26 VIRGINIA WOOLF'S BUST

The novelist (1882–1941) lived close by, at 52 Tavistock Square, with her husband Leonard, from 1924 until 1939, during which time they ran the Hogarth Press here. The house was bombed in 1940. Virginia visited the wreckage and recorded: 'I could see a piece of my studio wall standing: otherwise rubble where I wrote so many books.

Open air where we sat so many nights, gave so many parties.' The Tavistock Hotel now occupies the site.

The bust was sculpted by Stephen Tomlin in 1931 and placed here in 2004 by the Virginia Woolf Society of Great Britain.

☞ Take the exit by this bust and go down Bedford Way (parallel with Woburn Place) to Russell Square. The tube station is a few yards to the left.

To continue turn right to the next corner where there is a small green hut which is a:

27 CABMEN'S SHELTER

This Victorian shelter was one of many built from 1875 onwards to keep the drivers of horse-drawn carriages out of pubs. They were tempted into pubs during rain and snow rather than sit on the uncovered part of the carriage and get soaked, which meant it was difficult hailing one in such conditions. It was also when the Temperance Society was at its height and a Cabmen's Shelter Fund was set up, erecting the huts with 'good and wholesome refreshments at moderate prices' to lure them away from the taverns and keep them on the job. By law they had to be no larger than a horse and cart. Many were destroyed in the Blitz or later demolished during road widening, so this is one of only a handful that remain. It was originally in Leicester Square from 1901 until pedestrianisation in the 1960s and, restored on this site in 1987, it continues to serve snacks to cabbies and members of the public.

☞ Turn left here, round the Russell Square (which a few years ago was restored to the early 1800s historic landscape design by Humphrey Repton for Sir Francis Russell, 5th Duke of Bedford), past the back of Senate House on the right, where George Orwell worked during the war (see page 53), ahead into Montague Street to Great Russell Street. Turn right and a few yards on the right is the:

28 BRITISH MUSEUM

Great Russell St, WC1B 3DG ☎ 020 7323 1234 🖱 www.britishmuseum.org
🕐 daily 10.00–17.30; Fri 10.00–20.30

Bloomsbury's best-known museum and free to enter, this has a huge classical exterior by Robert Smirke. It contains one of the great

SEASONAL SPLENDOUR

Fresh air and breathtaking views can be enjoyed within the Freedom Pass zone whatever the season.

1 Happy Valley, with its downland and ancient woodland, is a year-round pleasure, but when the snow falls, the steep slopes become ideal toboggan runs, **walk 11**.
2 A spectacular spring sight: a carpet of bluebells in Banstead Woods, **walk 5**.

IN THE FOOTSTEPS OF THE FAMOUS

Within these pages find politicians and pop stars, fictional characters and philosophers, murderers and music hall legends and much more besides. Read about Little Titch and his 'big boot dance' or seek out the drinking-holes favoured by famous writers – we have peppered our walks with the colourful histories of the great as well as the downright dodgy.

1 It was Dickens who brought fame to The Old Curiosity Shop – it is still open today as a shoe shop, **walk 6**. **2** Lose yourself in the world of Winnie the Pooh for an afternoon.

Pictured here, Owl's house, of course, **walk 16**. **3** Samuel Johnson's cat stands guard outside his former residence in Gough Square, **walk 23**. **4** In Dartford, an ironwork stencil-style silhouette two-dimensional artwork portrays Rolling Stones singer Mick Jagger who was born in the town in 1943, **walk 19**. **5** Whilst this plaque may rightly mark Samuel Pepys's birthplace, the date given for his birth is actually a year out, **walk 23**. **6** The mural in the Marx Memorial Library, **walk 25**. (Picture courtesy of the Marx Memorial Library.) **7** A painting of Pepys hangs in the Worlds End pub in Tilbury in memory of his stay here in 1666, **walk 12**.

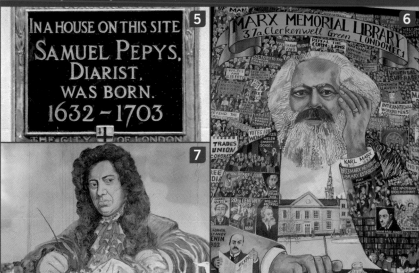

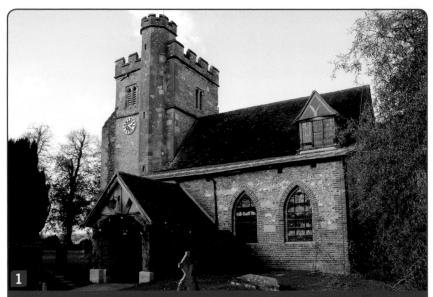

CHURCHES

From hidden art treasures to tales of ghosts and ghouls: the churches and cemeteries featured in these pages are well worth seeking out.

1 Little Missenden's Saxon church has a striking stained-glass window in the style of William Morris and Edward Burne-Jones, **walk 18**. **2** Find out about the devilish imp that plagued Old Barnes Cemetery in Victorian times, **walk 20**. **3** St Andrew Church in Holborn features in novels by both Charles Dickens and Iris Murdoch, **walk 23**.

museum collections of the world, and large enough to lose yourself in for a day or a week; if you just want to pop in, you might like to seek out the Rosetta Stone (which helped historians to decode hieroglyphics), or ponder whether the Elgin Marbles should be returned to their original place on the Parthenon in Athens. The huge former Reading Room was where Karl Marx researched *Das Kapital* (see page 235), within the vast domed courtyard of the two-acre Great Court; designed by Foster & Partners, it is Europe's largest covered square, and has a stylish café.

☛ Retrace your steps along Great Russell Street, past Montague Street, to on the right:

29 CHARLES JAMES FOX'S STATUE

Bloomsbury Square Gardens

The radical Whig MP known as 'the Intrepid Fox' (1749–1806) had a huge capacity for alcohol. Finding him surrounded by seven empty bottles of port, a friend asked if he had drunk them all unassisted. He replied: 'No, I was assisted by a bottle of Madeira.' Such heavy drinking meant he had rather a portly figure so, when his second in a duel advised him to stand sideways to reduce the target area for his opponent, Fox chuckled: 'Why? I am as thick one way as another.' The opponent, William Adam, invited Fox to shoot first, but, showing remarkable courtesy in the circumstances, he replied: 'After you.' Both missed, then Fox was hit in the groin, after which he again showed incredible civility in the circumstances by firing in the air. They then became firm friends. Politically he supported many progressive causes such as the extension of the franchise (when less than a quarter of a million people had the vote out of a population of six million) and the abolition of slavery.

☛ Go through the gardens about halfway and take the exit to the left, then turn right, and over the road into Sicilian Avenue opposite (a pedestrian arcade with some interesting shops). Turn right at the end into Southampton Row. Go past Holborn underground station on the left, and just past it turn left into Gate Street (a pedestrian alley). Here on the corner of Little Turnstile is:

30 THE SHIP

🍺 🏅 12 Gate St, WC2A 3HP

A great traditional alehouse hidden away in this back alley, The Ship dates back to 1549 and appropriately has its own 'Ship 1549' bitter (brewed by the Caledonian Brewery) along with other real ales such as Tribute and Bombardier. It also serves old-fashioned pub grub and has jazz on Sunday nights.

☛ Continue along Gate Street into Lincoln's Inn Fields, where Lord William Russell was publicly executed in 1683 for plotting the assassination of Charles II. Turn left and a short distance on the left is:

31 SIR JOHN SOANE'S MUSEUM

13 Lincoln's Inn Fields, WC2A 3BP ☎ 020 7405 2107 🖰 www.soane.org
🕐 Tue–Sat 10.00–17.00

Soane (1753–1837), the son of a bricklayer, was one of the great British architects, and this is his quite startling home, preserved by private act of parliament after his death so it would be retained as a museum and left unchanged (partly so his sons couldn't get their hands on it), and it's free to enter too. Three houses at numbers 12, 13 and 14 were knocked down to build the museum in two phases between 1808 and 1824. So many curiosities and relics are packed into this museum that you hardly know where to look: all manner of things – Greek and Roman relics, thousands of drawings, paintings, stained-glass windows and even mummified cats are stashed on the walls and in display cases. In the room where originals of Hogarth's celebrated paintings (the series *The Rake's Progress* and *The Election*) hang, the attendant unhooks the panels to reveal more works hidden behind, including a painting combining a number of Soane's architectural schemes that never reached fruition, plus a scale model of the Bank of England which he designed. In the central courtyard, itself cobbled with wine bottle bottoms, arches recycled from the House of Lords surround a melodramatic mausoleum to 'Alas, poor Fanny!' – his beloved dog. His tomb is in St Pancras Old Church (see page 59).

☛ A bit further along on the same side is:

32 RAMSAY & MARGARET MACDONALD'S HOME

3 Lincoln's Inn Fields, WC2A 3AA

James Ramsay MacDonald, the first Labour prime minister (see page 54), lived here from 1896 to 1916. He also attended regular debates in the Rainbow Tavern at nearby 15 Fleet Street.

☛ Ramsay's wife Margaret (1870–1911) is commemorated by a statue nearby. To get to it, retrace your steps a few yards and turn left into Lincoln's Inn Fields gardens, then take the path immediately right, where on the right is:

33 MARGARET MACDONALD'S STATUE

Margaret, who married James Ramsay MacDonald in 1896, founded the Women's Labour League and was a deeply committed feminist. Her statue is accompanied by nine children (of whom she had six).

☛ Go to the opposite (southern) exit of the gardens, turn right and a few yards on the left is the:

34 HUNTERIAN MUSEUM (ROYAL COLLEGE OF SURGEONS)

35–43 Lincoln's Inn Fields, WC2A 3PE ☎ 020 7405 3474 🖱 www.rcseng. ac.uk/museums/hunterian ☻ Tue–Sat 10.00–17.00

A must for lovers of the ghoulish and macabre, but definitely not for the squeamish (there are skeletons of foetuses and bottled organs). One of the oldest anatomical collections in the world, this free museum reveals 400 years of medical history right up to the latest advances in minimal access surgery. To give a taste (maybe an unpleasant one) there are: the distal end of the stomach of a horned dogfish (with the commencement of the intestine, pancreas and spleen), the sac of a hernia (with a partially constricted portion of a small intestine which killed a watchmaker) and part of a dog's skull (showing atrophy due to infestation of the brain with parasitic worms).

There are also photos of the war wounds and early plastic surgery used in World War I, and coronary bypass surgery in 2003.

John Hunter (1728–93) started the museum. After no early formal education, he trained as a surgeon and became very proficient at dissection and experimental research. In 1777 he tried to resuscitate the body of Rev. William Dodd, who had just been hanged for fraud and forgery. Hunter had previously revived people who had been drowned. Dodd's friends bribed the hangman to cut him down early and rushed the body to Hunter whose attempt to revive him in a hot bath failed. Dodd had written his best-selling autobiography in prison during his last two weeks, prompting his friend Samuel Johnson's famous remark: 'When a man knows he is to be hanged in a fortnight it concentrates his mind wonderfully.' Hunter's brother William had a medical school which received corpses from body-snatchers at 8–10 Windmill Street, off Tottenham Court Road, where over a hundred bodies were found hidden in a shed in 1776.

John Hunter died heavily in debt so the government purchased this museum in 1799 to bail his widow out of debt, and then gave it to the forerunner of the Royal College of Surgeons.

☞ Turn left out of the museum, and take the first left into Portsmouth Street, where on the left near the junction with Sheffield Street, is:

35 THE OLD CURIOSITY SHOP
13–14 Portsmouth St, WC2A 2ES

The novel of this name by Charles Dickens was serialised from 1840 to 1841 and was so popular in America that the ship carrying the magazine with the last instalment from London was besieged when it arrived in New York. The building is now a shoe shop but it maintains the original structure and name.

☞ Continue a few yards along Portsmouth Street and turn left into Portugal Street, then first right into Carey Street. On the next corner is:

36 THOMAS MORE'S STATUE
Corner of Carey St and Searle St

More (1478–1535) wrote the classic *Utopia* (meaning Nowhere Land) in 1516, in search of the best form of government. It describes an imaginary island of communal ownership, education for all men and women and religious toleration. Sadly, the latter was not extended to him and he was beheaded by Henry VIII for refusing to recognise him as head of the Church in place of the Pope. More studied at nearby Lincoln's Inn in 1497 and became a successful barrister. He later became an MP, speaker of the House of Commons and then Lord Chancellor.

☞ Continue along Carey Street where a few yards on the left is the:

37 SEVEN STARS
53 Carey St, WC2A 2JB

One of the oldest pubs in London, dating back to 1602, and one of the few buildings to survive the Great Fire of London. It is just behind the Royal Courts of Justice, so gets a fair passing trade of barristers and their clients. A small and busy pub, it is a free house (run by a feisty female called Roxy) with pub grub and real ales (including Adnams).

☞ Continue to the end of Carey Street, then turn left into Chancery Lane, then first right into Bream's Buildings. This takes you to Fetter Lane where you turn right. Here is:

38 JOHN WILKES'S STATUE

Wilkes (1727–97) like Thomas More was a defender of religious toleration, as well as freedom for all. The cry 'Wilkes and Liberty' was often heard in the streets of London. He was thus a thorn in the side of the establishment and was locked up in the Tower of London for sedition and blasphemy from 1768 to 1770. While he was incarcerated his supporters formed the Society for Supporting the Bill of Rights. Earlier he had been elected three times as MP for Middlesex, but was expelled each time by the house. One of his greatest opponents in parliament was the Earl of Sandwich, who said Wilkes would die of the pox or on the gallows. Wilkes famously rejoindered: 'That depends, my lord, on whether I embrace your principles or your mistress.'

☛ Continue along Fetter Lane and take the first left into West Harding Street, which becomes Pemberton Row. On the right go through an archway into a cobbled alley (signposted 'Dr Johnson's House') to Dr Johnson's House in Gough Square (see *Literary London* walk, pages 207–8), then to the opposite exit from the square into Wine Office Court on the right. A few yards on the left is:

39 YE OLDE CHESHIRE CHEESE

Wine Office Court, off 145 Fleet St, EC4A 2BU

The original pub of 1538 (the Horn Tavern) was destroyed in the Great Fire of London in 1666 after which it was rebuilt. A pub without natural light, it has an appealingly dingy atmosphere, with a real fire and several sawdust-covered floors connected by a rickety staircase. Many of its distinguished former customers are described in the Literary London walk (page 207), but others include Theodore Roosevelt (1858–1919) who was president of the USA from 1901 to 1909.

Chops and pies are served every day and Samuel Smith's beers are on hand pump.

☛ Continue down Wine Office Court a few yards to Fleet Street, named of course after the famous river-turned-sewer. Turn left and continue almost all the way down to Ludgate Circus. But just before you reach it turn right into a small passage called St Bride's Avenue. At the end is the entrance to:

40 ST BRIDE'S CHURCH

St Bride's Av, Fleet St, EC4Y 8AU

St Bride (or Bridget) was a woman who could transform water into beer, so it is appropriate that the journalists' church should be named after her. After it was bombed in World War II the restoration work involved excavation, which led to archaeological finds that showed it was nearly a thousand years older than previously thought – right back to the Celts and Romans of 2,000 years ago. There have been seven previous churches on the site, including the one designed by Sir Christopher Wren (1632–1723). His design of several tiers was used by a Fleet Street baker to create a wedding cake in the 18th century, so what you see before you here has been unknowingly replicated in millions of cakes the world over.

Moll Cutpurse (1584–1659), the female highway robber who lived in Fleet Street, is buried here. Her real name was Mary Frith and she was born with clenched fists, the sign of a wild and adventurous spirit. She grew to be a 'lusty and sturdy wench', who fought well with a distaff and disliked housework and tending to children. She escaped from domestic service and turned to crime, first as a pickpocket, then as receiver and forger and ultimately a highway robber. While working as a receiver of stolen goods in Fleet Street she often sold the items to those from whom they had been robbed. After robbing and wounding General Fairfax with a gun she was sentenced to death, but released after paying him £2,000, a considerable fortune at the time, proving how profitable her crimes were.

Many others connected with this church are included on the *Literary London* walk (see pages 204–5).

☞ Continue down to Ludgate Circus and turn right into New Bridge Street down towards the Thames, and on the left on the corner of Queen Victoria Street is:

41 THE BLACK FRIAR
174 Queen Victoria St, EC4V 4EG

A rare Art Nouveau pub interior, complete with stained-glass windows and furniture, and on the site of an old Dominican monastery, this has many jolly friars in sculptures, mosaics and reliefs. It was built in 1875, renovated in 1905, and in the 1960s was saved from demolition by Sir John Betjeman's campaigning. Real ale (including Sharp's Doom Bar, Fuller's London Pride and Nutty Black dark; other milds are guests during autumn and winter) and basic pub grub are available and there is seating outside.

☞ Next to the pub is Exit/Entrance No. 1 to Blackfriars tube station. Go down this and come out at Exit No. 6. This takes you to a landing stage on the Thames a few yards from Blackfriars Bridge. From the end of the landing stage you will see under the bridge (except at high tide) the sewer outlet which is:

42 THE MOUTH OF THE RIVER FLEET
This now tiny outlet was in Roman times 600 yards wide!

FREEDOM PASS

DISTANCE 5 MILES
DIFFICULTY EASY
TIME 2–2½HRS

7

EPPING FOREST:
CHINGFORD TO LOUGHTON

EPIC FOREST FIGHT

A MIRACULOUS SURVIVAL OF SEMI-WILDERNESS IN THE NORTHEASTERN SUBURBS, PRESERVED THANKS TO AN EPIC STRUGGLE AGAINST ENCLOSURE.

Epping Forest wasn't always called that. For centuries it was Waltham Forest. And despite its name it's not all wooded; there are also patches of heath, wetland, grassland, numerous rivers and streams. It's quite huge, large enough to lose yourself in comprehensively: this green corridor of elevated, rather infertile gravelly land, extends from Manor Park to beyond Epping, a total of over nine square miles. More than half of it is designated as a Site of Special Scientific Interest, and it comprises ancient woodland which has been covered with trees since Neolithic times. Parts of the forest are still grazed by cattle; rare-breed Pedigree English Longhorn keep the grass down to allow more flowers to flourish. These flowers in turn preserve butterflies and insects.

In medieval times it was a royal hunting forest, allowing only the king to hunt there; locals were allowed to exercise their commoners' rights and collect

DISTANCE/DIFFICULTY 5 miles. Easy.

TIME 2–2½hrs

MAP OS Explorer map 174

START Chingford railway station ✲ TQ392946

FINISH Loughton station (⊖ Central Line) ✲ TQ423956

TAKING A BREAK Robin Hood, Kings Oak, Victoria Tavern

GETTING THERE 🚃 To Chingford from Liverpool Street (26–28mins; 4 an hour) or ⊖ to Walthamstow Central (Victoria Line), then train to Chingford (11–12mins; frequent)

DIRECTIONS TO START Turn right out of Chingford station into Station Road wood and food from it. That's where things turned nasty in the 19th century as matters came to a head between landowners and commoners and the then Lord of the Manor started enclosing parts of the forest. In this walk we pay homage to local hero Thomas Willingale whose bold lopping saved the forest from suburbanisation. Although much of the forest was lost, an act

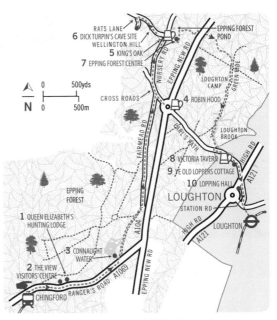

of parliament preserving the remainder was passed in 1878, since when the ownership of Epping Forest has passed to the Corporation of London.

Earlier, Henry VIII hunted in the forest and breakfasted in it while the second of his six wives, Anne Boleyn, was being beheaded. Another murderer, police killer Harry Roberts, used it as a hide-out in 1966, as did highway robber Dick Turpin a couple of centuries earlier.

☛ After turning right into Station Road follow it as it becomes Ranger's Road for about seven minutes or so to the Royal Forest pub, then a bit further on the left is:

1 QUEEN ELIZABETH'S HUNTING LODGE

Ranger's Rd, Chingford E4 7QH ☎ 020 8529 6681 🖱 www.cityoflondon.gov.uk
🕐 daily 10.00–17.00

This lodge was built by Elizabeth's father, Henry VIII, in 1542 to enable the royals to stand with their crossbows on the lodge balconies and shoot at the already captured deer which were driven to them by beaters. If they missed, the deer were brought down by hounds, so the beasts didn't have much of a chance. After each wave of deer had been slaughtered the carcasses were collected by carts to make way for the next set of victims.

To prevent the royals being 'soiled by contact with servants' they were partitioned off into separate quarters. The nobility were also protected from the 'annoying' cooking smells of the

A display at the Hunting Lodge.

venison wafting upwards into the banquet room, because the kitchen ceiling was specially filled with plaster containing human hair which acted as a filter. On display here are vicious 'man traps', placed in the forest to prevent commoners poaching the deer.

☞ Right next to the lodge is:

2 THE VIEW VISITORS' CENTRE

6 Ranger's Rd, Chingford E4 7QH ☎ 020 7332 1911 🖱 www.cityoflondon.gov.uk
🕓 daily 10.00–17.00

An imaginative and child-friendly centre which houses exhibitions of paintings of the forest mainly by contemporary local artists, examples of the forest wildlife such as dragonflies, poems by the 'Forest Poet' John Clare, including *Enclosure* which was his impassioned plea against fencing off common land. Local characters who saved Epping Forest from further enclosure are also celebrated – Thomas Willingale (see page 78) and George Burney who, with 100 workers, tore down fences in 1878 (a short biography of whom called *Forest For The People*, by Richard Morris, is on sale here). You can pick up a useful free map of the forest here.

☞ You are now on the edge of the forest. The more adventurous might take the Green Ride and Centenary Walk from behind the hunting lodge on tracks through the forest all the way to the King's Oak pub and the Epping Forest Centre. This route is shown on Ordnance Survey Explorer map 174, but the tracks are not well signposted. There is an emergency 24-hour call out line on ☎ 020 8532 1010 (so it is advisable to take a mobile phone with you).

The more cautious might like to stick to the following better-marked paths and roads to the same destination.

After turning left out of the hunting lodge continue along Ranger's Road for about another 15 minutes until you come, on the left, to:

3 CONNAUGHT WATER

Birdlife abounds here, and in 1882 Queen Victoria rode by in an open carriage, celebrating the Epping Forest Act which protected the forest from further enclosures. She declared: 'It gives me the greatest satisfaction to dedicate this beautiful forest to the use and enjoyment of my people for all time.' She then rode along Fairmead Bottom to High Beach (a route also followed in this walk).

☞ Just before reaching the water take a path to the right, which has lots of blackberry and holly bushes. At the end turn left into a track, Fairmead Road (not marked as such) which ends at a tea hut (a favourite haunt of bikers) on the junction with Cross Roads (again unmarked).

If you wish to stop off in a pub, turn right and a few hundred yards away on a roundabout on the A104 is the:

4 ROBIN HOOD

Epping New Rd, Loughton IG10 4AA

A traditional pub with flagstone floors, low-beamed ceilings and a restaurant. Real ales include Directors and Squirrel.

☞ To continue the walk from the Cross Roads turn left and after about 200 yards turn right into a road (signposted to 'High Beach') which is Nursery Road. Parallel with the road are bridleways or tracks through the forest which you can use. After about 15 to 20 minutes you will come to the:

5 KING'S OAK

Paul's Nursery Rd, High Beach, IG10 4AE

This is a child-friendly pub (there is a play area), which allows dogs, has fires and a pool table, and serves Greene King as well as hot food. You're following the footsteps of royalty, though not in a very appealing way: Henry VIII had breakfast in this pub on 19 May 1536 while he waited for news that his wife Anne Boleyn had been decapitated.

☞ Take the path directly opposite the pub (Wellington Hill) ahead, then left into Rats Lane, an isolated track which was the site (sadly not visible) of:

6 DICK TURPIN'S CAVE
Rats Lane, High Beach

The infamous highwayman (1705–39) had a butchery business at Waltham Abbey, just two miles northwest of here. He used to steal cattle or deer grazing in the forest, and then sell it in his shop until he was caught and forced to go on the run. He became a burglar and highwayman, and lived for a while in a cave on this site. He shared it with another highway robber called Tom King until they were captured by police. Turpin was aiming to shoot one of the constables but hit and killed King instead, before escaping and riding on his horse Black Bess all the way to York, only to be hanged there for shooting a cock after confessing to a murder and several robberies.

Another highwayman to use the forest was John Rann (1750–74), better known as 'Sixteen String Jack' on account of the eight silk ribbons he wore on each of the knees of his breeches, representing one for each of his acquittals until he was finally hanged. There is a pub named after him by the forest (Coppice Row, Theydon Bois CM16 7DS).

Another more recent fugitive who took refuge in the forest was Harry Roberts (born 1936), who in 1966 shot and killed two police detectives in Shepherds Bush, west London, and his accomplice killed a uniformed constable. They were resisting arrest in a stolen car. Roberts, who had been trained in the army on how to survive in the wild, spent 3½ months in the forest before being captured. He was sentenced to life imprisonment with a minimum of 30 years, which he has now exceeded by nearly 20 years, and is one of the country's longest-serving prisoners.

☛ Return to the King's Oak and go through its car park to on the right:

7 EPPING FOREST CENTRE
Paul's Nursery Rd, High Beach IG10 4AF ☎ 020 8508 0028 ◷ Wed–Sun 10.00–15.00

This has a range of maps and guidebooks about the forest, and souvenirs made from local wood. Next door to it is the Epping Forest Field Studies Centre, which caters for groups, including families, and provides outdoor education programmes.

Dogs, horses and humans mixing uneasily on one of the tracks in Epping Forest.

☛ After leaving the centre, turn right into an asphalt path between a 'Corporation of London, Epping Forest' board on the left, and a 'City of London, Epping Forest Centre' one on the right by the fence. This takes you past a pond on the left, after which you turn immediately right into a 'Horse Ride' track. When it forks turn left, down to a road. Cross over it ahead, and fork right by a small car park into another track. At the very end of this track, turn right, and it eventually goes downhill to a small winding stream at the bottom.

Turn left into the small earthen path along the right bank of the stream. Cross a small bridge over the stream, and follow the path to the right along its left bank. Ignore the first very small bridge over the stream, and cross the next one (a wooden one with a handrail and a 'Permissive Path' arrow), and left along the right bank. This takes you to an 'escape pond' used for flood control, with a grass bank around it. Take the steps up to the right, over the bank, down the other side to another road (Shaftesbury). Turn right and after a few yards turn left into Forest Road. After going over a speed bump the road has houses. Just after The Oaks pub, turn right into a small turning with a car park, to:

8 VICTORIA TAVERN

🍺 🏵 165 Smarts Lane, Loughton IG10 4BP

A recommended real ale pub which serves Adnams, Greene King and Timothy Taylor Landlord, as well as guest beers such as Old Speckled Hen. Walkers and well-behaved dogs are welcome and there is a play area for children outside, a real fire inside, and hot food served daily. The Victoria Tavern was built about 1868 as a beerhouse with extensive tea gardens and a field between Forest Road and Smarts Lane, which also housed visiting circuses and other entertainments for the thousands of visitors who came to Loughton by train for the forest. The field was sold in 1908 for housing.

One of the previous landlords, the late John Wilkes, was a bit of an eccentric who banned mobile phones, and if one went off he put it into the drink of the offender. He also had two huge St Bernard dogs in the bar, one friendly, the other not.

☛ Return to Forest Road and turn right to continue down it. After a while on the right is:

9 YE OLDE LOPPERS COTTAGE
56 Forest Rd, Loughton IG10 1EQ

A descendant of the great defender of commoners' lopping rights in the forest against enclosure, Thomas Willingale, lived here until dying recently. She was Gwendoline Gatherclowe, who was Willingale's great-great-granddaughter. Details of his campaign at the next stop.

☛ Continue along Forest Road until you come to a staggered crossroads with High Road. Go ahead into Station Road and a few yards on the right is the back entrance (with a sculptured relief of loppers) to:

10 LOPPING HALL
187 High Rd, Loughton IG10 4LF

A pilgrimage spot to pause and thank the saviour of Epping Forest as we know it: Thomas Willingale (1798–1870) led the battle in the 1860s to stop the further enclosure of the forest and protect the lopping' rights of commoners to collect firewood from trees in winter. His good deeds are commemorated by this hall, built in 1883.

The ancient rights of commoners to graze their cattle and other livestock, as well as lopping, were threatened in the 19th century by the lord of the manor, Rev. John Whitaker Maitland. The not very reverend Rev. managed to take advantage of legislation from 1851 onwards that allowed building and enclosure of woodlands and then tried to undermine the right of lopping. To protect this right the commoners had to lop one branch at midnight on 11 November each year and present it to the lord of the manor. On that night in 1860, Maitland tried to prevent this by inviting all the commoners to a supper at the King's Head pub (now Zizzi restaurant), on the corner of York Hill and Church Hill, in Loughton near here. After getting them all drunk he then locked them in before the midnight hour.

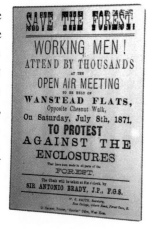

SAVE THE FOREST.

WORKING MEN!
ATTEND BY THOUSANDS
AT THE
OPEN AIR MEETING
TO BE HELD ON
WANSTEAD FLATS,
Opposite Chesnut Walk,
On Saturday, July 8th, 1871,
TO PROTEST
AGAINST THE
ENCLOSURES
That have been made in all parts of the
FOREST.
The Chair will be taken at Six o'clock, by
SIR ANTONIO BRADY, J.P., F.G.S.

But he had reckoned without Willingale, one of the commoners in the pub who had kept his senses – and his axe, which he used to break out at 11.30PM. He ran up to nearby Staples Hill and, on the stroke of midnight, lopped off a branch and returned in triumph with it to the fuming Maitland.

Maitland tried to get his revenge by prosecuting Willingale for 'injury to forest trees' but he was found not guilty. His son and two nephews were less lucky though, being jailed for similar offences at Waltham Abbey court.

When Maitland tried to enclose more land Willingale spearheaded a campaign of resistance which led to the formation of the Commons Preservation Society and successfully took legal action against Maitland. This paved the way for the Epping Forest Act of 1878 which protected it from further enclosures.

The right to lopping was finally abolished on conservation grounds, but compensation was granted and was used to build this hall – a fine legacy for Willingale. His name also lives on locally through Willingale Road and Willingale School.

Every November there is an 'Our Lopping Festival' of art, music, drama, films, crafts, talks and guided tours at Lopping Hall (www. loppinghall.org.uk).

☛ Continue down Station Road to a roundabout at the bottom, the other side of which is Loughton tube station.

DISTANCE 6 MILES
DIFFICULTY EASY
TIME 3HRS

RICKMANSWORTH TO BUSHEY

THE CANAL, THE OLD RAILWAY & THE QUAKER

WILD FLOWERS, KINGFISHERS AND A NOD TO WILLIAM PENN IN AN EXPEDITION ALONG THE GRAND UNION CANAL AND EBURY WAY.

We've carefully plotted this route to get the most scenic aspects of this green swathe near Watford. On the way you'll pass three rivers – the Chess, the Gade and the Colne – and encounter two nature reserves (Croxley Common Moor and Lairage Land). There are satisfying stretches along the towpath of the Grand Union Canal as well as the Ebury Way, which is a disused railway track that acts as a green corridor for wildlife. And there's the opportunity to visit the home of William Penn (founder of Pennsylvania) and to see a stained-glass window by the Pre-Raphaelite artist Edward Burne-Jones.

Foraging and fishing could reap some pleasing rewards. We saw a 4lb 7oz perch landed from the canal, and were told particularly large carp and chubb

DISTANCE/DIFFICULTY 6 miles. Easy.

DROP-OUT POINT After 3 miles and 4 miles

TIME 3hrs

MAP OS Explorer maps 172 and 173

START Rickmansworth tube station (Metropolitan Line) ❋ TQ057946

FINISH Bushey railway station (London Overground) ❋ TQ118953

TAKING A BREAK The Pennsylvanian, Coach & Horses, The Victoria

GETTING THERE ⊖ To Rickmansworth (Metropolitan Line)

DIRECTIONS TO START Turn immediately right out of the station, past the bus stops can be caught in the River Colne (where a massive 14lb barbel had recently been netted). Apples can be legally picked along the Ebury Way along with plentiful rosehips, blackberries and (if you pick them while they're young, and use rubber gloves to do so) good standard edible nettles. For recipes see *Food for Free* and others in *Useful publications* (page 11). For children there are plenty of horse chestnuts (conkers) in Oxhey Park.

☞ After turning right out of the station, turn right again under the railway bridge (Station Road), then left into the High Street. On the right a short distance away is:

1 THE PENNSYLVANIAN

115 High St, Rickmansworth WD3 1AN

This Wetherspoon's pub has all the usual Wetherspoon's real ales and depicts on its sign a portrait of William Penn (see below) and displays much information about him inside. Perhaps more bizarrely, an incomplete set of encyclopedias in the Norwegian language is on the shelves for drinkers' edification.

☞ Continue along the High Street to the junction with Church Street. Go ahead and turn immediately left by the library to:

2 THREE RIVERS MUSEUM (HOME OF WILLIAM PENN)

Basing House, 46 High St, Rickmansworth WD3 1RL ☎ 01923 775882/772325 🖰 trmt.org.uk ☺ Mon–Fri 14.00–16.00, Sat 10.00–16.00; closed Sun

William Penn (1644–1718), the Quaker who founded Pennsylvania, lived here from 1672 to 1677 after getting married to local resident Gulielma Springett.

It was at the age of 22 when he was in Cork that he became a Quaker and so was disowned by his family. A plaque outside the free museum describes him as a 'Quaker statesman and man of vision, founder of Pennsylvania and planner of Philadelphia, friend of the Indians, crusader for civil and religious liberty, designer of European peace.'

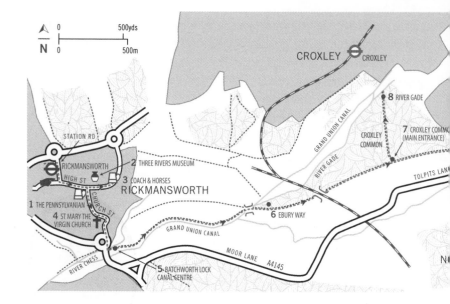

During his life in England he was jailed four times for his beliefs. He was imprisoned for heresy in 1688 after attacking the doctrine of the Holy Trinity. While incarcerated in the Tower of London he wrote a book, *No Cross, No Crown*, against organised religion and royalty. Shortly after being released he and a fellow preacher, William Meads, were charged with conspiring to cause

PENN IN AMERICA

In 1675 William Penn went with some fellow Quakers to the American colonies and settled by the Delaware river. This was land given to them by Charles II in payment of a debt to Penn's father. Penn wanted to call it just Sylvania (meaning 'wooded place') but Charles insisted on 'Penn' being added to the name. Although the king had given them the land, Penn recognised it really belonged to the native Americans, so he insisted on paying them and signing a treaty with them. Voltaire later wryly observed that this was the only treaty that was 'never sworn to and never broken'. He clearly insinuated that all the sworn ones had been broken.

Penn believed divine providence had provided them with the colony and so he had an obligation to make it into a model community. Laws were passed

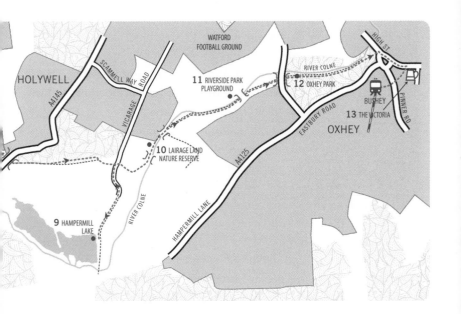

a riot. The judge directed the jury to deliver a guilty verdict and, when they refused to do so, he locked them up in Newgate Prison until they changed their minds. Then he jailed Penn and Meads. A higher court, however, ordered their release and established the precedent that juries could deliver their own verdicts without being coerced by judges.

guaranteeing freedom of conscience and religious toleration. The colony's capital, Philadelphia, was built and became known as 'the city of brotherly love'.

He returned to England for a while but fell out of favour in 1688 when William and Mary ousted James II (whom Penn had supported). Penn was accused of treason but not prosecuted. In 1699 he went back to Pennsylvania but mismanaged his finances, forcing him to sell his land, and before long he ended up in a debtors' prison. A group of supporters paid off his debts and he returned once more to England, where he suffered a stroke in 1712 which left him disabled for the rest of his life. He was buried in an unmarked grave at the Quaker cemetery in the village of Jordans, five miles west of Rickmansworth.

Penn was penned up again – once for preaching, and once for the evidently heinous crime of daring to wear a hat in court.

In a book called *Primitive Christianity Revisited* he wrote: 'True godliness doesn't turn men out of the world but enables them to live better in it, and excites their endeavours to mend it.'

You can get leaflets in the museum about famous people from the area, including William Penn and also Feargus O'Connor (1794–1855), who set up the nearby Chartist colony of O'Connorville (now called Heronsgate) in 1847 which gave farm land to workers through a lottery. Apart from providing the opportunity to work for themselves it also gave them the vote (which at this time was only given to those who owned a significant amount of property). The authorities declared the arrangement illegal and forced it to finally close in 1858. The colony is commemorated by a pub in Heronsgate village near Rickmansworth called The Land of Liberty, Peace and Plenty (🍺).

☞ After coming out of the museum, turn left, go along the High Street until you reach the junction with Wharf Lane and on the left is the:

3 COACH & HORSES
22 High St, Rickmansworth WD3 1ER

A great traditional pub with fires, food and real ale, it dates back to at least 1722 (and the building to the late 16th century). When an erstwhile owner and brewer Samuel Salter died in 1829 his will stipulated that a free cask of ale be put outside every day for passers-by and travellers. Unfortunately this attracted huge crowds of ne'er-do-wells who would guzzle it down in less than an hour and then get aggressive with each other, and so in 1857 the practice was discontinued.

☞ Retrace your steps to the junction with Church Street and turn left into it. Go past several picturesque old cottages to:

4 ST MARY THE VIRGIN CHURCH
Church St, Rickmansworth WD3 1LB

The original church was built between 1191 and 1216, then set on fire by Protestant rioters at the start of the 16th century, and rebuilt in 1826 and again in 1890. Since 1979 it has been the subject of an unusual sharing arrangement between the Church of England and the Methodists.

At the east end of the church is a magnificent stained-glass window installed in 1896. It is by Pre-Raphaelite artist Edward Burne-Jones and depicts Christ hanging from the Tree of Life.

☞ After coming out of the church, turn right and go through the churchyard, which rejoins Church Street, and takes you to a roundabout. Go straight over it to Batchworth Bridge which crosses first the River Chess, which you can see over the wall to the left (it goes north to Chesham and merges into the River Colne to the south), then the Grand Union Canal. Take the steps on the left down to the river and the canal where on the left is:

5 BATCHWORTH LOCK CANAL CENTRE
99 Church St, Rickmansworth WD3 1JD ☎ 01923 778382 🖱 www.rwt.org.uk
🕑 weekends Easter–Oct

A fascinating little place, where you can pick up plenty of information leaflets, including some relevant to this walk, especially maps of the Ebury Way and Croxley Common Moor.

☞ Cross the short bridge over the river to the canal and follow the towpath. On the left is a traditional tea stall (Café @ Lock 81) with a seating area overlooking the

Motoring up the canal near Rickmansworth.

River Chess on one side and the canal on the other. There is now a 10–15 minute walk alongside the canal where many colourful houseboats are moored. (It was in this stretch that we saw the 4lb 7oz perch caught by artist Paul Quest, who said it was the biggest he had caught in his life and it appeared just before he was about to go home.) Then you come to the first bridge, with a sign to 'Ebury Way' pointing left. Go up the steps, then turn right and cross over the bridge. You are now on:

6 EBURY WAY (DISUSED RAILWAY TRACK)

The railway track between Rickmansworth and Watford was built by Lord Ebury in 1862, and carried passengers (until 1951) and freight until it finally closed altogether in 1981. It is designated 'Ebury Trail' on the Ordnance Survey map but all the signposts declare it as 'Ebury Way'.

It is a three-mile track which is now reserved for cyclists and ramblers, lined by a variety of trees (notably ash, oak, apple and horse chestnut) and running between the River Gade (north of the track to the left) and the River Colne (south to the right). Both rivers wander away from the track and are mostly not visible from it. But you have

Ebury Way disused railway track between Rickmansworth and Watford.

a chance to see the Gade soon in Croxley Common Moor, and the Colne during the last part of the walk.

☞ Shortly after going under a railway bridge you will see on the left a nature reserve (fenced off at this stage) but after a few minutes you come to the first entrance to it (through double kissing gates), and a bit further along Ebury Way to the main entrance (signposted 'Public Footpath No 17'). This is:

7 CROXLEY COMMON MOOR NATURE RESERVE

Designated as a Site of Special Scientific Interest and periodically used by model aircraft enthusiasts to fly their machines, this is a wonderfully unspoilt hundred-acre area of grassland within the floodplain of the River Gade. It is renowned for its wild flowers, with some 130 grassland species, as well as invertebrates and some rare insects. The considerable number of anthills support plants such as large thyme and the ants themselves are food for green woodpeckers.

☞ A five-minute walk along the footpath through the moor takes you to the:

8 RIVER GADE

Kingfishers are a common sight on its bank here, and numerous fish can be seen darting between the reeds.

✋ The bridge over the river ahead is the first drop-out point, for Croxley (Metropolitan Line) tube station.

☞ Otherwise return to Ebury Way and continue along it. After about 10–15 minutes you will come to a bridge under a road (Tolpits Lane).

✋ Two minutes later is a path on the left signposted to Watford (Metropolitan Line) tube station.

☞ Otherwise continue straight ahead along Ebury Way. After a further ten minutes you will come to a crossing of paths. Left is a path to the bottom of Vicarage Road (home of Watford Football Club), and right is 'Public Footpath No 2' to Hampermill Lane, which is a detour to:

9 HAMPERMILL LAKE

This is a haven for wildlife, especially birds such as great crested grebes, pochards, shovelers, tufted ducks, Canada geese, herons and swans. It has excellent views across the wide valley. The lake is owned by Merchant Taylors' public school so there is no right of access to it, but if you have binoculars you can view the wildlife from the public path.

☛ Retrace your steps to the crossroads and continue along Ebury Way. After about two minutes, a path on the left is signposted to:

10 LAIRAGE LAND LOCAL NATURE RESERVE

Lairage means 'grazing land': these meadows and reedbeds attract abundant wildlife, including butterflies, dragonflies, green and great spotted woodpeckers, and are home to masses of yellow water lilies. The path off Ebury Way leads to a kissing gate on the right, then a bridge over a stream to the nature reserve. The River Colne and marshland prevent you from returning to Ebury Way at the far end, so after you have wandered around you will have to retrace your steps.

☛ Back on the Ebury Way you very soon cross two bridges over the river then go through:

11 RIVERSIDE PARK PLAYGROUND

This community park provides excellent facilities for all ages, including a skateboarding park, ball game areas, gardens and seating. As you

Street art at the Riverside Park skate park.

go through it you will see on the right it has been comprehensively decorated with colourful and imaginative graffiti.

☞ After crossing another small bridge over the river, turn left into a cycle and pedestrian track along its bank beside a small green. At the other end, cross over a road (Wiggenhall Road), and go ahead to the path signposted 'Public Footpath No 56 to Bushey Arches' to the bank of the River Colne on your left. You are now in:

12 OXHEY PARK

This stretch of the Colne Valley Linear Park contains kingfishers, blue tits, chaffinches, coots, woodpeckers, poplars, willows and big ducks. Unhappily burst footballs, discarded supermarket trolleys and other detritus also adorn the river. More graffiti is on display but by less gifted artists than those who have embellished the Riverside Park playground.

☞ After about five or six minutes along the bank of the River Colne you come to a path on the right (signposted to 'Bushey Station') which takes you uphill to a road (Lower High Street). Then turn right and immediately bear left (under the Bushey Arches railway viaduct) to Chalk Hill. At the first set of traffic lights on the right is:

13 THE VICTORIA

39 Chalk Hill, Bushey WD19 4BU

A fine traditional pub with three fires, three dartboards and food, plus Young's, Timothy Taylor Landlord and guest ales, plus football and local history memorabilia.

☞ After refreshing yourself, turn left out of the pub's side entrance, then right at the first set of traffic lights, and ahead to Bushey station. Go to Platform 2 to use your Freedom Pass on the London Overground to Euston (three trains an hour, 43 minutes to Euston). Faster main-line trains to Euston (about 20 minutes) stop here but the Freedom Pass is not valid on them (although you can pay a small charge to take you to the valid zone).

HOLLY, IVY, CHESTNUTS & SHARKS' TEETH

PAST A STRIKING MONASTIC RUIN IN LONDON'S FAR SOUTHEAST, THROUGH WOODLANDS AND ACROSS A HEATH PATROLLED BY BIRDS OF PREY.

If you like roast chestnuts with your Christmas feast the woodland here is the place to get them, as well as holly and ivy for the decorations. When we went in October the sweet chestnut shells were seemingly everywhere on the ground and we met more than one person gathering bagfuls of them. There were also some of the largest mushrooms and toadstools (at least a foot tall) we have ever seen. Apart from the holly and ivy there are also various berries and wild flowers and you may well spot kestrels or hear the tapping of green woodpeckers.

Lesnes Abbey's 800-year-old ruins might not rank among the likes of Fountains or Rievaulx but have a tremendous sense of history, and next door you

---

DISTANCE/DIFFICULTY 5½–6 miles. Easy except for two quite steep climbs of about 200 and 350 paces.

DROP-OUT POINT After 2½ miles and after 4 miles

TIME 2½–3hrs

MAP OS Explorer map 162

START Abbey Wood railway station ✾ TQ473790

TAKING A BREAK Ye Olde Leather Bottle, Abbey Arms

GETTING THERE 🚇 To Abbey Wood station (from Charing Cross, Waterloo East, or London Bridge, 30–35mins; 2 an hour)

DIRECTIONS TO START Cross over the bridge (from London direction) and go straight out of the exit (past the Abbey Arms on your right)

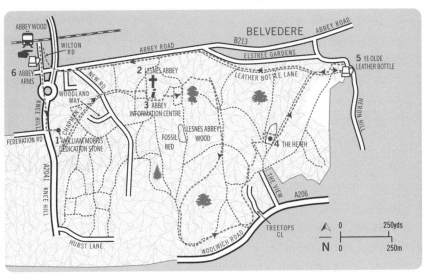

can go further back in time and peruse an eye-opening array of fossils, including sharks' teeth, from the time when this area was the sea bed.

After the walk, you might like to pay a visit to William Morris's extraordinary Red House (National Trust, check opening times on 🖱 www.nationaltrust.org.uk) three miles away in Bexleyheath. Take the B11 bus in Abbey Wood Road near the station in the direction of Bexleyheath for an 18-minute journey to the Upton Road/Broadway stop – it's then a five to ten-minute walk using an A–Z or a satnav to the property on Red House Lane (DA6 8JF). Morris's memorial features near the start of this walk.

👉 After passing the Abbey Arms by the station, continue uphill along Wilton Road (you will see the woods ahead of you). The road will become Knee Hill. Keep going straight, over a roundabout (still on Knee Hill) then, when you see Federation Road on the right, turn left into a grass footpath. Then immediately bear right going uphill between trees in the same direction as the road. After a few yards you will see on the right:

1 WILLIAM MORRIS DEDICATION STONE

The socialist poet, designer and craftsman William Morris (1834–96) passed this spot regularly in the 1860s when walking between Abbey Wood station and his home in Bexleyheath about three miles away. This was Red House in Red House Lane, which he created and designed in 1859, then lived in for five years when it was completed in 1860. Pre-Raphaelite Brotherhood artist Edward Burne-Jones described it as 'the beautifullest place on earth'. It contains many of Morris's earliest designs, furniture and decorative schemes, plus wall paintings and a stained-glass window by Burne-Jones. The garden was also designed to 'clothe the house'.

It includes a herb garden, vegetable garden, two flower beds and various fruit trees including apple, pear and cherry.

Morris resided there with his new wife, Jane Burden (one of Rossetti's models), until 1865 when he was forced to sell it for financial reasons. While living here their two daughters, Jenny and May, were born.

He loved entertaining friends at the Red House, and would pick them up in a wagon from Abbey Wood station and take them through 'the rose-hung lanes of woody Kent'. The wagon was designed by his friend Philip Webb (who also helped design the house), based on a traditional market cart.

His friend and dissolute poet Algernon Swinburne lived in Red House along with a groom, housemaid, cook and nurse. The house and garden are now owned by the National Trust.

More details of Morris can be found on the *River Wandle* and *Literary London* walks (see pages 118 and 213).

☞ Continue up the path (where we found the huge mushrooms on the right), to the top, then left into a wide tree-lined track going downhill. After about five minutes along this track you will come to a lane (New Road) which you cross over and take the footpath ahead (just to the right of Monks Close, signposted to 'Lesnes Abbey'). After a few yards you will come to:

2 LESNES ABBEY RUINS

This was founded in 1178 as an act of penance by one of those who murdered Thomas Becket (then the Archbishop of Canterbury, now the patron saint of brewers) at Canterbury Cathedral in 1170. This was Richard de Luci (1089–1179), Chief Justiciar (a judiciary officer) of Henry II when he came to the throne in 1154, who controlled the country during the king's absences. Born in Normandy (where the king had to crush a rebellion) Luci was Sheriff of Essex, and owned Chipping Ongar where he built Ongar Castle. He helped change the constitution, against the will of Becket, so that clerics convicted of felony in ecclesiastical courts could be punished by the secular authorities rather than by the church. Becket excommunicated Luci twice as a result (in 1166 and 1169), and when he refused to lift it the second time he was stabbed to death with swords. It was Luci's regret at his involvement in this that led to him founding the abbey. He became its canon, then died in the following year and was buried in its grounds.

During the dissolution of the monasteries over 300 years later, in the reign of Henry VIII, it was pulled down by Cardinal Wolsey around 1525. Sixteen years later it was bought by Henry Cooke who built a mansion on the grounds, which was finally demolished in 1845. London County Council bought it in 1930 and Bexley Council took it over in 1986.

☞ Next to the abbey ruins is:

3 ABBEY INFORMATION CENTRE

As well as plenty of background information on the abbey itself, it's well worth looking in here to peruse relics from the nearby Fossil Bed from about 54½ million years ago during the Eocene epoch when this area was under the sea. They include sharks' teeth, seashells, fish and a pony-like mammal. You can visit the fossil bed but must not remove more than two kilograms of material nor dig more than two feet down. Large groups should first get permission from Bexley Council (🖱 www.bexley.gov.uk).

A rather sad notice proclaims: 'As a result of theft all lead has been removed from the roof' (leaving us to wonder whether it had been removed by the thieves or the authorities).

In the surrounding grounds are an ancient burial site, an ornamental garden and a wildflower enclosure (picking of bluebells and wild flowers at this historic site is strictly prohibited).

☞ After going through the abbey's remains, continue straight over, bearing slightly left (uphill), past picnic tables with a view (to the left) over the Thames towards Dagenham and its wind turbines. Follow the path as it bends to the right and you will pick up the 'Green Chain Walk' signs ahead. Follow the main path (not taking the Green Chain Walk when it branches off), which goes up and down with moderate climbs of up to 200 paces.

Eventually you go through a tunnel of holly trees and past the back gardens of houses on the right, then past a heavily fenced private area guarded by a particularly noisy rottweiler dog, and round to the left to a metal gate on the right and into a main road (with a signpost to 'Belvedere Sports & Social Club'). This is Woolwich Road, a few yards from Treetops Close to the left.

✋ You can get the 99 bus on the same side of the road to Erith, or on the other side to Plumstead.

☞ Otherwise follow the path round to the left through the woods (with back gardens on your right). Ignore steps uphill to the right and continue downhill bending to the left. At the bottom of a small valley you will reach a junction of paths where you turn right. After a while you will see a fenced-off area on the left.

At the next fork go straight ahead (bearing right). Eventually you reach a crossing of paths, signposted 'Green Chain Walk' with 'Lesnes Abbey ¼ mile' to the left, and the 'Leather Bottle pub ¾ mile' to the right: take the right turn, up the hill, stepped in parts, steepish for about 350 paces. Keep following the 'Green Chain Walk' signs at the top. Here you enter:

4 THE HEATH

This was common grazing land for ponies, cattle and sheep for many centuries, between the marshes of Woolwich, Erith and Bexley. In those days, heather turfs were cut for fuel, fodder and livestock bedding. It is this open heath which is now a favourite spot for birds of prey.

☞ Keep following the 'Green Chain Walk' signs (you will soon see houses ahead where you will turn right and keep following the signs until you reach a public road). This road is Kingswood Avenue, where you turn right and after a few yards you come to a crossroads with St Augustine's Road to the left downhill, and Heron Hill to the right uphill. Turn right and a few yards on the right is:

5 YE OLDE LEATHER BOTTLE

131 Heron Hill, Belvedere DA17 5HJ

Built as a farmhouse in 1643, this is a good community pub which allows children and dogs, and has a pool table and dartboard. Hot food is served every day 12.00–18.00. It does not serve real ales but has bottled Old Speckled Hen.

It was first licensed as the Bottle in 1740, and became the Leather Bottle in 1803 ('Ye Olde' being more recent).

You can skip the last part of the walk by going down St Augustine's Road to Abbey Road where there are buses (229 and 469) back to Abbey Wood railway station (four or five stops).

To continue the walk turn left out of the side of the pub, following the footpath signed 'Footpath 11', right after a short distance, then immediately first left, to a path round the edge of the woods (which is 'Leather Bottle Lane' on the map but not signposted). This takes you to Abbey Road by Lesnes Abbey Wood Recreation Ground (by which time a sign shows it has become 'Byway 7'). Here you can turn left through a kissing gate back into the wood and follow the line of Abbey Road back to Knee Hill at the roundabout to Abbey Wood station.

Opposite the station is the:

6 ABBEY ARMS

31 Wilton Rd, Abbey Wood SE2 9RH

A down-to-earth pub with cheap beer, a pool table, a jukebox, live sports on television and a beer garden with play facilities for children. The staff and customers are friendly, but some of the notices are not. One sign forbids glasses being taken into the toilet. Another had been amended from 'illegal' to 'legal' by customers so that it read on our first visit: 'Anyone caught taking legal substances will be barred instant.' On our return '(il)legal substances' had been changed to 'drugs' and 'instant' replaced by 'and the police informed'. An additional sign now warns: 'Anyone caught smoking on these premises will be barred.' You might expect the next sign to pop up to be a warning against people defacing the pub's warning notices.

A RACING CERTAINTY

VARIATIONS ON AN EQUESTRIAN THEME, WITH A WANDER PAST
THE DERBY COURSE AND A CHANCE TO GO RIDING TOO.

Pretty much everything on this walk is related to the art of racing and training horses. You'll see the historic course where the famous Derby has been run since 1780, and – even if there's no race in progress – racehorses can be seen training from early morning to noon on any of the three sand gallops laid out on the side of the downs. They make a spectacular sight. And you get a decent view of the racecourse from the featured pub. The whole area is public but there are always council employees to ensure that dogs are kept under control and to make sure people don't wander along the gallops rather than just crossing them. The scenery opens up to magnificent views of the rolling countryside, which is made full use of by leisure riders and dog walkers. For the really keen, arriving by car and with plenty of plastic sheeting to protect the inside of their vehicles, thoroughbred horse manure is available free for gardeners from riding stables, though even the most intrepid Freedom Passer is unlikely to be able to make use of such a tempting offer.

DISTANCE/DIFFICULTY 6 miles. Easy–moderate.

TIME 3hrs

MAP OS Explorer map 146

START Epsom Downs station ✳ TQ228598

TAKING A BREAK Tattenham Corner

GETTING THERE 🚌 To Epsom Downs station from London Victoria (47–55mins; 2 an hour, none on Sun)

DIRECTIONS TO START Turn right out of station into Bunbury Way

---

Continue along Bunbury Way, which is quite a long cul-de-sac with a couple of mini-roundabouts, for about six or seven minutes. At the end is Langdale Lane South where you cross to the other side and turn left into a public bridleway (signposted with blue arrows) round the edge of a golf course. When you come to a road (Heath Road) cross it and continue following the bridleway round the golf course, to another road (Grandstand Road) on your left. You will see the Epsom Racecourse Grand Stand ahead. When you reach a roundabout there is a pub on the right called the Derby Arms (established 1875).

Directly opposite is:

1 EPSOM DOWNS RACECOURSE

KT18 5LQ

Turn right in the forecourt and on the right is a statue of Generous, the winner of the 1991 Derby. It was unveiled by the Queen in 1995. A bit further along on the right is a plaque marking the spot where Lord Kitchener reviewed 20,000 soldiers of the 2nd London Division on 22 January 1915.

A few yards further ahead is a gate adorned with Lester Piggott pictures and information boards. This famous jockey (born in 1935) rode a record nine Derby winners in his long career from 1948 to 1995. Five of them are pictured here: Nijinsky, Roberto, Empery, The Minstrel and Teenosa. In his remarkable career he rode 4,493 winners on the flat (among them a record 30 Classics) and 20 over jumps in this country, as well as 1,200 in 26 other countries.

A dog walker we met on the course told us that at one Derby a naked man streaked on to the track in full view of the television cameras. He then fled to the surrounding countryside, hotly pursued by the police. 'He was finally caught by the Cock at Headley' (a nearby pub), chuckled our informant.

☞ You may open the gate with the Lester Piggott pictures and information as it is a right of way. Go through it and follow the path round the track to the front of the Rubbing House pub, and turn left into the downs by a noticeboard proclaiming 'Welcome to Epsom and Walton Downs' and warning you that racehorses train there (06.15–12.00 Mon–Sat and 08.00–09.30 Sun), and it is dangerous to get too close to them.

Ramblers beware!

When the path forks go to the right for a short gradual climb which takes you over the race track and another warning notice about racehorses travelling at speed in the mornings.

Follow the path down the other side, over two more gallops and a track, into Walton Downs ahead. Keep going ahead over another gallop to white railings over the track and the far edge of the Downs. Follow the track ahead which goes slightly uphill for a long way through fields and hedgerows, and widens into a lane (Ebbisham Lane). This takes you eventually past Downsview Farm and then Wingfield Farm, both on the right, and then on the left:

2 WILDWOODS RIDING CENTRE

Ebbisham Lane, Walton-on-the-Hill, Tadworth KT20 5BH ☎ 01737 812146
🖱 www.wildwoodsriding.co.uk

'Picnic rides' are a speciality of this centre, where novices can go for a horse ride on the Epsom Downs at 11.00, stop off for lunch, and then ride back again at 15.00. Anthea, who runs it, started at the age of 12, working at Ewell Riding Stables in return for rides. She also worked at other jobs to save enough to buy her first pony at the age of 14, which was stabled in her back garden. She started the school here at 17, now has over 25 horses and ponies, and gives riding lessons at all levels. Her mother has written a book about the centre, *Legs, Legs, Legs,* under the name Justine Dowley-Wise.

☞ Continue along the lane a few yards and on the left is a place where gardeners can pick up free horse manure already bagged up.

Turn right opposite here through a gap in the hedge and over a stile with a yellow-arrowed 'Public Footpath' sign. This takes you through a paddock, and over another stile to the left, into a public bridleway where you turn right and go downhill. This goes between more paddocks, trees and hedgerows, and becomes a chalk path with rosehips, old man's beard and deadly nightshade bushes either side. Hazelnuts and crab apples can also be found in season. The bridleway continues downhill through arable fields, thickets, holly bushes and woods, until there is a cottage at the bottom on the left. A few yards further along, on the right, you are back on the downs. Turn right and follow the edge by the gallops for a mile or so, bearing left. This takes you to Epsom Lane North on the right, which leads into Tattenham Corner Road. Here on the right by a roundabout is the:

3 TATTENHAM CORNER
Epsom Downs KT18 5NY

The pub is part of the Beefeater chain, where dogs are not allowed but children (and grandchildren) are welcome (as long as they don't play ball games). It serves real ales such as Fuller's London Pride and Hobgoblin, and is quite a large modern comfortable pub overlooking the race track.

☞ After coming out of the pub, turn left and take the first left (apart from a private road), and a little way on the right is the Tattenham Corner railway station (where you can get trains to East Croydon and London Bridge).

11	DISTANCE 6 MILES DIFFICULTY EASY TIME 2½–3HRS	NORTH DOWNS: COULSDON COMMON, CIRCULAR

HAPPY VALLEY

VINTAGE SURREY DOWNLAND, WITH A VISIT TO A SAXON CHURCH WITH AN ASTONISHINGLY SPOOKY MEDIEVAL WALL PAINTING.

You couldn't be much closer to Croydon, but this walk on the North Downs is remarkably rural in character, and was a favourite stamping ground of the novelist D H Lawrence. Happy Valley is indeed a feel-good patch of land, comprising downland and ancient woodland acquired by the local authority under the Green Belt Scheme back in 1937, and evidently saved from the developer's bulldozer in the nick of time when so much of London's fringes had succumbed to suburbanisation. When it snows, it's a veritably happy valley for children as the steep grass slopes become ideal toboggan runs. Farthing Down, owned by the Corporation of London, adjoins it and has many of the same qualities. Despite both areas' municipal ownership, they are very much managed as open countryside.

DISTANCE/DIFFICULTY 6 miles. Easy except for two steep climbs of short duration.

DROP-OUT POINT After 3½ miles

TIME 2½–3hrs

MAP OS Explorer map 146

START Coulsdon South station ✵ TQ299591

FINISH Coulsdon Town station ✵ TQ301597 (if visiting The Pembroke; otherwise finish at Coulsdon South station)

TAKING A BREAK The Fox, The Pembroke

GETTING THERE 🚆 To Coulsdon South station from London Bridge (24–27mins; 4 an hour, daily) direct, or London Victoria changing at East Croydon (33–37mins; 4 an hour, 2 an hour on Sun)

DIRECTIONS TO START Take Farthing Downs exit from Platform 2 of the station

Two historical goodies come in the form of an exceptional Saxon church with a remarkable wall painting, and a 300-year-old pub.

☛ Turn left from the 'Farthing Downs' exit into Reddown Road. When you reach the end turn right (Marlpit Lane) and immediately right into Downs Road. After a few yards bear left off the road and into:

1 FARTHING DOWNS

Stone Age hunters, Iron Age farmers and Saxon warriors all roamed this area. There are low banks where fields were ploughed 2,000 years ago, and circular mounds of 7th-century Saxon graves.

Novelist D H Lawrence and his friend Helen Corke also rambled on these downs in 1911 when they were both teachers in Croydon. She likened the downs to 'the smooth, rounded back of a huge animal' which they walked along 'in mutual isolation from humankind.'

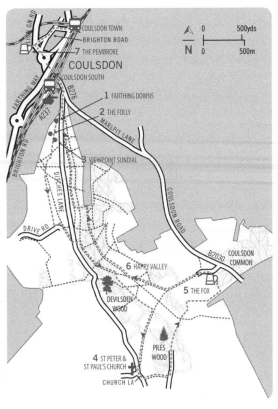

There is an ancient notice warning of a £5 penalty for assaulting constables or keepers, or resisting them, or inciting others to do the same. A ranger told us not everybody respected local warning signs. A couple of kids, he said, removed a 'Road Closed' sign to use as a sledge, which led to a car ploughing ahead and ending up in a roadside ditch where it was abandoned. We later saw a 'Sledges for sale' sign.

Sussex cattle graze with sheep all year round to enable wildlife to flourish on the chalk downland and keep invasive scrub at bay; dogs must be kept under control and on certain bridleways walkers are asked to give way to horseriders. There's also a burgeoning deer population, which has trebled in recent years.

The chalk grassland supports a wide range of plants (including pyramidal orchids and dropwort), insects (including half of all English butterfly species, and ants which make nests up to three feet tall), birds, lizards and slow worms; an information board gives the details.

During World War II, anti-glider ditches were dug over it to prevent enemy invaders landing by glider.

☛ Take the footpath which forks left going slightly uphill. When you reach the top of the hill you will see seven trees in a circle. This is:

2 THE FOLLY

This is a circle of seven beech trees marking the highest point on the Farthing Downs (600 feet above sea level). Nowadays there is one large tree, three medium-sized ones, two saplings and a stump. The original ones were planted either by Thomas Harley (later Lord Mayor of London) in 1760 of which only one remains, or by Edward Bangham MP in 1783 of which only two remain (one being just the stump after being killed by lightning). The Corporation of London has made up the number to seven again with new trees, in the middle of which a signpost points to Coulsdon to the north, Purley to the east, Hooley to the west and Chaldon to the south.

☛ Just past The Folly a few yards to the left of the footpath is a:

3 VIEWPOINT SUNDIAL

This shows you that the church in Chaldon is is 2.53km ahead, Happy Valley is 0.79km to the left and The Folly is all of 0.04km behind you. It also identifies other places you can see.

☛ Continue along the footpath until you reach Farthing Downs Cottages. Turn left in front of the cottages, and then right where the path is signposted

Sundial-style viewpoint stone on Farthing Down.

'Public Footpath 71, Devilsden Wood/Happy Valley' and also 'Downlands Circular Walk' and 'London Loop'. Later bear left to Happy Valley, then follow the 'Permissive Path, Chaldon Church, 1 mile' bearing right round the edge of fields by woods, through a gap to the right into the woods, and left to 'Public Footpath, Chaldon Church, 1 mile', into fields, then right into woods again at the 'Public Footpath, Chaldon Church ½ mile' sign. This takes you through fields into a lane. Turn left and after a few yards bear right to:

4 ST PETER & ST PAUL'S CHURCH
Church Lane, Chaldon CR3 5AL

The Saxon foundation of this restored church was recorded as being there in AD727, and the present building was started in the late 10th or early 11th century. The remarkable feature here is the stupendous wall painting, dating from about 1200 on the west wall, and surely guaranteed to put the holy wind up the medieval congregation; there is nothing else like it in England. It depicts the 'Ladder of Salvation of the Human Soul' with 'Purgatory and Hell' and was painted by a travelling artist monk. Sinners being punished include a blacksmith making a horseshoe without an anvil, a mason without a chisel,

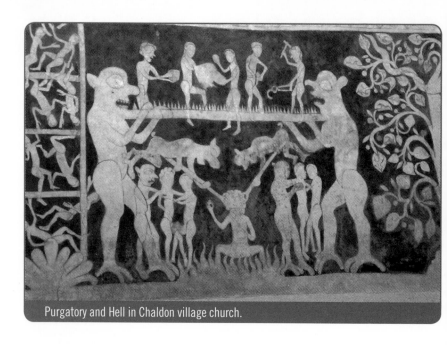
Purgatory and Hell in Chaldon village church.

a potter without a wheel and a usurer held by pitchforks in flames by demons. Other demons are encouraging a couple to surrender to lust. But there are also gates for the righteous to enter.

The pulpit of 1657 is one of the few surviving ones from the time of Cromwell. Lt Col William Edward Shaw, who served in the Indian Mutiny of 1857 and died in 1900 was a churchwarden here, are commemorated by a brass plaque on the west wall. Two sons of the rector were killed at the Battle of the Dardanelles in August 1915, Capt. Austin Belcher and Lt Humphrey Belcher, are commemorated with a plaque on the north wall (altogether 23 locals were killed in the two world wars).

The closed circuit television seems incongruous in such an ancient church, but increased security proved necessary after a 750-year-old bell was stolen in 1970 for scrap metal. A plaster cast of it is in the south aisle.

Turn left out of the church back to the lane, then turn right and immediately turn left into the public footpath signposted to 'Piles Wood'. This takes you through a field and soon between woods on the left bordered by a long and high holly hedge and horses on the right. Follow this when it goes left into a track between gardens on the right and woods on the left. Follow it ahead into woods, signposted 'Public Bridleway, Happy Valley'. At the next fork bear right, following a 'Downland Circular Walk' arrow. At a crossing of paths continue ahead following the public bridleway signposted 'Coulsdon Common ¼ mile'. This takes you up a steepish hill for a short climb and emerges into a lane. Go through a kissing gate a few yards on the left by a 'Coulsdon Common' noticeboard. Take the grass track which forks to the left, then after a short distance go through a kissing gate on the right. This takes you to a village green. Turn left and on the left is:

5 THE FOX

Coulsdon Common CR3 5QS

This pub dates back to 1720 and has a log fire for winter and a beer garden for the summer (or for frozen smokers). It has hot meals and real ales include Fuller's London Pride and Young's, plus guests including Charles Wells DNA and Sharp's Doom Bar. Dogs (on a lead) and children are allowed, and there is an old anvil outside to which to tie them (the dogs, not the children).

A plaque on the pub wall reveals this was the site of the Joint Services for Linguistics listening post for covert national security work from 1952 to 1954 during the cold war. The plaque was erected in 2007 by the Royal Air Force Linguists' Association and states the linguists at Coulsdon Common Camp were 'trained for covert work, their vigilance contributing to national Security during the Cold War'.

If you want to finish the walk here, turn right out of the pub and cross the village green to a bus stop for the 404 to Coulsdon South station (18-minute journey; hourly) or the 466 to Purley Oaks station (20-minute journey; 4 an hour) or East Croydon station (35-minute journey; 4 an hour).

To continue the walk turn left out of the pub to the public footpath signposted 'Farthing Downs' as well as 'London Loop' and 'Happy Valley' taking you naturally to:

6 HAPPY VALLEY

This ancient woodland and downland grass area is designated a Site of Special Scientific Interest and is run by Croydon Council.

A notice tells us that coppicing of the trees since 2001 has helped to dramatically increase the number of butterflies (and led to the return of the silver-washed fritillary), and to preserve dormice which are now rare and a protected species. The coppicing allows light to the woodland floor which helps bluebells and other plants to flourish, creating glades for butterflies and other insects and an ideal habitat for birds and small mammals. This takes place on a 15-year-rotation basis. After the cutting, temporary fencing is erected to deter deer from eating the hazel as it grows.

Follow the path which becomes arrowed 'Downland Circular Walk' again. The path comes out into open fields with a sign 'Public Footpath, Farthing Downs ¾ mile'. A bit further on is a public footpath sign 'Drive Road ½ mile'. Go down the hill (very popular with sledges and toboggans in the snow). At the bottom, fork right along the flat. At a crossing of paths follow the path ahead signposted 'Chaldon Way 260 yards' and through a kissing gate. Just before you reach the houses ahead, turn left up the hill, which is steep for a short distance,

View from the top of Farthing Down.

through another kissing gate, through woods a few yards to another gate on the right which takes you back into Farthing Downs. Follow the footpath ahead uphill.

Near the top of the hill turn right along a bridleway just before the narrow road which runs parallel with it. The bridleway becomes marked with red arrows for the 'Happy Valley & Farthing Downs Nature Trail' and the green arrows of 'Corporation of London Permissive Ride'.

This takes you through a gate and back to Downs Road. You can turn into Reddown Road then turn right, back to Coulsdon South station.

If you want refreshment and are willing to walk another 700 paces to a real ale pub then continue along the main road (Marlpit Lane) ahead, go under two railway bridges and a flyover to a roundabout. Take the footpath to the right of the roundabout and follow it to traffic lights where you fork right (Lion Green Road). When you reach a mini-roundabout turn left into Chipstead Valley Road where on the other side is:

7 THE PEMBROKE
12 Chipstead Valley Rd, Coulsdon CR5 2RA

A large modern Smith & Jones pub which provides hot meals and snacks up to 22.00 and allows children. A wide range of real ales include Greene King and Fuller's London Pride and guests including Old Speckled Hen, Abbot and Sharp's Doom Bar.

☛ Turn left out of the pub, and about 200 yards on the right is Coulsdon Town station (still shown on some maps by its previous name of Smitham). Here trains take 30 minutes to London Bridge (3 an hour, 2 on Sundays) and 33–40 minutes to Victoria (2 an hour every day).

TILBURY'S SEAL OF APPROVAL

EXPANSIVE SKIES ABOVE THE ESTUARY-SIDE PATH,
BETWEEN TWO FORTS.

With the salty whiff of the Thames estuary to accompany you, this is a breezy, cobwebs-blowing walk along the river, and beside the Essex marshes – a desolate landscape reminiscent of Pip's first encounter with the convict in *Great Expectations*. This is certainly a walk for those seeking solitude, passing as it does a derelict power station and with views of shipping across to the Kent side. Seals make regular appearances in the water – a survey by the Zoological Society of London recently recorded over 700 grey and harbour seal sightings hereabouts. At either end are the two imposing forts, presented in very different style: Tilbury Fort, admirably maintained by English Heritage,

DISTANCE/DIFFICULTY 3½ miles. Easy.

TIME 1½hrs

MAP OS Explorer maps 162 and 163

START Tilbury Riverside Terminal ✵ TQ645751

FINISH The Ship, East Tilbury ✵ TQ684776

TAKING A BREAK World's End, The Ship

GETTING THERE 🚆 To Dartford station from Charing Cross (43–49mins; 8 an hour, daily)

DIRECTIONS TO START From Dartford station take any bus to Gravesend. 🚌 480, 490 (34mins, 6 an hour). Then Gravesend River Ferry to Tilbury Riverside Terminal (15mins, 2 an hour; Freedom Pass not accepted £ 🪙).

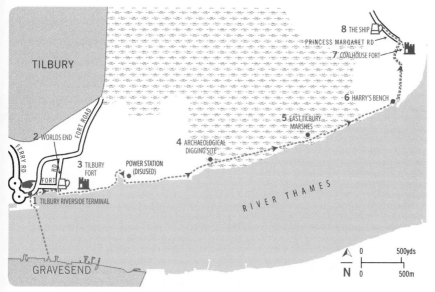

is a fascinating journey back through time, in a building that began in Henry VIII's day and played a role in both world wars. In contrast, Coalhouse Fort opens just one Sunday a month, and is a volunteer-run labour of love, well worth catching if you can.

There will likely be birdwatchers and anglers to chat to; one fisherman we spoke to had caught three cod here on the same day, and another a bass weighing 6lbs, both at low tide; their previous catches included whiting, eels, plaice and halibut.

1 TILBURY RIVERSIDE TERMINAL

Nearly 500 West Indian immigrants landed here on 22 June 1948 from the ship *Empire Windrush*. This historic occasion was illustrated by now-famous photographs of them coming down the gangplank and is now commemorated at the terminal by a plaque, yet at the time there was some hostility to their arrival. The ship had been on its way from Australia to England when it docked in Kingston, Jamaica, to pick up several locals who had fought in the RAF during the war and were returning from leave. Cy Grant was such a person who had been a prisoner of war in Germany and was a fully qualified lawyer but had to perform as a calypso player to earn a living in London. An advert offered a fare of £46 to those who wanted to work in England and many others took up the offer, including calypso star Lord Kitchener. They were put up in a shelter at Clapham, near Brixton employment exchange, where many sought work and settled. A square was renamed Windrush Square in Brixton to mark the 50th anniversary in 1998.

☞ Turn right out of the ferry terminal, then climb up some steps to the right, over the river wall, and follow the riverbank a short distance to:

2 THE WORLDS END

Fort Rd, Tilbury RM18 7NR

A historic timbered pub in the style of a ship's hold with a real fire, where Samuel Pepys (1633–1703) stayed in 1666 and wrote about it in his famous diary. He was on his way to Holland to help bring Charles II back to England and restore the monarchy. His diary covering this period shows he enjoyed many sexual encounters in pubs, often with the barmaids. Charles II did not reward his loyalty and Pepys was locked up in the Tower for a year for treason and piracy before the charges were dropped.

In 1667, the year after his stay here, the Dutch raided the Thames and the Medway, and towed away the *Royal Charles* ship and destroyed

The Worlds End pub featured in Samuel Pepys's diary.

three others. They reached Lower Hope Point at East Tilbury, a couple of miles from here. Ultimately the Dutch, William III (of Orange) and his wife Mary did successfully invade and take the throne (uniquely jointly) under the pretext of ousting the Catholic king, James II. William then formed the Bank of England to finance more wars.

There is much memorabilia about Pepys in the pub, which provides both snacks and hot meals. Its real ales are Abbot, Greene King IPA and guests, which can be enjoyed in the bar or the beer garden.

☛ Behind the pub, a few yards further along the river, is:

3 TILBURY FORT

RM18 7NR ☎ 08703 331181 📱 www.english-heritage.org.uk

🕙 Apr–Oct Wed–Sun, Nov–Mar weekends only; for times for see website £ 🪙

Henry VIII built a blockhouse (known originally as Thermitage Bullwark) here with a rampart and ditches in 1539 to defend against a French invasion.

The fort was rebuilt and strengthened with new ditches and ramparts from 1670 to 1685 by workers from Essex and Kent. From around 1716 it was used to store and supply gunpowder, with a special wharf being constructed for that purpose; by 1830 it could store over 19,000 barrels of gunpowder.

After the defeat of Bonnie Prince Charlie at Culloden in 1746 over 300 Jacobite prisoners were rounded up and shipped here from Inverness. But 57 died *en route* from starvation and disease and within a month of arrival another 45 died of typhus. The survivors were tried in London in 1747. Some were executed, but most were transported to Barbados and Antigua as slave labour on sugar plantations. A memorial stone to their suffering is in the river wall outside the Water Gate.

As battleships took over the role of defending the estuary early in the 20th century, the fort became a barracks for soldiers on their way to the front in World War I. It was also used for storing explosives and ammunition.

TILBURY FORT & THE ARMADA

On 9 August 1588 Elizabeth I made what is perhaps her most quoted speech at Tilbury Fort against the Spanish to her 'Citizen Militia' makeshift English army. Wearing a breastplate and sword she told the troops that she was 'resolved, in the midst and heat of the battle, to live or die amongst you all; to lay down, for my God and for my kingdom, and for my people, my honour and my blood, even the dust. I know I have but the body of a weak and feeble women; but I have the heart and stomach of a king, and of a king of England too; and think foul scorn that Parma or Spain, or any prince of Europe, should dare to invade the borders of my realms: to which, rather than any dishonour should grow by me, I myself will take up arms.' A few days later news reached Tilbury that the Armada had been beaten and was retreating in flight. Then the army disbanded on 17 August.

When air raids by German Zeppelins started in 1915 the fort was equipped with anti-aircraft guns and searchlights, and it became known as 'Screaming Lizzie'.

During World War II the building became an anti-aircraft operations room, directing fire from guns along the river against German bombing raids, but some of the barracks still suffered from bombing. To prevent enemy troops being dropped, a series of trenches were dug in the surrounding marshland.

The army kept it until 1950 when the Ministry of Works took it over as a historic monument. Major restoration work was carried out in the 1970s. It was opened to the public in 1982 and is now cared for by English Heritage.

☛ As you leave the fort continue following the riverbank, which is often crowded with anglers. After passing horses grazing by the moat of the fort you will come to the wall around Tilbury Power Station. This is labelled as 'Footpath 146', which you follow to the right around the wall by the river, past blackberry bushes, teasel thistles and rosehip bushes. You can find much strikingly artistic shaped driftwood of varying shapes washed up on the shore or in the mud. There are plenty of accessible beaches, as well as a jetty for delivering coal (where we saw a heron). At the end of the wall on the left is an:

4 ARCHAEOLOGICAL DIGGING SITE

It may not look anything more than a load of rubbish: but look carefully and you never know what might pop up hereabouts. Among the detritus of plastic bottles and modern junk on the riverbank, someone once unearthed an extremely rare Victorian glass bottle at this very spot. It sold for a whopping £3,000.

☛ Continue past more beaches and keep to the river, ignoring any tracks off to the left (especially where there are warnings of quicksand). On the left, fenced off, are:

5 EAST TILBURY MARSHES

These are a favourite place for migrant wading birds, hawks, kestrels and other birdlife as well as hosts of rabbits.

☛ As you continue along the riverside, the fence around the marshes gives way to farmland and more rabbits. Soon you will come to a 'Footpath 146' sign and a Thurrock Council warning: 'We advise people not to climb on any structure beyond the high tide mark as you risk being stranded when the tide comes in.' Beside it is:

Crows perch on a derelict wharf beside the Tilbury Marshes.

A poignant collection of treasures at Harry's Bench.

6 HARRY'S BENCH

'In memory of a very special boy, 28.02.1997 to 29.08.2003', this bench bears a picture of him and is surrounded by toys, statues and a school tie. There is a 'Special Brother' plaque dedicated to him which reads: 'Brother, thank you for being my friend, for giving me memories to treasure until the end. Dear brother, rest in peace.' This is a good place to imagine him and have a picnic in his memory before leaving the river.

☛ Follow the tarmac path away from the river, which leads a short distance to:

7 COALHOUSE FORT

Princess Margaret Rd, East Tilbury RM18 8PB 🖱 www.coalhousefort.co.uk
🕑 Last Sun of the month, Mar–Sep 11.00–17.00 and most bank holiday Mon.
Plus paranormal investigations most Sat nights £ 🪙

A blockhouse was built by Henry VIII on this site in 1540 against a feared invasion by 'Catholic powers'. In 1792 a gun battery was built during the war with France. The existing fort was built between 1861 and 1874 to protect the country against a potential invasion from French warships and housed up to 200 soldiers with barracks, kitchens, a hospital and a forge. A new battery was built in 1893 and gunfire could break windows half a mile away. It was used again during both world wars. In the last war its occupants laid minefields, fired anti-aircraft guns and detected enemy ships from its radar tower. It closed in 1956, but since 1983 has been open to the public and is run entirely by volunteers.

It has two play areas for children and there are several picnic tables around the fort overlooking the moat and the river. This is also a Site of Special Scientific Interest with grasslands and reedbeds, visited by wildfowl in winter, wading birds and rare water voles.

☛ Follow the road (Princess Margaret Road) past the Norman church of St Catherine's (which has red-hot poker plants in front of it) and after a few minutes on the left is:

8 THE SHIP
Princess Margaret Rd, East Tilbury RM18 8PB

A picturesque free house which serves a series of guest ales including Fuller's London Pride, Eagles IPA and Bombardier, and has a dartboard in the public bar. It serves bar snacks as well as hot meals and has a beer garden, a decked terrace and a play area. Signs warn against leaving your horse in the car park or entering the lounge bar in boots or working clothes, but once you're inside the staff are most friendly.

☛ The 374 bus stops outside the pub every hour for a 25-minute journey to Grays rail and bus station. From there you can pay for two stops on the train to Rainham (where your Freedom Pass will take you the rest of the way) or a little more for one stop to Tilbury (where you can go back the way you came). To get back to London all the way on your Freedom Pass you will have to take any bus (routes 22, 44, 66, 73, 83, 100, 201 or 265) from Grays station to Lakeside, and then the 372 to Rainham railway station (20 minute journey; 3 an hour, 2 an hour on Sun). From Rainham your Freedom Pass is valid.

> ## UPDATES WEBSITE
> Why not post your comments and recommendations, and read the latest feedback and updates from other readers online at 🖱 www.bradtupdates.com/freedompass?

WANDERING ALONG THE WANDLE

A THROWBACK TO THE TIME OF COUNTRY ESTATES, WATERMILLS AND WILLIAM MORRIS ON A RIVER EXPLORATION.

Nowadays the Wandle makes a distinctly leisurely nine-mile journey through southwest suburbs from Croydon to the Thames at Wandsworth, but a century or so ago its current was once much stronger, enough to power 68 water wheels. You'll see evidence of these at Merton Abbey Mills, now a market, and within Morden Hall Park, one of two striking former country estates on the route. Yet again, London reveals its villagey side, particularly at the gorgeous scene around Carshalton Pond and in the form of the abundant wildlife in local nature reserves such as the exotically named Wilderness Island.

DISTANCE/DIFFICULTY 9 miles. Easy.

DROP-OUT POINT Nine places

TIME 4½hrs

MAP OS Explorer map 161; a map showing the whole route can be downloaded from 🖰 www.merton.gov.uk/wandle_trail.pdf

START Colliers Wood station ✻ TQ268704

FINISH Hare & Hounds pub, Croydon ✻ TQ311653

TAKING A BREAK Merton Abbey Mills, The William Morris, Deen City Farm, Surrey Arms, Lord Palmerston, The Greyhound, Pavilion Café (Beddington Park), Hare & Hounds

GETTING THERE ⊖ To Colliers Wood

DIRECTIONS TO START Turn left out of the station

Proceed along Merton High Street past the Charles Holden pub on the right and keep going straight, over a dual carriageway (Christchurch Road) past Merton bus garage (on the right) until you see the river on the left and then a footbridge over it to Sainsbury's. Instead of crossing the bridge, turn right along the riverbank (signposted 'Abbey Mills ¼ mile'). Almost immediately is a plaque embedded in the ground on the left informing you this is:

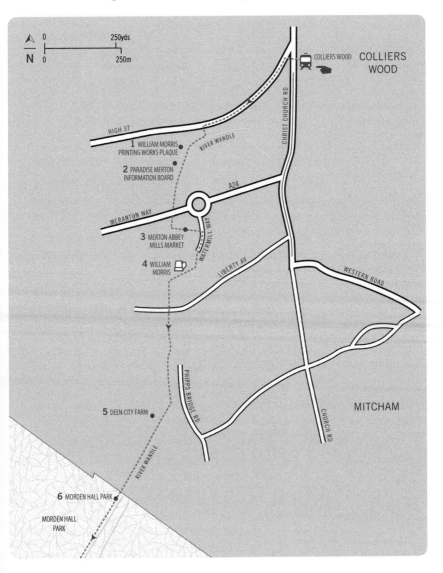

1 THE SITE OF WILLIAM MORRIS'S PRINTING WORKS

Here the socialist, author and artist William Morris (1834–96) took over the calico printing works in 1881. This he turned into a craft workshop where he perfected his 'indigo discharge' printing technique on textiles. His aim was 'honest, original work, done with enjoyment, not mechanical imitation done by routine... executed in a pleasant and healthy surroundings, not in squalid dens... and properly rewarded, not sweated'. He produced stained glass, textiles, tapestries, carpets, dyed and printed chintz, silk and wool products, much of which was sold to Arthur Liberty of Regent Street (who bought the works in 1904 after the death of Morris). Some examples of his work are displayed in the pub named after him later on the walk.

Morris lived about four miles away on the riverside at Hammersmith where, in 1881, the year he took over the workshop, he saw homeless ruffians outside his comfortable house and observed: 'It was my good luck only of being born respectable and rich that has put me on this side of the window among delightful books and lovely works of art and not on the other side, in the empty street, the drink-steeped liquor shops and foul and degraded lodgings.'

Another of his remarks sheds light on why he aimed for work to be an enjoyable experience at his workshop: 'If I were to work ten hours a day at work I despised and hated, I should spend my leisure time I hope in political agitations, but I fear – in drinking.'

His political agitation was in favour of the Marxist Social Democratic Federation and its journal *Commonweal*, which he both edited and advertised in the streets wearing a sandwich board. When it split in 1884, he and the journal supported its more anarchistic successor, the Socialist League. His classic socialist utopian novels *A Dream of John Ball* and *News from Nowhere* were published initially as serials in *Commonweal* from 1886 to 1890.

Morris also branched out into book publishing and designed his own typeface.

☛ On the other side of the path is an information board about:

2 PARADISE MERTON

Emma Hamilton described this area to her lover, Admiral Lord Horatio Nelson, as 'Paradise Merton' on moving here in 1801 when it was a small village. They lived in nearby Merton Place (off what is now called Nelson Road). The River Wandle fed a canal through her grounds which she referred to as The Nile. There were fish and water fowl in her garden. It was a retreat of Nelson and their daughter Horatia. Nelson died in 1805 in the Battle of Trafalgar, after which Emma descended into debt (despite a plea from Nelson before he died for public support of her) and she had to sell the house in 1808. Pubs and roads around the area are named after them.

☞ Continue along the path over two roads and then across a footbridge (signposted 'Merton Abbey Mills & Phipps Bridge') over the river to:

3 MERTON ABBEY MILLS MARKET

This lively indoor retail place occupies a former textile mill established by Huguenot weavers in the 18th century, and later taken over by William Morris for his Morris & Co. workshops, which manufactured textiles, stained glass, tapestry, dyes and carpets; it later became the Liberty Print Works. This in turn takes its name from the largely vanished Merton Priory nearby, where Thomas Becket was a pupil and where Henry VI was crowned in 1437; it was demolished by Henry VIII. The Mills now house a fishmonger, craft shops (including pottery classes at The Wheelhouse), a farmers' market, restaurants and (on the first Sunday of every month) a car boot fair. Here you will also find:

The mill wheel at Merton Abbey Mills.

4 THE WILLIAM MORRIS

20 Watermill Way, Merton Abbey Mill SW19 2RD

Examples of the works of William Morris produced nearby are on display in this modern pub. It serves food and real ales (Liberty Ale brewed by Westerham and Adnams), and you can drink on the patio overlooking the river.

☞ After refreshing yourself, cross the footbridge by the pub over the river and turn left along the opposite bank, following the 'Wandle Trail' signs. After a while you will come to a road, and after you cross it you will see the Deen City Farm and Riding School ahead. Go past a notice about Phipps Bridge (the original of which dates back to 1572). If you have time you can turn left and cross over to see part of the old Merton Priory Wall, as well as remains of Wandle Villa and The Lodge.

Otherwise continue ahead and after a short distance on the right is:

5 DEEN CITY FARM

39 Windsor Av, Merton Abbey SW19 2RR ☎ 020 8543 5300
🖱 www.deencityfarm.co.uk ⊙ Tue–Sun, 10.00–16.30

Children may get seriously distracted at this free-to-enter farmyard and riding school: it has pony rides, a maze, a farm shop, a plant and vegetable stall and a café. The animals include geese, turkeys, ducks, pigs, horses, cows, goats, llamas, rabbits, guinea pigs, hamsters, gerbils, ferrets and an owl.

☞ After visiting it, follow the riverbank until you come to a crossing over a tramway. Keep going and take a path to the left, through bogs and swamplands, to a noticeboard announcing this is:

6 MORDEN HALL PARK

A surprisingly large expanse of wetlands, woodland and meadows, this former country estate is a tad wilder than its name suggests. You might find kingfishers, newts and grey herons here, and mallards and moorhens on what's probably the river's most scenic moment. A restored waterwheel stands redundant as a reminder of the Wandle's industrious past, beside a modern hydro-electric turbine. The walled garden centre has an aquarium and pet departments, craft workshops with furniture restoration and handmade pottery. The site is now owned by the National Trust, with free access, and special events, including an annual country show, are held frequently.

☛ Follow the path ahead signposted 'National Trust Snuff Mill ¾ mile'. Then fork left at the sign 'Snuff Mill ½ mile'. Follow the path over wooden bridges, and just before a metal bridge turn right at the signpost 'Snuff Mill & Rose Garden ¼ mile'. This naturally takes you to:

7 SNUFF MILL & ROSE GARDEN

☎ 020 8545 6850 🖱 www.nationaltrust.org.uk

Here are historic snuff mills, which were owned by the philanthropist Gilliat Hatfield who left them to the National Trust in 1941. The western snuff mill has been renovated and functions as a learning centre. A spectacular rose garden has over 2,000 roses which bloom from May to September.

☛ Return to the metal bridge, cross over it and follow the path signposted 'Phipps Bridge ¼ mile'. This takes you through an avenue of trees.

Morden Hall Park.

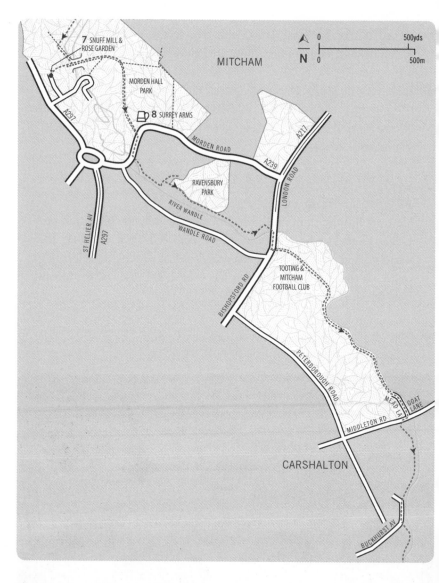

When you come to a fork and if you are getting tired you can go left (signposted 'Phipps Bridge Tram Link ¼ mile'), for trams to Wimbledon or Croydon.

To continue the walk take the right fork, following the path signposted 'Hackbridge 2½ miles, Carshalton 3 miles'. This takes you to Morden Road. A few yards to the left on the same side of the road is the:

8 SURREY ARMS

Morden Rd, Mitcham CR4 4DD

A traditional and friendly pub with two bars, a pool table, a dartboard and a jukebox but no cask ales.

☛ Turn right out of the pub.

✋ In a few yards on the same side is Bus Stop Q for the 201 to Mitcham, Herne Hill and Morden.

☛ To continue the walk, go past the bus stop along Morden Road, and after a hundred yards or so turn left (signposted to 'River Wandle'). Cross over a footbridge, take the path to the left (by a large grinding stone) between the river on the right and a stream on the left, keeping to the riverbank into Ravensbury Park.

Do not cross the next bridge over the river (which leads to a dead end), but follow the path to the left, keeping on the left bank. After a couple of hundred yards cross a steel bridge (No. 70) and you will have rivers on both sides. They merge where you cross another footbridge to the left bank of the combined river. When you approach a road the path forks.

✋ If you wish to end the walk, take the left fork into Riverside Drive. Turn left to Bus Stop Y on the same side for the 280 to Mitcham, Brixton and Tooting. Turn right to Bus Stop Z on the other side for the 280 to Morden and Sutton.

☛ To continue the walk take the right fork to Bishopsford Road, cross over it, turn right and then immediately left through a circular gate with the number 74 on it, into a footpath, with a fence on the left. This goes past Tooting and Mitcham Football Club's ground on the right. When you come to the end of the football pitches, fork to the right around them and you will soon be back on the left bank of the river. When you come to the 'Willow Cottages' terrace on the right in Watermead Lane go past them to a T-junction (Goat Road to the left, and Middleton Road to the right).

✋ To get to this drop-out point turn left and walk a few hundred yards to the main road with The Goat pub on the corner. Here you can get the 127 bus to Tooting Broadway and Purley, or the S1 bus to Banstead and Mitcham. Mitcham Junction railway station is just a few minutes' walk away (turning left out of the pub along Carshalton Road).

☞ To continue the walk when you come out of Watermead Lane, turn right (into Middleton Road) and immediately left over a pedestrian crossing. Take the path and cycle track ahead to the left, then left again at the signpost to Buckhurst Avenue. When you reach Bridge 86 on the left, don't cross it but keep to the right bank of the river. A blue plaque embedded in the ground warns you to 'Avoid frogs and toads after dark.' You will come to Culvers Avenue (with Millside ahead).

✋ To the left on the other side of the road is Bus Stop V for the 80 to Belmont, Sutton and Morden.

☞ To continue, turn left into the road, then take the first right into Culvers Retreat (signposted 'Wandle Trail, Poulter Park'). At the end of this cul-de-sac take the path to the left (signposted to 'Hackbridge Road'), cross over a footbridge, turn right past a weir to reach another road (Hackbridge Road).

✋ To the left on the other side is Bus Stop S for the 127 to Purley and Tooting, and the 151 bus to Worcester Park and Wallington.

☞ To continue the walk, cross the bridge to the right and turn left into the path back to the river (signposted to 'Wilderness Island' and 'Carshalton Ponds'), where there are two huge magnificent plane trees. You will come to another road (River Gardens) which you follow ahead to the left (signposted 'Wilderness Island') and it goes into Mill Lane, which you also follow ahead. You will shortly come to a bridge to the left (opposite the junction with Strawberry Lane), over the river into:

9 WILDERNESS ISLAND
River Wandle, Carshalton

This tranquil nature reserve has ponds and wetlands as well as mature woodlands and wildflower meadows, which are a habitat for orange-tip butterflies, frogs, fish and wetland birds. Sedges and grasses have been planted to encourage water voles to live here. A notice warns: 'Only kingfishers are allowed to fish on the island.' The kingfisher population has indeed increased in recent years. It is well worth exploring the island before resuming the walk.

Continue along Mill Lane, under a railway bridge, to Butter Hill bridge on the left. You can cross it for a short cut, but we preferred the longer route so continued along the right bank of the river (signposted to 'Carshalton Ponds'). After a short distance take a path off to the left from Mill Lane to follow the river (signposted 'Wandle Trail').

If you need refreshing, turn right when you come to Papermill Close, then turn left and on the right is the:

10 LORD PALMERSTON

31 Mill Lane, Carshalton SM5 2JY

This traditional two-bar pub sells pizza and serves real ales such as Greene King and London Glory.

Back to the river, continue along it until you come to a bridge over it (signposted 'Carshalton Ponds') into:

11 GROVE PARK

Here you'll find ducks, geese, squirrels, palm trees and a crazy golf course.

Take the path forking right and follow the left bank of the river. At the ponds turn left (signposted 'Carshalton Ponds & Beddington Park') and left again when these signs are repeated. This takes you to:

12 CARSHALTON PONDS

Part of the Carshalton Village Conservation Area, this forms a delightfully villagey tableau with pre-suburbia houses around it. The ponds are not natural but were created in the early 17th century, possibly as a landscape feature for a nearby house.

For those so inclined, there is a bus stop here for the 127 to Morden.

Around the ponds are the following four places which are worth visiting if you have time:

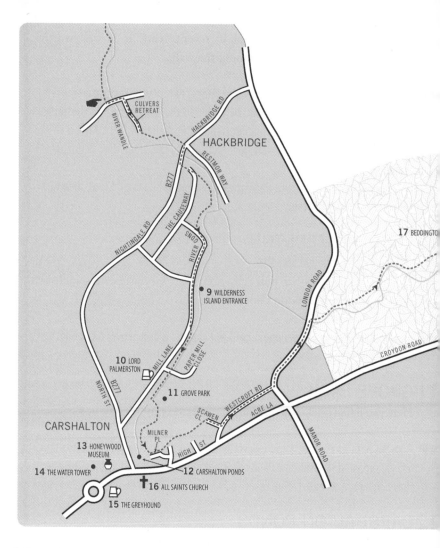

13 HONEYWOOD MUSEUM

Honeywood Walk, Carshalton SM5 3NX ☎ 020 8770 4297 🖱 www.
friendsofhoneywood.co.uk 🕘 Wed–Fri 11.00–17.00, Sat–Sun 10.00–17.00

An Edwardian billiards room and a collection of Edwardian toys take
pride of place, and there are exhibitions telling the history of the house
and the people who lived here. Unusually a stream flows beneath it, one
explanation being it was a commercial cold bath in the 17th century
when cold water was considered a cure for many ailments.

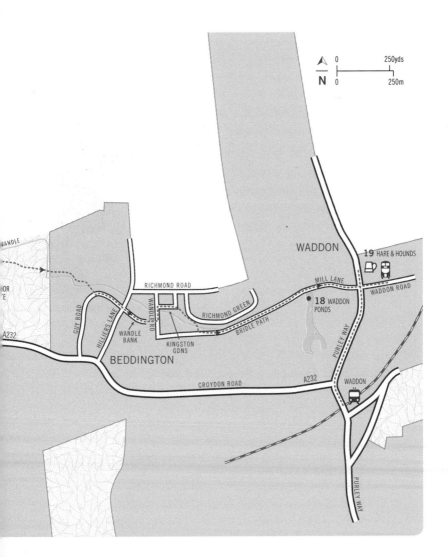

14 THE WATER TOWER

West St (junction with Festival Walk), Carshalton ☎ 020 8647 0984
🖱 www.carshaltonwatertower.co.uk ⊕ Apr–Sept Sun 14.30–17.00 £

A listed early 18th-century garden building, where a water-powered pump supplied water to the fountains and garden. It also has an orangery and a remarkable 18th-century bathroom complete with a tile-lined plunge bath. In the garden is the Hermitage and Folly Bridge.

ANGLING IN THE WANDLE

The river has been cleaned up after being heavily polluted in the past when it was treated as a sewer, and is now clear enough for fish to breed and flourish, including trout, chubb, dace, barbel, roach and gudgeon. One angler we met netted six chubb in six hours, while another caught a rainbow trout weighing 1½ pounds. And a third (Derek Purton of Waddon) caught a dace within five ounces of the English record, plus a brown trout weighing two pounds. You do, however, need an Environment Agency rod licence to fish in the river.

Keen angler Derek Purton on the banks of the Wandle.

15 THE GREYHOUND

High St, Carshalton SM5 3PE

This Young's pub is a listed building. A plaque states:

> This public house was known as the Greyhound as early as 1700. It was a sporting centre and the venue where racehorses were inspected prior to competing on Banstead Downs. The old inn was rebuilt around 1840 and a separate existing building, "The Two Rooms" incorporated.

On its corner is Anne Boleyn's Well, which burst from the ground when Anne Boleyn kicked against a stone there as she rode by.

The ghost of a traveller who froze to death on the doorstep in the 1800s haunts the Swan Bar which is part of the original coaching house. The bar has a log fire (which the ghost presumably appreciates rather belatedly).

Look out for the mosaic of a greyhound in the floor of this bar; it's thought to be over 200 years old and was crafted by an Italian artist.

FASCINATING FLORA

A botanist's delight! Favourites such as bluebells and daffodils can be seen as well as poetic-sounding flowers like honeysuckle, cowslips and buttercups, and the rather less appealing stinking bore... It's well worth taking the time to admire the little things as well as the striking vistas.

1 Honeysuckle in Ashtead Common Nature Reserve, **walk 22**. **2** Pitcher plants in the greenhouse of Darwin's garden, **walk 1**. **3** Cowslips on the edge of Banstead Woods, **walk 5**. **4** Insects at work on Downe Bank where Darwin studied the special relationship between the orchids that grew there and their pollinators, **walk 1**. **5** Cornflowers in Heartwood Forest, **walk 3**.

THE GREAT OUTDOORS

From rolling countryside to pristine woodlands – you don't have to travel far to find some truly rural terrain. Spectacular views and cosy, historic pubs along the way are just some of the reasons to try out our more rural rambles. Recreational activities include village cricket, sailing, sledging, fishing and foraging. Herons, deer, foxes, red kites – even otters – can all be seen in the wild; and rare breeds can be seen in captivity.

5

1 The strikingly beautiful valley between Cudham and Downe, **walk 1**. 2 Dancing trees on the heath by Lesnes Abbey Wood, **walk 9**. 3 A friendly face at the WRAS Animal Centre: Buck, an old English feral goat, **walk 17**. 4 A patchwork of colour, Heartswood Forest, **walk 3**. 5 View from the top of Box Hill, **walk 2**. 6 Hunting and shooting scene on the wall of the George and Dragon pub in Downe, **walk 1**. 7 On the road to Little Missenden, **walk 18**. 8 Parakeets making themselves at home in Dartford, **walk 19**.

6

7

8

1 Folly Bridge over the River Darent in Farningham was built to contain cattle in the 18th century, **walk 19**. **2** Wood sculptor Friedel Buecking carving animal figures in Trent Country Park, **walk 17**. **3** Guards are placed around the new saplings at Heartwood Forest to protect them from deer and rabbits, **walk 3**. **4** Deer in Richmond Park, **walk 20**.

16 ALL SAINTS CHURCH

High St, Carshalton SM5 3PD

This occupies what was originally a pagan site. Although the building was much restored in 1891, the tower was built before the Norman Conquest. It has several magnificent stained-glass windows including one dedicated to the locals who died in World War I, with their names listed below, and another created in 1743 showing the Magi worshipping the baby Jesus. There is also a table tomb from 1400 showing a Tudor knight by the north wall.

☛ To continue the walk turn left before the ponds and follow the signs to Beddington Park. Fork right past the crazy golf course on the right, take the path to the left and over a bridge at the end with Westcroft Leisure Centre ahead. Turn right and then left into Westcroft Road (signposted 'Wandsworth Trail, Beddington Park'). At the end of the road, round to the left is the Rose & Crown on the corner of Butter Hill. Opposite the pub is a small pond with a fountain in the middle, which you walk past with the main road on your right, following the signpost to 'Beddington Park'.

✋ To end the walk here, go to Bus Stop GM for the 151 to Wallington or Worcester Park.

☛ To continue the walk keep along the main road (London Road) until you come to a road bridge over the river. Just before the bridge take the public footpath (signposted to 'Croydon Road') to the right which leads to, on the left:

17 BEDDINGTON PARK

This landscaped park was once a deer park, part of Carew Manor, a Tudor mansion. It has many attractive features including an avenue of trees, a long lake, and the Pavilion Café in the centre where you can get homemade cakes and other snacks every day from 09.00 to 16.30. But if you have any canine companions, heed the notice warning that dogs are being stolen from the park.

☛ Follow the footpath until the path forks and take the left fork. Then at a crossing of paths, turn left, down to a footbridge which you cross over a lake and then turn right (signposted to 'Waddon Ponds') along the left bank.

An egret patiently watching the River Wandle below for fish.

Stick to the same side of the river (ignoring a footbridge) even though the track gets a little overgrown, through woodlands, until you come to the the Riverside Animal Centre. Then turn right over the bridge and left along the right bank (signposted to 'Waddon Ponds'). Go through a car park and take a path through grass to the right (away from the river) with the back of Carew Manor (now a school) to the right. Cross over the next footbridge, then bear right though grass, and pick up a tarmac path going right, back to the river by a waterfall and continue along the left bank. Further along cross two footbridges close to each other and turn left into Guy Road (signposted 'Wandle Trail, Waddon Ponds').

✋ You can opt to leave the walk here: at the end of Guy Road on the junction with Hilliers Lane, turn right to Bus Stop B for the 455 and 463 to Croydon.

☛ To continue the walk, cross over Hilliers Lane and follow the footpath ahead (signposted to 'Bridges Lane') along the river's right bank to Bridges Lane, past a row of picturesque cottages and then left into Wandle Road, cross over the river and turn right into Kingston Gardens. Cross another footbridge and follow the signs to Waddon Ponds. Before long you will indeed reach, on the right:

18 WADDON PONDS

Large willow trees surround the water gardens, and a variety of waterfowl including ducks and coots can be seen on the water. The name Waddon comes from 'woad', which grew on the chalk hills and was used by ancient Britons to extract blue dye for use as body paint; traces dating from the Bronze Age and the Iron Age have been found. The Domesday Book lists a mill at the northern end of the ponds used for grinding corn; this was in use up until 1928.

➤ After strolling around the ponds continue along the path that you came from, along Mill Lane to Purley Way. Close to the junction you will see to the left on the other side the:

19 HARE & HOUNDS
325 Purley Way, CRO 4NU

The pub has a beer garden, a children's play area, food served all day, three pool tables, a dartboard and a small library. The Ruddles beer is very reasonably priced.

A 'Croydon Monster' stalked the streets here in 1803 and attacked over 50 people, escaping each time by leaping over 12-foot walls. He was dressed in a black mask and cape, according to a feature in the *Croydon Guardian* in 1992.

➤ After leaving the pub, turn left and left again into Waddon Road, to Bus Stop EX where you can get the 410 to both West Croydon and East Croydon railway stations (about 8 and 12 minutes respectively). Or you can continue down Purley Way, past Waddon Road, a short distance to Epsom Road on the left where on the left is Waddon railway station, where you can get trains to London Bridge and Victoria.

FREEDOM PASS

14

DISTANCE 4 MILES
DIFFICULTY EASY
TIME 2HRS

RIVER THAMES:
STAINES TO CHERTSEY

PICNICKERS' PARADISE

THAMES-SIDE PLEASURES IN LONDON'S FAR WEST.

Munching a sandwich and pouring a drink while contemplating the beauties of the Thames makes a nicely laid-back way of passing by an afternoon, and happily for picnickers there are plenty of strategically placed seats and tables along the riverside as well as on the Penton Hook Island to help you make the most of it. You can pick wild fruit and look out for a wide variety of birds besides the swans (you might be lucky to spot a kingfisher and then celebrate in the pub of that name). Salmon swim up the river with the aid of a special channel for them and a wide variety of fish lure anglers.

From Staines bus station take the Friends Walk exit, then turn left, go under the railway bridge and on the right is the River Thames. Turn left along the Thames Path. Garden lovers will appreciate a variety of flowers on display from the riverside cottages, chalets and bungalows. There are plenty of benches to sit on along the route.

DISTANCE/DIFFICULTY 4 miles. Easy.

TIME 2hrs

MAP OS Explorer map 16

START Staines bus station ❊ TQ036714

FINISH Chertsey Bridge ❊ TQ055666

TAKING A BREAK The Kingfisher

GETTING THERE ⊖ To Hatton Cross station (Piccadilly Line, Heathrow Branch)

DIRECTIONS TO START The bus station is next to Hatton Cross station exit.
🚌 203 to Staines (23mins; at least 3 an hour, 2 an hour on Sun).

After about half an hour you will come to Penton Hook Lock where a friendly lock-keeper occupies the lodge which was built in 1814. Cross over the lock to:

1 PENTON HOOK ISLAND

This is managed by the Environment Agency to protect wildlife and allow fish to spawn and travel upstream in a special channel bypassing the weir. A salmon ladder was opened in 1995 (completing the link from Teddington to Whitchurch) and the fish spawning channel in 1999 (which also acts as a nursery for young fish). Fishing is not allowed by the lock but is on the rest of the island with a permit.

This is also a good habitat to look for the endangered water vole; kingfishers and herons nest here too. Be sure to look out for the beautiful banded demoiselle damselfly, which is attracted by the water crowfoot that grows in the channel, the gatekeeper butterfly (also known as the hedge brown although golden in colour) and dragonflies. Five species of willow are seen around the island and on the river.

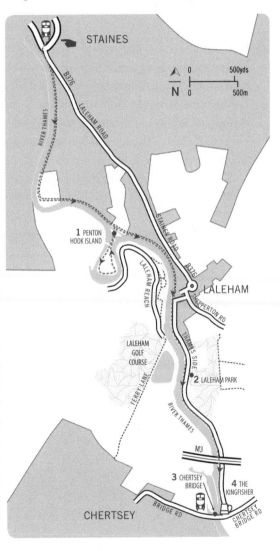

There are picnic tables on the island and fruit to be picked for making preserves, such as blackberries, crab apples and rosehips.

☞ After walking around the island continue along the Thames Path. You will see traditional boat-builders' yards on the opposite bank of Laleham Reach, and before long you will come to:

2 LALEHAM PARK

This is a large open green with more picnic tables. It used to be part of the Laleham Manor grounds owned by the Lord Lucan family, which included the 7th earl who went missing in 1974 after being suspected of murdering his children's nanny. The 3rd earl didn't exactly cover himself in glories either, as he led the disastrous Charge of the Light Brigade in 1854.

Noticeboards highlight the bird species, which include cormorants, great crested grebes and mallards. You might spot the improbably brightly coloured parakeets, which originate from Asia and were kept as pets in Victorian times but some escaped and bred until 1855 but then died out. In the 1970s they returned (being released by rock star Jimi Hendrix to add more psychedelic colour to London just before his death, according to one theory) and there are now tens of thousands in this area around Kingston and Twickenham.

☞ Continue along the river past Laleham Park Camping Site, under the M3 motorway, past Chertsey Lock to:

3 CHERTSEY BRIDGE

A bridge has spanned this point since around 1300, linking Dumsey Meadow on the Middlesex side with Chertsey in Surrey. When the present seven-arched span was erected in 1785, the counties got in a muddle with their contract and stipulated the number of arches to be built; this the contractor duly supplied, but the bridge failed to reach the bank on either side, so the authorities had to fork out more money for its completion.

Next to the bridge is the:

4 KINGFISHER
Chertsey Bridge Rd, Chertsey KT16 8LF

A traditional pub which has an outdoor seating area by the river and a log fire inside. It serves hot food including Sunday roasts. Real ales on our visit included Fuller's London Pride, Adnams and Sharp's Doom Bar.

Cross the bridge over the river and catch the 557 bus on the same side of the road for the 55-minute journey back to Hatton Cross tube station. It is only once an hour (and does not run on Sunday), but you can wait by the bus stop in the Boat House, a modern pub.

TWO ECCENTRICS ON THE THAMES

Dylan Thomas (1914–53), the fiery, alcoholic, tragic but hugely talented Welsh poet, lived on a houseboat on the river here at Chertsey on his first visit to London in 1933. It was owned by his older sister, Nancy and he had come to meet fellow poet Pamela Hansford Johnson, who became his first serious girlfriend. He was barred from the Café Royal, in London's Regent Street, for 'scraping his tongue with the menu and presenting the detritus to another diner'. He met his future wife, Caitlin Macnamara, a showgirl and dancer, in the Wheatsheaf pub in Rathbone Place, Fitzrovia, and they got married at the third attempt after twice spending the marriage licence fee on drink. His masterpiece was *Under Milk Wood*, the only copy of the manuscript of which he inadvertently left in the George pub, Great Portland Street, Fitzrovia, after a drunken binge. Luckily it was rescued by the landlord.

Viv Stanshall (1943–95), the eccentric leader of the Bonzo Dog Doo-Dah Band, also lived on a houseboat at Chertsey from 1977 to 1983 and produced part of his album *Sir Henry at Rawlinson End* on it. Later he and his second wife lived on a floating theatre called The Old Profanity Showboat which gave performances on tour. Viv and his friend Keith Moon (drummer of The Who) were great pranksters. Viv once entered a tailor's shop and admired a pair of trousers. As planned Keith followed him in and admired the same pair of trousers. In a struggle to gain possession of them, they tore them in half with one leg each, to the chagrin of the tailor. There then entered a one-legged actor they had hired who declared: 'Ah! Just what I was looking for!'

FREEDOM PASS

15

DISTANCE 8 MILES
DIFFICULTY EASY
TIME 4HRS

RIVER LEE:
TOTTENHAM TO WALTHAM ABBEY

DRAGONFLIES & GUNPOWDER

A WATERY SLICE PAST POWDER MILLS TO A NORMAN ECCLESIASTICAL WONDER ON LONDON'S NORTHERN FRINGE.

This river (variously spelled Lee or Lea) has been used for transport for over 2,000 years carrying everything from gunpowder into London to horse manure (from London to local farms). The story of gunpowder crops up twice on this walk, as you pass the factory site where Lee-Enfield rifles were made and have the chance to visit the gunpowder mill that served some of the nation's military needs for several centuries.

Seeds blown off the barges have seen wild flowers from Asia and North America growing in the meadows along its banks; a summer spectacle is the exotic-looking, eye-catching bee orchid, so named because of its extraordinary

---

DISTANCE/DIFFICULTY 8 miles. Easy.

DROP-OUT POINT After 2, 4 and 6 miles

TIME 4hrs

MAP OS Explorer map 174

START Tottenham Hale tube station ✳ TQ345895

FINISH The Crown, Waltham Abbey ✳ TL383005

TAKING A BREAK The Navigation Harvester Inn, The Greyhound, The Narrowboat Café, The Crown

GETTING THERE ⊖ To Tottenham Hale (Victoria Line) or 🚌 from Liverpool Street (11mins; daily, at least 4 an hour)

DIRECTIONS TO START Turn left out of the station

---

likeness to that insect (nature's curious method to attract bees to the flower; the petals even smell like female bees, thus emitting enticing signals to male bees to come and mate).

On the way you'll also see colourful barges, and almost adjacent to the waterway are several huge reservoirs which supply a tenth of London's water, as well as providing a haven for aquatic birds and otters. Near the largest heronry in Greater London is a dragonfly sanctuary, while your binoculars might help you spot peregrine falcons, the rare Savi's warbler, kestrels and other species.

The walk ends at Waltham Abbey, where the superb Norman church is the burial place of King Harold after his demise at Hastings in 1066.

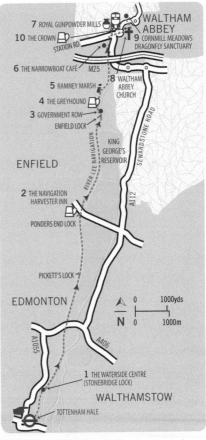

☞ After turning left out of the station, take the first left into Ferry Lane. Just after Mill Mead Road take the second footpath on the left, signposted 'Lea Valley Walk' (after the first one which is Pymme's Brook), down to Tottenham Locks, and continue ahead on the bank of the River Lee Navigation on your right.

After about half a mile or so you will reach Stonebridge Lock. A few yards past it is:

1 THE WATERSIDE CENTRE

Stonebridge Lock, Tottenham Marshes N17 0XD

A useful place to know about if you want to hire canoes or cycles. For general info, see the Friends of Tottenham Marshes information board and another board explaining how the Lea Rivers Trust is building holts for otters to rest and shelter in during the day.

☞ After visiting the centre return to the lock, cross over it and turn left. After passing Chalk Bridge, you will go past Edmonton bus garage and two business parks (opposite which we saw elders in flower, and coots building a nest) and then under the North Circular Road.

✋ At Cooks Ferry Roundabout, Harbet Road, on the North Circular Road you can catch the 34 or 44 buses to Walthamstow, Chingford, Palmers Green or Turnpike Lane.

☞ Continue following the river, past a signpost 'Pickett's Lock 1 mile, Enfield Lock 4 miles'. After passing Pickett's Lock you will see to the left a golf course on the opposite bank, and plenty of ivy, wild roses, hazels and hawthorn hedges.

✋ When you reach Ponders End Lock, walk up the ramp from the canal to Wharf Road, turn left and walk a short distance to the junction with Lea Valley Road. Here there are bus stops on both sides of the road where you can get the 313 bus to Chingford in one direction or Enfield in the other.

☞ If you would just like a refreshment stop before continuing, walk up the ramp to Wharf Road, turn right, over the canal and first right on the other side for a short walk to:

Leaving the dog in charge of the houseboat on the River Lee.

2 THE NAVIGATION HARVESTER INN

4 Wharf Rd, Ponders End EN3 4XX

A former pumping station built in 1899, this building was converted in 1995 and is now a large Harvester dining pub with a beer garden overlooking the canal (but no real ales).

Return to Ponders End Lock and continue along the river. To the right you will see sheep and a few horses grazing on the raised grass banks of King George's Reservoir. When you reach Enfield Lock, cross over a bridge with a signpost 'Waltham Abbey 2 miles' and follow it to the other side of the canal. On the right is:

3 GOVERNMENT ROW

Enfield Island Village

The Royal Small Arms factory was sited on the island in 1816, and was originally driven by waterwheel. Here the famous Lee-Enfield rifles were manufactured up to 1987. Government Row was built below the level of the canal bank in 1857 to house the arms factory workers, and the proximity of the waterway enabled barges to carry materials such as coal.

A bit further along on the left is:

4 THE GREYHOUND

425 Ordnance Rd, Enfield Lock EN3 6HR

A family-friendly pub owned by local brewery McMullens, the Greyhound serves real ale, food and has a pool table and a dartboard.

Opposite the pub is the third drop-out point on this walk: from Causeway Bridge opposite the pub, you can catch the 121 bus to Southgate and Palmers Green or the 491 to Edmonton. Or you can turn left out of the pub and along Ordnance Road a few hundred yards to Enfield Lock railway station (which is just within the Freedom Pass zone) for trains to Liverpool Street (27 minutes; 2 an hour).

Otherwise continue along the canal past:

Reeds in the sun along the banks of the River Lee.

5 RAMNEY MARSH

Passed on your left, this ancient pasture surrounded by river and marshes has been used since medieval times to graze sheep.

☛ Continue along the canal, with narrow boats moored with names such as *Wet Dream* and *Pub Crawl*, past Ramney Marsh Lock (built in 1768 and then rebuilt in 1864 from brick and stone from the demolished Westminster Bridge). If you would like to fish between here and Tottenham Lock, you need to join the River Lea Angling Club, annual membership £15, or £10 for over 65s (☎ 07842 033356).

Follow the river under the M25 and soon you will come to:

6 THE NARROWBOAT CAFÉ

Hazlemere Marina, Highbridge St, Waltham Abbey EN9 1BA

Good solid hot meals and light refreshments are available here all day along with laundry and shower facilities.

☛ Cross over the next bridge on the right (signposted 'Waltham Abbey ½ mile, Royal Gunpowder Mill ¼ mile' over both the canal and Horsemill Stream into Highbridge Street, Waltham Abbey. Take the first on the left opposite the 24-hour McDonald's into Beaulieu Drive. After nearly half a mile you will come to the:

7 ROYAL GUNPOWDER MILLS

Beaulieu Drive, Waltham Abbey EN9 1JY ☎ 01992 707370
📱 www.royalgunpowdermills.com 🕐 10.00–17.00 (last entry 15.00);
check website for opening dates ££ 🪙

The story of gunpowder and weaponry is vividly explained at this museum on the 170-acre site that formed a crucial supply centre for over 400 years. Gunpowder was produced here from 1561, then the government took over in 1780. During the Napoleonic Wars the gunpowder was taken in sailing barges down the River Lea to the Thames and on to Woolwich Arsenal. By World War II there were over 3,000 workers at the mill, making Dambuster bombs and other weapons. The Ministry of Defence withdrew in 1991 since then it has become a museum and 'Secret Island' attraction with archery and rifle ranges. Note the alders and willows, descendants of trees planted to make charcoal for the gunpowder production. Herons nest in the surrounding grounds along with a large flock of siskins (small finches).

☞ Return to Highbridge Street, turn left, continue past a roundabout and on to:

8 WALTHAM ABBEY CHURCH (CHURCH OF HOLY CROSS & ST LAWRENCE)

Abbey Church Centre, Abbey Farm House, Abbey Gardens, Waltham Abbey
EN9 1XQ ☎ 01992 767897 📱 www.walthamabbeychurch.co.uk
🕐 daily 10.00, 11.00, or 12.00–16.00

Few Norman churches can compare with this in all England: the magnificence of its 12th-century nave is in a similar class to Durham Cathedral though on a lesser scale. The abbey was begun before the Norman Conquest, and was consecrated by Harold on 3 May 1060; the present church represents less than half of the size of the original abbey before it was dissolved under Henry VIII. The east end window was designed by Pre-Raphaelite artist Edward Burne-Jones, and the church's bells inspired Tennyson's poem *Ring Out Wild Bells*.

Pick up signposts to 'King Harold's Tomb' round the church to the back. Harold was cured of paralysis after praying here and then attended it regularly. Just before the Battle of Hastings in 1066 he vainly prayed here for victory, but instead was killed by (according to most interpretations of the Bayeux Tapestry) an arrow in his eye. William the Conqueror refused Harold's mother permission to claim his body, but it was later identified by his mistress, Edith Swan-neck, who brought it back to Waltham, where he was buried, only to be moved several times as the church was extended. As well as the tomb and memorial stone behind the church, there is a statue of him on the southwest corner. The herringbone masonry on the east wall was paid for by Harold.

Richard II took refuge here during the Peasants' Revolt, and Thomas Cranmer stayed here when discussing Henry VIII's desire for a divorce and the need to split from the Roman Catholic church.

The church is surrounded by extensive gardens with archaeological treasures such as a 14th-century gatehouse, seats, picnic tables and a green.

☛ From Harold's Tomb go away from the church diagonally left to a gap in the cloister wall, follow the path ahead to Abbey Church Centre, turn left and then right round the side of the centre to a lane which goes across a wooden bridge over a stream, under a road subway, through a kissing gate into fields with a 'Welcome to Lea Valley' sign. Bear right through a grass track to:

9 CORNMILL MEADOWS DRAGONFLY SANCTUARY

At this Site of Special Scientific Interest, 23 species of dragonfly have been recorded (that's half the UK species). The meadows are seasonally flooded, and the site includes ponds, woodland and hay meadows, with an arboretum and heronry nearby. You can follow a waymarked trail of blue arrows to find out more.

☛ Return to the church, retrace your steps towards the canal, take the first right (Romeland) and tucked round the corner is:

10 THE CROWN

Romeland, Waltham Abbey EN91 1QZ

Another McMullens real ale pub, this friendly place has ancient timber beams, a dartboard and lots of Tottenham Hotspur football memorabilia (including much from their glory days in the 1960s such as a picture of Dave Mackay holding Billy Bremner of Leeds by the scruff of his neck).

☛ Turn left out of the pub, then right into Highbridge Street. When you come to the roundabout turn right and on the right is the Highbridge bus stop where you can catch the 213 to Epping (Central Line), the 505 to Walthamstow (Victoria Line) or Chingford (rail), or the 250 and 255 to Loughton (Central Line).

DEATH IN THE CHURCHYARD, LIFE BY THE LAKE

PLENTY FOR ALL AGES ON THE THRESHOLD OF BRITAIN'S HOLLYWOOD:
RARE-BREED ANIMALS, CRICKET AND YACHT RACES,
AND A VISIT TO WINNIE THE POOH'S WORLD.

Death stalks in the local churchyard in Elstree where three victims of infamous brutal murders are buried. It sets a sombre, even macabre tone for this entertaining walk, but things cheer up markedly after that. The route takes in Aldenham Country Park, teeming with life in various ways, with wildlife abundant on and around the scenic reservoir, and a notable collection of rare breeds of farm animals that visitors are allowed to feed.

DISTANCE/DIFFICULTY 5 miles. Easy.

DROP-OUT POINT After 3 miles

TIME 2hrs

MAP OS Explorer map 173

START Elstree Church ❀ TQ179954

TAKING A BREAK The Fishery

GETTING THERE 🚌 To Elstree & Borehamwood station from St Pancras (22mins; daily, 2 an hour)

DIRECTIONS TO START In station forecourt go to the bus stops on the left. 🚌 107 from Stop A (3 an hour every day) or the 306 from Stop B (3 an hour, except Sunday 1 an hour) to The East public house (5mins).

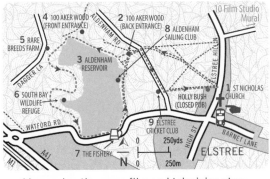

Children can enter into the world of Winnie the Pooh in a themed woodland and play area, and there's a child-friendly pub too. Elstree is a name that can't be uttered without evoking the world of film-making, and the walk's finale is a mural honouring the many film and television stars who have worked at the local studios.

☛ Go back a few yards after alighting from the bus and on the same side is:

1 ST NICHOLAS CHURCH
High St, Elstree WD6 3EW

Buried here are no fewer than three murder victims and one of the country's most eccentric explorers was baptised here.

The first murder victim was Martha Ray, born in Elstree in 1742, who was shot in the head by her spurned lover on 7 April 1779. She gave birth to five children by the 4th earl of Sandwich, a member of the Hell Fire Club, who was 24 years older than her. She had a brief affair with a young army captain (later to become a vicar) called James Hackman. He later became excessively jealous and followed her to a Covent Garden theatre. When a stranger offered to escort her to her carriage, Rev. Hackman (as he now was) stepped forward with two pistols, shot Martha through the crown of the head with the right, and aimed the left at his own head, but the bullet glanced off merely wounding him. He was sentenced to death and was publicly hanged in front of a large crowd at Tyburn, and his body publicly dissected. Many pamphlets and poems about the crime were published as well as a novel, *Love and Madness* by Sir Herbert Croft in 1780. Martha's body was entombed inside this church under the chancel floor. In 1820, her coffin was discovered when the church was being renovated and she was reburied outside the vestry door (the back entrance), where it remains to this day.

The second victim interred here is William Weare, murdered locally in 1823 and buried about 20 yards to the east of the vestry door. He was a solicitor and a heavy gambler and won £300, a fortune in those days, for a game of billiards or cards from John Thurtell, who strongly suspected Weare of cheating. So Thurtell invited him to a cottage belonging to his friend William Probert, three miles from Elstree village, for 'a weekend's shooting'. They took Weare to the Waggon & Horses pub in Watling Street, Elstree, where he was shot in the face by Thurtell, but the bullet glanced off his cheek bone. Thurtell then cut Weare's throat with a knife, then battered him to death with his pistol. Thurtell, Probert and their accomplice Joseph Hunt dumped the body in a pond. Afterwards they enjoyed a supper of pork chops, drank, sang and shared out the victim's property. Probert gave evidence against Thurtell in return for immunity from prosecution. Thurtell faced the noose 'nonchalantly' in 1824.

His was the last public execution in Hertfordshire. Hunt was also sentenced to death, but this was commuted to transportation to Australia, where he eventually became a police constable. Probert was shunned for his treachery and hanged a year later for stealing a horse from a relative.

The third murder victim whose final resting place is here was Eliza Ebborn, from Watford. A married woman aged about 31, she was killed by a 24-year-old shoemaker, George Stratton, on 13 August 1882 in Elstree; she was buried four days later in the then new extension to the old churchyard. His death sentence was repealed and he was committed to an institution on grounds of insanity.

The eccentric explorer Richard Francis Burton (1821–90) was baptised in the church on 2 September 1821. During his career in the army of the East India Company, one of his assignments was to investigate (under cover) a brothel in Karachi believed to be used by soldiers after young boys, which led to his long-term interest in sexual practices. He became circumcised in order to disguise himself as a Muslim when going on a pilgrimage to Mecca as an explorer. In Somalia he was impaled by a javelin through his (facial) cheeks and had to escape with it still in his head, leaving him with a scar for the rest of his life. He could speak numerous languages, and translated the

Kama Sutra. In his travel books he also described sexual techniques in different regions of the world, hinting he had participated in them, so breaching sexual and racial taboos of the time. When baptised he was living with his uncle, Francis Burton, at Barham House (now called Hillside) in Allum Lane, which is on the bus journey from the station. The house was owned by Burton's grandfather, also Richard Baker (who is buried in the church).

☞ After visiting the church continue downhill a few yards and cross the road to the Holly Bush pub (which has closed down). Down the side of the pub are signs for two footpaths through the fields.

Take the one bearing right through the centre of the fields going downhill. Follow the 'Public Footpath' signpost and later a 'London Loop' one which takes you to Aldenham Road. Cross straight over through a kissing gate into a footway by a noticeboard for 'Aldenham Sailing Club' and another 'London Loop' sign (it is part of its Section 15). A few yards on the right is a kissing gate which is:

2 WINNIE THE POOH'S 100 AKER WOOD (BACK ENTRANCE)

This is not signposted as such, but you can enter 100 Aker Wood here and follow its route backwards. You will see more of the lake, however, if instead you continue along the path a short distance to:

3 ALDENHAM RESERVOIR

Part of Aldenham Country Park, the reservoir was hand dug by French prisoners of war from 1795 to 1797 for the Grand Union Canal Company to control water levels after the building of the canal. Mute swans, mallard, coots and moorhens are often seen on the lake, and there are populations of damselflies and dragonflies. The lake contains massive roach, carp, pike, bream and tench, but areas of angling are restricted and only for members of the Verulam Angling Club.

☞ Turn right by the reservoir and follow the Lakeside Path round its edge. This takes you across a footbridge over a stream to a car park (where a farmers' market is held on the last Saturday of each month, 10.00–14.00). The path to the right leads via a woodland path over a stream by 'Pooh Bridge' to the main entrance of:

4 WINNIE THE POOH'S 100 AKER WOOD

Free to enter and also part of Aldenham Country Park, this is a themed park for children to explore many of the places from the classic stories by A A Milne. They have been recreated from the book's illustrations by E H Shepard (which themselves were based on real locations in Ashdown Forest in Sussex) and include Pooh Bear's House, the Sandy Pit where Roo plays, a Nice Place for Picnics, the Bee Tree, the way to the North Pole, an area with Big Stones and Rocks, Rabbit's House, Christopher Robin's House, the Pooh Trap for Heffalumps, Piglet's House, Where the Woozle Wasn't, a Floody Place, Owl's House, Eeyore's Gloomy Place and Pooh's Thoughtful Spot. Quiz sheets are available with prizes, and Pooh sometimes walks around. It is indeed a nice place for picnics.

☛ Back at the car park, the other path continues round the lake and after a short distance on the right is the:

5 RARE BREEDS FARM

Aldenham Country Park, WD6 3BA ☎ 01438 861447
🖱 www.aldenhamcountrypark.co.uk ⊙ daily 09.00–17.00; last entry 16.30 £
The rarest breed here among the assortment of pigs, turkeys and the like is the whiteface woodland sheep, which is even rarer than the panda. They also have golden Guernsey goats, whose total numbers dwindled to just 30 at the end of war after most had been eaten by the islanders and German invaders. The modest entrance fee includes a bag of animal feed which you can give to the poultry, pigs and cattle; elsewhere you can observe bees in a special hive, ride on ponies

(at weekends and holidays) and walk through an orchard of very special apples and pears. On certain days a cheery handler tells you about raptors such as the eagle owl, peregrine falcon and European goshawk and lets you get close to them.

☞ Retrace your steps a short distance and turn right into a path signposted 'Nature Trail' and 'Lakeside Path' around the reservoir. After a while you come to:

6 SOUTH BAY WILDLIFE REFUGE

A notice tells you this is the quietest waterside part where plants and animals live undisturbed, as fishing and sailing are not allowed here. The trees by the water's edge are mainly alder and willow, and the smaller bankside plants include sedges and rushes. In the water are water bistort and water crowfoot. Swans, great crested grebes, water voles and shrews live and breed here. In the summer are damselflies, dragonflies, swallows, swifts and martins. In the autumn and winter there are Canada geese and cormorants.

☞ Further along the path it goes away from the reservoir to a farm where one signpost is the 'Nature Trail', which you have just taken, and the other to continue in the same direction on the 'Lakeside Path', which you follow. Eventually you will come to a wooden kissing gate on the right which takes you into Watford Road, where almost opposite is:

7 THE FISHERY

Watford Rd, Elstree WD6 3BE

A traditional child-friendly pub which serves real ale from the McMullen brewery in Hertford, and food from 12.00 to 21.00 every day. There is also a terrace lounge with a view over the lake.

✋ If you wish to end the walk here turn right out of the pub, walk a few yards round a bend, and cross the road to the bus stop for the 306 back to Elstree & Borehamwood station (3 an hour during the week, 1 an hour on Sunday). If it's late summer, while waiting you can pick blackberries by this stop.

☞ Otherwise continue along the Lakeside Path. After a short while you will come to:

8 ALDENHAM SAILING CLUB

Aldenham Country Park, WD6 3BD ☎ 020 8207 3782 🖱 www.aldenhamsc.co.uk

One of the oldest sailing clubs in the country, this has operated since the 1920s and has 16 boats for hire. On Sundays (10.00–14.00) and Wednesday evenings in summer you can watch races on the reservoir. The event we witnessed was contested by yachtsmen from the ages of 17 to 74. One of its most distinguished members was yachting author and journalist Ian Proctor (1918–92), who designed over a hundred sailing dinghies and cruisers, of which 65,000 were built. This earned him the title of 'Yachtsman of the Year' in 1965.

☞ Continue along the Lakeside Path a short distance and on the right is the path to the right (signposted 'London Loop' and 'Aldenham Road') where you first came to the reservoir. Follow this back to Aldenham Road. The shortest way back to the Holly Bush and the bus stop for the return journey is uphill through the fields you came down originally. But if this is very muddy and/or you would like to watch some village cricket, then turn right along Aldenham Road, and a short distance on the right is:

Sailing dinghies racing on Aldenham Reservoir.

9 ELSTREE CRICKET CLUB

Aldenham Rd, WD6 3BD

There is a good chance of seeing a village cricket match here at the weekends, especially Saturdays. Elstree Cricket Club was formed in 1878 and has two teams, one playing on Saturday, the other on Sunday. The ground is also used by Hatch End Cricket Club (founded in 1933) which plays on Saturdays. Both clubs welcome spectators.

☞ Almost opposite the cricket club is a path through a gap in the hedge, signposted 'Public Footpath 2 and 4', which is less muddy and goes up the side of the fields back to the Holly Bush. The bus stop for the return journey is on the same side of the road, near The East pub, for the 107 or 306 back to the railway station. In the station forecourt is a:

10 FILM STUDIO MURAL

Elstree is a name inextricably linked with film-making: the mural features stars Elizabeth Taylor, John Mills, Roger Moore and Vincent Price (as Dracula) who have all made movies here. It all started in 1914 when Neptune Studios (now the BBC Elstree Centre) was set up, and throughout the 20th century films and television brought thousands of jobs and millions of pounds to the area, which became known as the 'British Hollywood'. The main studios are nearby at Clarendon Road (BBC) and Shenley Road, where over 800 feature films have been made since 1927. Eventually six different studios operated within two miles of each other. By 1980, six of the top ten box office earners were made here. Barbara Windsor, best known for her role as pub landlady Peggy Mitchell in the BBC TV soap *EastEnders*, earns a special display for her three films made here (*Too Hot to Handle* in 1960, *Crooks in Cloisters* in 1964 and *The Boy Friend* in 1971). Early movies were directed by Alfred Hitchcock and later ones included the *Indiana Jones* and *Star Wars* series.

17 DISTANCE 4½ MILES
DIFFICULTY EASY
TIME 2HRS

TRENT COUNTRY PARK,
CIRCULAR

A DRAGON & QUEEN GUINEVERE'S GHOST

THROUGH A FRAGMENT OF A FORMER HUNTING FOREST AND
PAST A HAUNTED MOAT, ON THE TRAIL OF WINSTON CHURCHILL,
RUDOLF HESS AND DICK TURPIN.

This walk in the old county of Middlesex starts at Trent Country Park, where the former mansion now forms part of Middlesex University's campus. Lucky students, you may think: and in the interwar years it hosted the likes of Lawrence of Arabia and Charlie Chaplain at lavish society parties. The man who put his stamp on it after taking on the property, Philip Sassoon, also created what is the perfect chilling-out spot: an exquisite little Japanese Water Garden, where you might like to contemplate the strange cast list of characters that you encounter on the way.

☛ After leaving by the Cockfosters Road exit, turn right, go past the cemetery and holly bushes, and after about four minutes turn right through gates by the 'Trent Country Park' notice, into:

DISTANCE/DIFFICULTY 4½ miles. Easy with two short moderate climbs.

TIME 2hrs

MAP OS Explorer map 173

START Cockfosters tube station ❈ TQ281963

TAKING A BREAK Wildlife Animal Centre café, Cock & Dragon

GETTING THERE ⊖ To Cockfosters station (Piccadilly Line)

DIRECTIONS TO START Leave by the Cockfosters Road exit

---

1 TRENT COUNTRY PARK

This expanse of open land encompasses farmland, a golf course and an equestrian centre. In the 14th century it was formed part of Enfield Chase, one of Henry IV's hunting grounds. After the English Civil War, the Cromwellian government tried to sell it off to pay its troops. This didn't go down at all well with the peasants, who revolted as they realised they would lose their rights to graze animals, gather firewood and collect acorns to feed their pigs. They ambushed and killed soldiers, and kidnapped a sergeant.

In 1909 the ownership of the estate passed over to Sir Philip Sassoon (cousin of the World War I poet Siegfried Sassoon) who entertained film star Charlie Chaplin and Winston Churchill at the mansion here. During World War II the house became a prison for 84 captured German generals and other officers, among them Hitler's deputy Rudolf Hess. They were pampered into a false sense of security, with special rations of whisky and allowed to walk in the grounds. However, their conversations were bugged, with many anti-Nazi German refugees acting as 'secret listeners', and from this much evidence was gained about war crimes and the unsuccessful attempt to assassinate Hitler on 20 July 1944.

Since the peasants were disfranchised in the 17th century, things seem to have turned full circle and the park is now public property once again.

The hornbean trees growing here were, in the past, used to produce tough wood for the manufacture of a variety of products, from windmills to cogs, chopping blocks, and screws.

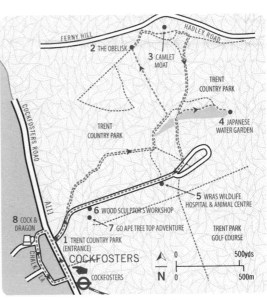

☞ After going through the gates, follow the road ahead through the park past a pond on the right. Soon you will reach a fork around a monument informing you the gardens were built in 1706. Take the left fork, past a café on the left in a car park, then left off the road into a track, by a 'London Loop' noticeboard (it is part of Section 17), through woods. Just before reaching a field the path bends right by the woods, then goes over a wooden bridge across a stream, out of the woods along the side of a field towards more woods. Turn left just before these woods and go downhill a short distance. The path then bends right by a large oak tree, then goes left uphill; you will soon see fish ponds on the right.

When you reach a signpost pointing several ways, turn sharp left where the sign points to 'Obelisk', through fields up towards woods. This moderate climb takes you across a wooden bridge over a tiny stream, through a gap in the woods, to the top, where you turn right by:

2 THE OBELISK

This tall stone erection is engraved 'To the memory of the birth of George Grey, Earl of Harold, son of Henry and Sophia, Duke and Duchess of Kent, in 1702.' All is not quite what it seems: in fact George was born in 1732 and died less than six months later.

☞ Follow the path around the edge of the woods, which forks right just before reaching Hadley Road. After a few yards go through a kissing gate on the left to:

3 CAMLET MOAT

'Camlet' is a shortened version of 'Camelot': indeed apparitions of a figure like Guinevere (King Arthur's legendary queen) are said to have been seen in a Holy Well here, as documented in *London's Camelot and the Secrets of the Grail* by Christopher Street. The moat is said to be haunted by Geoffrey De Mandeville, the Earl of Sussex and Hertfordshire, who was killed by an arrow in 1144 during

It is thought that Camlet Moat was originally dug out over 2,000 years ago.

a rebellion against King Stephen. He hid treasure down a very deep well in the area which his ghost is said to guard.

The moat is classified as an Ancient Monument, and is of Celtic origin so could be over 2,000 years old, and there are remains which indicate there was a drawbridge in Roman times, and habitation during the reign of William the Conqueror. It probably became used for hunting around 1140, and anyone found poaching was detained in a lodge, the ruins of which were used as a hiding place by highwayman Dick Turpin while on the run from the law. Part of the original wooden drawbridge was found recently and dated to about 1357.

After going through the kissing gate follow the path to the right with the moat on your left, over a wooden bridge with a fence on the right, then after a few yards go through a wooden gate on the right, then a few yards ahead left into a track.

When this reaches another crossing of tracks follow the signpost pointing to 'Lakes and Water Garden' and 'Animal Centre'. This is a wide track between trees, which leads to an open green area with another sign to 'Animal Centre' ahead and downhill.

At the bottom is a 'London Loop' arrow pointing ahead, and a few yards further is the signpost pointing several ways. Follow the sign pointing left to 'Water Garden' through a gap in the hedge and along a ditch to a large pond. Turn left, cross a small bridge over the ditch, and follow the pond's edge. When the edge of the pond turns right there is an information board. Take the steps to the left down to the:

4 JAPANESE WATER GARDEN

The plants in this idyllically peaceful place – the ideal spot for a picnic – may be local rather than exotic, but the inspiration here is Japanese, a mini-world of harmony and balance, with water the key feature to promote feelings of serenity and well-being. It is the creation of Sir Philip Sassoon, and he made sure it all fitted in with the contours. A restoration project in 2011–12 desilted the two overgrown lily ponds and planted new oxygenating water plants and lilies in the ponds; the rhododendron beds were newly planted with ornamental shrubs and trees, while overgrown areas were cleared.

☛ Retrace your steps to the signpost at the crossing of paths and take the one to the left signposted 'Oakwood Station'. This takes you across a bridge over a waterfall between two ponds and through woodland, and then through a kissing gate, to a short moderate climb with a fence on your left.

At the top, just after a notice warning about patrolling guard dogs, is another kissing gate which takes you into the grounds of Middlesex University's Trent Park Campus. Turn right into the lane, then after a few yards through a traffic control gate, to a small roundabout, in the centre of which is an 18th-century stone memorial to Jemima Crewe, Duchess of Kent (who died in 1728). Go over the roundabout, bearing right, and a few yards on the left is the:

5 WRAS WILDLIFE HOSPITAL & ANIMAL CENTRE

Trent Country Park, EN4 0PS ☎ 020 8344 2785 🖱 www.wras-enfieldwildlife. org.uk ◷ daily 10.00–17.00 (until 30mins before dusk in winter) £

The WRAS (Wildlife Rescue & Ambulance Service) is devoted to rescuing wounded and sick wild animals within their Wildlife Hospital, and the modest entrance fee goes to funding their work.

Within the Animal Centre on the site you can get close up to a whole range of creatures, including a feral goat called Buck, a Chinese water deer, bats, owls, hedgehogs and birds of prey. There is also a tea shop and a playground.

☛ Turn left out of the shop continuing along the road, through another traffic control gate, to a wide straight road, lined with trees, through the park. You can take a grass track a few yards to the right parallel with the road. By this path is a sign informing us about the butterflies in these hay meadows. These include the small tortoiseshell butterfly (the caterpillars of which feed on stinging nettles) and the common blue butterfly (whose caterpillars feed on bird's-foot).

Towards the end of this road, on the left, is a:

6 WOOD SCULPTOR'S WORKSHOP

🖱 www.friedelbueckingwoodsculptor.co.uk

Friedel Buecking has been a sculptor for 30 years and for the past ten has used this area as an open workshop to sculpt various animals from wood with a chain-saw. These are on display and on sale.

☛ Adjacent to this workshop is the:

7 GO APE TREE TOP ADVENTURE OBSTACLE COURSE

☎ 0845 094 8634 🖱 www.goape.co.uk/adventure £££

Mainly for children and young adults this includes being strapped into a harness and using zip wires, Tarzan swings and rope ladders to go around the woods.

☛ Walk a few more yards to the monument and follow the sign pointing left to 'Cockfosters Station.' This takes you back to Cockfosters Road. Turn right out of the gate and take the first left after a few yards into Chalk Lane. A short distance on the right is the:

8 COCK & DRAGON

🍺 14 Chalk Lane, Cockfosters EN4 9HU

This large comfortable pub dates back to 1798, and is named after the alleged slaughter of a dragon in the 17th century by a local villager called Jason, who so saved a Princess Louise.

A recommended real ale pub, it serves Greene King IPA and Sharp's Doom Bar, seasonal and guest ales and, in winter, mulled wine. Hot English and Thai food is served and there is a beer garden and a decked area for smokers.

We overheard one drinker telling another the ancient joke about comedian Max Miller standing on a station platform. An old lady asked him: 'Is this Cockfosters?' He replied: 'No, Miller's the name, ma'am. And kindly keep your hands to yourself.' Clearly one from his infamous blue book.

☛ Turn right out of the pub and bear left (following a 'London Loop' arrow) along Chalk Lane, past the playing fields of Cockfosters Bowling Club, Cockfosters Football Club and a cricket pitch all on the left, and back to Cockfosters Road. A few yards to the right is the subway to Cockfosters tube station.

MIDSOMER MURDERS TRAIL

INTO THE REALMS OF FICTION, WITH TV WHODUNITS AND
THE WORLD OF ROALD DAHL, IN THE CHILTERNS LANDSCAPE.

Beyond Amersham, this route runs village to village along the Misbourne valley, keeping company with the perch-laden River Misbourne ('bourne' meaning stream that disappears from time to time). We have seen red kites twice over the farmland and lakes, as well as numerous spottings of buzzards and herons. Watercress grows here in one or two places, a reminder of what used to be a major industry on the river, along with fish and milling.

The scene will be familiar to many views of ITV's *Midsomer Murders*, which were shot (with both guns and cameras) in this area of the Chilterns. Indeed *Missenden Murders* was considered as its original title. It started in

DISTANCE/DIFFICULTY 10 miles. Easy–moderate.

DROP-OUT POINT After 4½ miles

TIME 5hrs

MAP OS Explorer maps 172 and 181

START Amersham station ✹ SU964982

FINISH Black Horse, Great Missenden ✹ SP890020

TAKING A BREAK The Eagle, Crown Inn, Red Lion, Full Moon, George Inn, New Akesh Indian restaurant, Black Horse

GETTING THERE ⊖ Metropolitan Line from Baker Street, or 🚆 from Marylebone (journey time 35mins; daily, 1–2 an hour) to Amersham tube/railway station

DIRECTIONS TO START Turn left out of station's main exit

1997 and is still going strong, and on the walk you'll pass many of its locations. Roald Dahl's connections with the area are celebrated in great style at the excellent child-oriented museum devoted to him and his works at Great Missenden, the village where he lived and died.

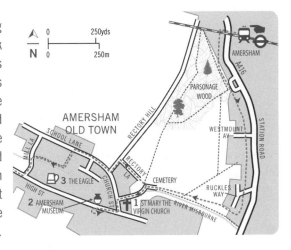

After leaving the station go downhill a few yards, turn left again under the railway bridge, down Station Road. After about 15 minutes, just before reaching the bottom of Station Road, turn right into a footpath marked 'Chiltern Heritage Trail', leading between fields and Tesco's car park (and the River Misbourne, which is very narrow at this point). When you reach a cemetery (St Mary's) you can make a short diversion over the small bridge across the river to:

1 ST MARY THE VIRGIN CHURCH

Church St, Old Amersham HP7 0DB

The church dates from about 1140, but long before then the site was used for baptisms by missionary monks of St Augustine (AD354–430), the patron saint of brewers and 'the alleviation of sore eyes'. A community play about the so-called Aylesbury Martyrs has been performed many times in the church. This concerns a dark episode in the 16th century when Henry VIII was still a Catholic, when the Lollards (early Protestants) were persecuted and 14 of them were burned for heresy. When one of them, William Tylesworth, was to be burnt in 1506 his daughter Joan was ordered to ignite the fire. Another, Thomas Chase, was tortured to death.

It was here that John Knox (1514–72), the leading Protestant and founder of Presbyterianism, preached his last sermon before fleeing from the new Catholic queen, Mary Tudor, in 1554. Many of the rectors were from the Drake family (descendants of admiral Sir Francis Drake's cousin). One of them, Rev. Arthur Tyrwhitt-Drake, died from an apoplectic fit at the end of his wedding service in the church in 1831 at the age of 31 and is commemorated by a memorial in the Drake Chapel.

Church funds have been raised by a variety of means over the years, the strangest perhaps being in 1539 when 'youngsters took turns tripping up passers-by, and tying them up until they agreed to make a payment' (from *St Mary's Church, Amersham: A Brief History and Guide*, by M J C Andrews-Reading).

☞ Nearby (left into Church Street and first right into Market Square then High Street) is:

2 AMERSHAM MUSEUM

49 High St, Old Amersham HP7 0DP ☎ 01494 723700
🖱 www.amershammuseum.org £

Housed in a 15th-century building the museum has exhibits from 2,000 years of local history.

☞ Return to the riverbank and continue along it. After the river goes underground keep following the path, until it forks. Take the left fork (Rectory Lane), and continue until you come to a road (Rectory Hill). Turn left and immediately right into School Lane. When you come to playing fields on the left (Barn Meadow Recreation Ground) go through them to the bottom where you will rejoin the river by some weeping willows. Turn right and follow the river. After a few yards there is a small footbridge over the river to the back of:

3 THE EAGLE

145 High St, Amersham HP7 0DY

Known as 'the poachers pub' in the 19th century (because of its discreet rear exit) it was licensed originally to sell only beer, cider and perry. Part of the building is 17th century but it did not become an alehouse until the middle of the 19th century. A traditional pub with real ale (including Adnams and Fuller's London Pride) and home-cooked food, it has a beer garden overlooking the river and meadow.

Continue along the riverbank. When you come to a road (Mill Lane), the river goes underground again under some cottages. Turn left here and immediately right. Follow the road uphill and take the path on the left which goes away from the road between trees and takes you up to the A413. Then turn right and after a few yards turn right into a footpath marked 'South Bucks Way'. This takes you down to the river again. Turn left under the road bridge, and follow the path away from the river to another road and Shardeloes House (not open to the public). Go through its grounds, fork right (following 'South Bucks Way' signs still), past the:

4 AMERSHAM CRICKET CLUB

Shardeloes, Missenden Rd, Old Amersham HP7 0RN

This club has been playing since the 1830s or even earlier. In the 1840s their star batsman was Rev. John Tyrwhitt-Drake and later his nephew, Rev. Edward Tyrwhitt-Drake, who went on to play first-class cricket for Cambridge University, specialising in slow left-arm underarm bowling; he was described as 'the prince of Buckinghamshire cricketers'. It has four Saturday teams and welcomes visitors.

Follow the perimeter fence until you come to a gate on the right (still marked 'South Bucks Way'). You will soon rejoin the river which goes to (on the right):

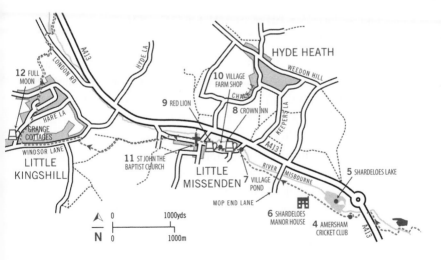

5 SHARDELOES LAKE

When the lake was being dug around 1750, remains of a Roman villa were found. Apart from swans it is visited by many species of bird and, in the first six months of 2013 alone, local twitchers spotted water rail, reed bunting, spotted flycatcher, mandarin duck, fieldfare, common teal, grey heron, shoveler and carrion crow.

☛ As you go round the lake, up on the hill to the left you will see:

6 SHARDELOES MANOR HOUSE

The present building was constructed in 1758 for William Drake, MP for Amersham, with Robert Adam designing its interior, and stands on the site of an earlier manor where Elizabeth I stayed in 1592. The Drake and Tyrwhitt-Drake family were Lords of the Manor whose wealth grew up to the 19th century, only for their fortunes to decline; Squire Drake had to sell most of his property in 1928 and the house was auctioned off in the 1930s. It later became a maternity home, then fell into disuse and was scheduled for demolition in 1953 but a local campaign saved the day, and it was converted into flats which were sold off in the 1970s.

☛ Keep following the 'South Bucks Way' signs through the fields and farmland until you come to a country lane. A few yards to the right is:

7 LITTLE MISSENDEN VILLAGE POND

You can spot plenty of large trout in this duck-patrolled body of water. The village's name comes from 'missen' (an old colloquial pronunciation of 'middle') and 'den' (an Anglo Saxon word meaning a valley). So it means 'middle valley', as the village is between the Chess Valley and Hughenden Valley. One of its most infamous residents was Dr Benjamin Bates (1736–1828), who moved about 1774 into the Manor House, built around 1600. A member of the notoriously scandalous Hell Fire Club, he was described as one of its leading members by E Beresford Chancellor in his 1925 book *The Lives of the Rakes: Volume IV, The Hell Fire Club*. Various debaucheries were practised by club members, whose motto 'Do what thou wilt' was later adopted by the satanist Aleister Crowley (1875–1947).

Little Missenden.

👉 A few yards to the left is the:

8 CROWN INN

🍺 Little Missenden HP7 0RD

A recommended real ale pub which sells Adnams, Directors, Rebellion and Tribute. The landlord is a keen golfer and he arranges visits to local clubs for those who stay overnight in his converted barn which has three rooms.

👉 A few minutes' walk further along the lane, on the right, is the:

9 RED LION

🏅 Little Missenden HP7 0QZ

This claims to have been visited by many monarchs from George II to Elizabeth II, and Prince Harry recently dropped in for ham, egg and chips.

The Red Lion has so far featured in three episodes of *Midsomer Murders*, and dates back to 1649 when it was a coaching inn for the Uxbridge to Aylesbury route. When the railway was completed in 1900, many people travelled from Amersham to spend a few days in the countryside, often staying at this pub (it still does bed and breakfast). The evidence of these guests is seen in the form of the unique table mats that show entries from its visitors' book of those days. One from Dalston Rambling Club, dated 4 August 1913, states they 'had a very enjoyable tea, so much so that the members of the Choral Class could not refrain from singing some glees'. The pub still has a piano which attracts local musicians who play live on Saturday nights. Real ale includes Sharp's Doom Bar and Wadworth 6X, and there's a dartboard; walkers are requested to remove muddy boots.

Adjoining the pub is a large fish-pond, which attracts swans, ducks and ducklings (one of which we witnessed stopping a lorry on the road). The landlord for nearly 30 years, Alan How, keeps a pet fox, pigs and rare chickens.

☛ Next to the pub is the:

10 VILLAGE/FARM SHOP

This has often been filmed on *Midsomer Murders*. Free-range sausages are a speciality plus old black-and-white postcards of the village.

☛ Continue along the road until you come (on the right) to:

11 ST JOHN THE BAPTIST CHURCH

Little Missenden HP7 0RA 🖱 www.lmchurch.org

The River Misbourne flows past the back of this Saxon church, the oldest part of which dates back to AD975. Two *Midsomer Murders* have been filmed here, and film star Diana Rigg (who appeared in the television series *The Avengers* and the James Bond film *On Her Majesty's Secret Service*) attended school services here.

Roald Dahl loved the church and gave it a medieval cherub's head (on the high left corner of the chancel arch) and a wooden figure of St Catherine (a copy of which is on the north wall). Particularly striking is its stained-glass window 'Faith, Hope and Charity', in the style of William Morris and Edward Burne-Jones.

King John, while Prince, gave two bells to the church. He often stayed in the nearby royal hunting lodge at Ashwell Farm, Little

Kingshill, where reports of wild parties with loose women and alcohol were rife.

The church is the main venue of the famous Little Missenden Music Festival which started in 1961 and is still going strong, every October. It includes classical music, jazz, folk, poetry, art lectures and children's events.

✋ You can opt out here if you time it right – buses from the village run only twice a week in each direction! Alternatively, you may wish to walk back to Amersham, stay overnight in one of the two pubs, or phone the local taxi firm which is Kingshill Cars (☎ 01494 868699/07852 898699).

👉 If you do carry on, continue along the road, just past Highmore Cottages on the left, to a kissing gate on the left signposted 'Chiltern Heritage Trail', cross a paddock diagonally through to the far side and another kissing gate, over a public bridleway and then keep ahead on the path marked 'South Bucks Way'. This takes you uphill with a hedge on your right and a field by a wood on the left. The path winds right, then left between a pylon and a hedge downhill towards more woods. After just a few yards there is an easily missed 'Public Footpath' yellow arrow quite high on a telegraph pole, pointing right through the middle of a large arable field. The path is not clearly delineated, but go through the field bearing slightly left to the far side to more woods bordered by a hedge.

Here 'Chiltern Society Footpath Walk' yellow signs point both ways: follow the one pointing right, round the edge of the field following the hedge. It winds to the right, then the left and left again to a gap through the hedge, marked with a Buckinghamshire County Council 'Public Footpath' yellow arrow. There is also a 'Town Path Bridlepath Association' notice facing the other way. This takes you along a tree-lined path to a lane (Windsor Lane, just to the left of the junction with Deep Mill Lane).

Turn left following the 'South Bucks Way' and 'Chiltern Heritage Trail Walking Route' signs along the lane for about ten minutes, past Little Kingshill Village Hall on the left, to the village green and playground on the right (by a desolate bus stop for the 27a).

Turn right along the far side of the village green, marked 'South Bucks Way', to a path between houses. This takes you to the:

12 FULL MOON

Hare Lane, Little Kingshill HP16 0EE (opposite Grange Cottages)

A traditional independently run pub which serves Adnams, Fuller's London Pride, Young's, guest ales and hot food, and has a large beer garden.

👉 Continue along the charming Hare Lane. After a short distance take the left fork into New Road. When you reach the corner of Wychwood, follow the path just to the left of the road between a holly bush and a fence marked 'South Bucks Way'. When you come to a road, cross it and continue along the path ahead between the fence to Cullen House and a holly bush. This takes you to a kissing gate into a field, follow the path bearing right and ahead round the edge of the field. After a while the path goes right, through a gap in the hedge and under a railway bridge. Keep following the path, turning left at the 'Public Footpath' sign beside some fenced-off playing fields on the left.

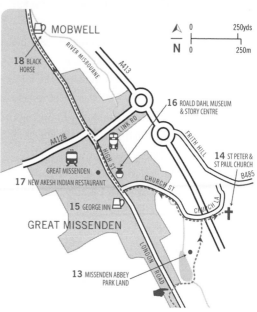

On the right is a sign by a back garden: 'Our dog loves children but couldn't eat a whole one.'

Follow the path as it turns left round the other side of the playing fields to a kissing gate on the right to a road. Turn left into the 'Chiltern Society Footpath' between trees parallel with the road for a short distance back to the road, which you cross, and follow the path ahead, which takes you to a kissing gate into a meadow. This is:

13 MISSENDEN ABBEY PARKLAND

William de Missenden founded Missenden Abbey in 1133. It was dissolved in 1538, when most of it was demolished. It was rebuilt in

1787 and bought in 1947 by Buckinghamshire County Council to use as an adult education centre. A fire in 1985 destroyed most of it but the council rebuilt it, uncovering part of its medieval structure in the process. Now it belongs to Buckinghamshire New University and can be hired for receptions of up to a hundred guests.

☞ After entering the meadow go past an old footbridge by a pond (part of the River Misbourne) and through the middle of the field ahead (sometimes containing cows and bulls) to the far side and another kissing gate with yellow arrows and a few wooden steps up to a bridge over the main road. On the other side of the bridge is:

14 ST PETER & ST PAUL'S CHURCH

Church Lane, Great Missenden HP16 0BA 🖱 www.missendenchurch.org.uk

The world-famous author Roald Dahl (1916–90) is buried in the churchyard. He had, according to his daughter, 'a sort of Viking funeral' as befitted his Norwegian parentage. On his insistence his snooker cues, a bottle of burgundy, chocolates, pencils and a power saw were all buried with him. More of him later. The church itself was built in the 14th century and restored in the 19th century.

☞ Go back over the road bridge, bear right and take the path to the left of the lane (Church Lane) between trees running alongside it marked 'Public Footpath' and 'South Bucks Way'. Follow it to the left when it comes to a narrow lane with pretty cottages on the right. It soon becomes a charming street (Church Street) which takes you to the junction with High Street.

On the other side to the left is the:

15 GEORGE INN

94 High St, Great Missenden HP14 0BG

A historic coaching inn which dates back to the 14th century, and still has the coaching arch and courtyard. The timber beams were made from the remains of a wooden galleon.

It has a log fire, real ale (including Sharp's Doom Bar and Rebellion Mutiny), pool table and dartboard. Friendly and down to earth, it has four rooms available for bed and breakfast.

☞ Turn left out of the pub and a short way on the right is:

16 ROALD DAHL MUSEUM & STORY CENTRE

81–83 High St, Great Missenden HP16 0AL ☎ 01494 892192

💻 www.roalddahlmuseum.org ⏰ Tue–Fri 10–5, Sat–Sun 11–5 ££ 💰

A wonderful homage to one of the most-read children's authors of all time (not to mention his huge success with adult fiction too). This museum is aimed at 6–12 year olds, but visiting adults have found their own creativity inspired by observing the children's interactive story-telling and craft sessions, and the colourful displays about the author's life interest young and old.

Many characters in Great Missenden inspired Roald Dahl's books, which sold over 100 million copies in about 50 languages. In 1986 he turned down an OBE, wanting instead a knighthood so his wife could become Lady Dahl.

Born in Wales of Norwegian parents, Dahl served in the RAF during the war, becoming a wing commander. He shot down five planes, earning the title of 'ace', and began writing in 1942. He moved to Gipsy House in Great Missenden in 1954, where he wrote in the small hut at the end of the garden, next to a traditional gypsy wagon he had bought as a playhouse for his children. The hut was described as a dingy but cosy refuge. A dirty plastic curtain covered the window, and he sat on a faded armchair inherited from his mother, writing with pencils and paper as he could not type. Next to him on a table he kept a ball made from silver wrappings off the many chocolate bars he had consumed in his youth, which may have helped inspire one of his most famous books, *Charlie and the Chocolate Factory*, published in 1964. Also on the table was one of his arthritic hip bones, which perhaps helped him write one of his short stories, *Lamb to the Slaughter*, in 1953. In this a woman beats her husband to death with a leg of lamb, then feeds it to the detective investigating the killing, who therefore destroys the evidence. This was televised in the ITV series *Roald Dahl's Tales of the Unexpected* which ran from 1979 to 1988, and which he introduced on screen.

There is an on-site café (Café Twit, no less) selling delicious homemade cakes and Roald-Dahl inspired drinks – try a Whizzpopper hot chocolate if you're not counting calories…

☛ Continue up the street and a short distance on the left is:

17 NEW AKESH INDIAN RESTAURANT
56 High St, Great Missenden HP16 0AU ☎ 01494 866953
We were hungry and tired after our long trek and found this a good-value restaurant.

☛ Continue along the High Street, past the sign to the railway station on the left and up Aylesbury Road, where eventually after about a walk of about 15 minutes on the right is the:

18 BLACK HORSE
Aylesbury Rd, Mobwell, Great Missenden HP16 9AX
The River Misbourne flows by the dog-friendly pub which has a large play area for children and a five-a-side football pitch, plus a large patio where barbecues are served in summer. It has an open fireplace and real ales include Sharp's Doom Bar; there's a dartboard. Hot-air balloons (🖱 www.adventureballoons.co.uk/buckinghamshire-balloon-flights) take off and land regularly from the fields next to this pub in the summer.

☛ For your return journey you can travel either free on your Freedom Pass by bus, or pay for a rail ticket for one stop. Retrace your steps to the High Street, where you can get the 55 bus from Great Missenden Library, HP16 0AL, which is just below Station Approach on the other side. It only goes every 2–3 hours (weekdays only) and takes 17 minutes to Amersham station where you can use your Freedom Pass again.

Alternatively you can follow the sign off the High Street to Great Missenden railway station, in Station Approach, and pay for a ticket to Amersham where again your Freedom Pass is valid.

> ## UPDATES WEBSITE
> Why not post your comments and recommendations, and read the latest feedback and updates from other readers online at 🖱 www.bradtupdates.com/freedompass?

19	DISTANCE 7 MILES DIFFICULTY EASY TIME 3½HRS	RIVER DARENT: FARNINGHAM TO DARTFORD

FROM DICKENS TO THE ROLLING STONES

ALONG THE DARENT VALLEY FOOTPATH TO ENCOUNTER AN INTRIGUING CAST OF KENTISH CHARACTERS

Although it ends in central Dartford, this walk gets some pleasingly rural stretches along the Darent as it winds through meadows, pastures, farmlands and woodlands. What is special about the walk is that it follows the river practically the whole way, except for a few very short stretches, as it flows through the Darent (sometimes spelt Darenth) Valley which is designated an

DISTANCE/DIFFICULTY 7 miles. Easy.

DROP-OUT POINT After 3, 4½ and 5 miles

TIME 3½hrs

MAP OS Explorer map 162

START Lion Hotel, Farningham ❄ TQ546671

FINISH Hufflers Arms, Dartford ❄ TQ542744

TAKING A BREAK The Chequers (Farningham), The Lion Hotel, The Bridges, The Chequers (Darenth), Brookland Lakes café, The Paper Moon, Wat Tyler, The Hufflers Arms

GETTING THERE 🚆 To Swanley station from London Victoria (25–31mins; 3 an hour Mon–Sat, hourly Sun)

DIRECTIONS TO START Take exit out of station by Platform 1 into Station Approach, go to the end of the road to the junction, turn right to the bus stop on the same side of road. 🚌 478 for a 7-minute journey to Farningham (hourly service, none on Sunday). Get off at the Lion Hotel stop.

Area of Outstanding Beauty. You'll see where Dickens fished for trout, where Mick Jagger and Keith Richards of the Rolling Stones met up, and where Wat Tyler gathered support during the Peasants' Revolt in 1381. Among a good number of pubs is one run by a former heavyweight wrestling champion of the world.

Go back a few yards from where the bus came from, to the corner, where you will find:

1 THE CHEQUERS

87 High St (corner of Dartford Road), Farningham DA4 0DT

Rolling Stones memorabilia adorns this pub, in celebration of local boys Keith Richard and Mick Jagger who hail from nearby Dartford. A cosy traditional place, this serves Harveys Sussex Bitter, Fuller's London Pride and other real ales, plus food including cheese and onion rolls. It also has a dartboard.

Retrace your steps past the bus stop down to, on the left:

2 THE LION HOTEL

High St, Farningham DA4 0DP

This pub dates back to the 16th century and was once visited by Charles Dickens when he was trout-fishing on the adjoining

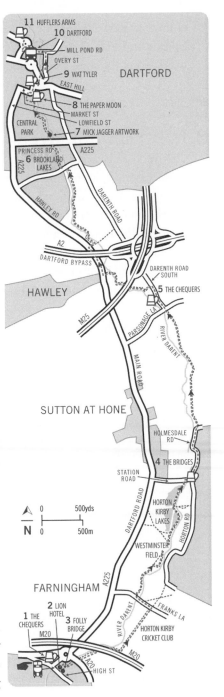

riverbank. Real ales include Harveys Sussex Bitter, Shepherd Neame Spitfire and Fuller's London Pride; you can drink in the beer garden overlooking the river, and hot food is available.

☞ Opposite the pub is the:

3 FOLLY BRIDGE OVER THE RIVER DARENT

This was built between 1740 and 1770 to prevent cattle from wandering downstream while crossing the ford, and is a strikingly ornate example of its kind. Water mint and wild watercress grow by the banks of the Darent, and herons, swans and kingfishers may be seen on and around the river. The Darent's name derives from a Celtic word for Oak River and has been settled since 6000BC. Edmund Spenser (1552–99) refers to the Darent in his poem *Fairie Queen* as 'the still Darent, in whose waters cleane/Ten thousand fishes play, and decke his pleasant streame.'

☞ Turn left along the river on its left bank following the 'Darent Valley Footpath' signs. Soon you cross a wooden footbridge to the other side and continue along the right bank through meadows and pastures, and under a bridge carrying the A20 road then under another beneath the M20. Shortly afterwards the path goes right over a footbridge then left through a stile between two fences. Soon you reach Horton Kirby Cricket Club ground on the right. Here turn left into a lane (Franks Lane) and go a short distance to a bridge over the river, then turn right and continue along its left bank, with trees by the river and fields on the left. Soon you go through a stile into a football field (Westminster Field). By the pavilion on the right, turn right through a gate back to the river and continue a short distance along the left bank. The path returns to the football field and then right, past Horton Kirby Lakes on the left, and back to the left bank of the river past rapids. When you reach a road (Station Road) and a large railway viaduct parallel to it, turn right and cross the bridge over the river and on the corner on the left is:

4 THE BRIDGES

📍 Horton Rd (corner of Station Rd), South Darenth DA4 9AX

A fine traditional pub run by former world wrestling heavyweight champion, Wayne Bridges and his wife Sarah, the former British heavyweight bodybuilding champion. There are many photographs

Former champions Wayne Bridges and his wife Sarah run The Bridges pub.

of them and their showbiz friends who have visited the pub, along with local history pictures, firemen's helmets, musical instruments and horse brasses. It serves crusty cheese and onion rolls, hot food and real ales (Sharp's Doom Bar plus guests).

Wayne (real name Bill) fought professionally from 1964 to 1988, often on television, and became the first British wrestler for over 60 years to become world heavyweight champion in 1979. He later lost the title but regained it in 1981 when beating the American giant known as 'The Mississippi Mauler' at the Wembley Arena. In those days Wayne weighed over 17 stone. His famous opponents included Masambula, the African Witchdoctor, Pat Roach (who later starred in the television series *Auf Weidersehen Pet*), the Wild Man of Borneo (Gungha Singh), Crusher Verdu, Wild Angus and Romany Riley (a fellow native of Kent). Sarah became the British heavyweight female bodybuilding champion in 2003, after being bitten by a dog who broke her finger, confining her to hospital and disrupting her training just three weeks before the competition. She is a professional and the biggest in the world by height and size. She is also a judge for the UK Bodybuilding Federation, gives nutritional and training advice to wrestlers, and has starred in films including *The Good Thief* (2001).

If you want to leave the walk at this point, go back over the bridge across the river, along Station Road a short distance to Farningham Road railway station (a small charge will cover you to Swanley and back into the Freedom Pass zone).

☞ To continue the walk, turn left out of the pub along Horton Road, under the railway viaduct, a short distance to the Jolly Millers pub.

✋ Opposite the Jolly Millers is a bus stop for the 414 to Dartford railway station (32-minute journey, 2 an hour, none on Sunday). You can use your Freedom Pass on the bus and the train.

☞ Otherwise bear left at the pub back to the river, turn right and follow it along the right bank along Holmesdale Road. As the road bends right, away from the river, turn left at The White House (signposted 'Darenth Valley Footpath'), over a stile between fences into an arable field. The path goes back to the river for a while, then away from it, then down steps to a path fenced off from a private lane on the left, which takes you to another road (Parsonage Lane). Go straight over it ahead into Darenth Road South. A short distance on the left is:

5 THE CHEQUERS

Darenth Rd South, Darenth DA2 7QT

Another traditional family-friendly pub with a beer garden, The Chequers does hot food, including a Sunday roast. Real ales are Sharp's Doom Bar, Fuller's London Pride and a guest.

☞ Continue along Darenth Road South to the end of the made-up road, then left through a kissing gate, signposted 'Darenth Valley Footpath', through a field and back to the river on its right bank. Follow it under the M25, sticking to the right bank of the river, for a short distance then cross a wooden footbridge over the river to the left bank, then left away from the river to a road (Hawley Road, A225) with Mill Road ahead. Turn right along Hawley Road (signposted 'Darenth Valley Footpath').

✋ A short distance on the right is the Shirehall Road Bus Stop in Hawley for the 414 bus to Horton Kirby. You are now just 2½ miles from Dartford station. To get the bus there you need the bus stop on the other side of the road.

☞ Continue along the Hawley Road a short distance under the A2, and after a few yards turn right over a stile (signposted 'Darenth Valley Footpath') into a field and fork left, back to the river and continue along its left bank on an asphalt path. After a short distance cross over a wooden bridge to the right bank of the river and through woodlands. When you come to a road, turn left, over the road bridge across the river, and then right, following the left bank of the river. This takes you on a path between the river and the:

6 BROOKLANDS LAKES

This is a private fishing lake but has waterside trails open to the public, and is described by Kent County Council as 'a peaceful place for a lakeside stroll'. There is also a café (08.00–15.00; closed Sunday). Those wishing to fish can buy a day ticket; carp up to 30 pounds have been caught here, but have to be returned to the water.

☛ Walk round the edge of the lake as it bends left, then turn off to the right (signposted 'Central Park') through The Princes Tunnel. If this is locked take the steps on the left up to the road (Princes Road), cross the road diagonally right to the path on the other side, then follow it through zigzags down to Central Park and back to the left bank of the river. Here there is a:

7 MICK JAGGER ARTWORK

Central Park, Dartford

This ironwork stencil-style silhouette two-dimensional artwork portrays Rolling Stones singer Mick Jagger. He was born in Dartford in 1943 and attended the local Wentworth Primary School, where fellow Rolling Stone, Keith Richards, was also a pupil but a year behind. Mick Jagger lived at nearby Denver Road, and later attended the local grammar school. The Mick Jagger Centre live music venue is in Shepherds Lane, Dartford DA1 2JZ.

☛ Continue along the riverbank, where we saw parakeets in a willow tree, until it is fenced off. Then take the path to the left, past a playground, through a gate, to an ornamental bridge, and then right to the park exit. Turn right into Market Street (with Dartford Museum on the right) and up to the corner of the High Street. On the right is:

8 THE PAPER MOON

🍺 55 High St, Dartford DA1 1DS

A Wetherspoon's community pub, the name of which reflects the town's history of papermaking, this holds regular dart competitions.

Its eight real ales include Adnams, Greene King Abbot, Ruddles and Kent Boss's Brew.

☞ Directly opposite (on the corner of Bullace Lane) is the:

9 WAT TYLER

80 High St, Dartford DA1 1DE

A historic pub named after the Peasants' Revolt leader of 1381 who drank here on the march to London. Dartford was one of the early towns to rise up on 5 June of that year, initially against the hated poll tax.

A plaque on the pub wall proclaims Wat and his followers 'called at this ancient tavern (so it is said) to quench their thirst with flagons of ale' before marching to London to see the king and demand 'that you make us free for ever, ourselves, our heirs and our lands and that we be called no more bond or so reputed'. The young king, Richard II, playing for time, promised he would grant them freedom.

The king met Tyler again at Smithfield on 15 June. When the king asked Tyler to disperse his followers the latter swore he would not leave until he had a charter signed and sealed, which abolished serfdom and divided all land among the commoners. The king agreed to this as long as he was able to retain his crown. Tyler celebrated by drinking a jug of ale in one go, but was then stabbed several times by the Mayor of London, William of Walworth. His supporters carried his wounded body to the nearby St Bartholomew's hospital for the poor. But Walworth followed and dragged him out and beheaded him. He then took the head on a pole to the king who thanked him and knighted him.

Many of the peasants were then slaughtered by the king's soldiers but some escaped and returned to this pub (then called the Rose and Crown).

Four hundred years later, Thomas Paine (who fought in both the American and French revolutions) said of Tyler: 'All his proposals made to Richard were on a more just and public ground than those which had been made to John by the Barons... If the Barons merited a monument to be erected in Runnymede, Tyler merits one in Smithfield.'

Sadly the only legacy he has in Smithfield is the dagger which killed him, held in Fishmongers Hall.

☞ Turn right into the High Street, past Dartford Parish Church, a short distance to the river. Turn left into St Saviours Walk and along the left bank. This takes you under a subway, up to the left and along the river, still on the left bank, over a wooden bridge to the right bank, through a car park to Overy Street. Turn left, under a railway bridge, and first left into Mill Pond Road. This takes you over the river, which then bends parallel with the road. This takes you to a roundabout.

Continue following the 'Darent Valley Footpath' signs to the right, which then take you left into St Saviours Walk, and back to the river. After a few minutes cross a wooden bridge, signed underfoot 'Darent Valley Footpath'. A bit further on turn left under a railway bridge into Mill Pond Road, to a roundabout. Take the first turning (Hythe Street), and a few yards on the left are steps up to:

10 DARTFORD RAILWAY STATION

This is where Mick Jagger and Keith Richards met, on Platform 2 on 17 October 1961. Mick, aged 18, was on his way to the London School of Economics where he was a student, and Keith, aged 17, was on his way to Sidcup Art College, where he was a student (after being expelled from Dartford Technical School for truancy). Keith was carrying his guitar and Mick his rhythm and blues records. They recognised each other from Wentworth Primary School and got chatting and discussed music on the train.

Richards (who had lived in Morland Avenue until it was hit by a V1 flying bomb, and then in Chastillian Road and the Temple Hill council estate) joined Jagger's group, Little Boy Blue and the Blue Boys, but a year later they met Brian Jones and Ian Stewart to form the Rolling Stones.

A blue plaque is being planned to commemorate this meeting.

☞ From here you can get trains to Victoria or Charing Cross. But if you would like to have a drink first, take the third turning off the roundabout into Hythe Street (Lower). There on the left is:

11 THE HUFFLERS ARMS

Hythe St (Lower), Dartford DA1 1BN
A cosy community family-friendly pub with a dartboard, a pool table and a jukebox, but no real ale.

BROOKSIDE &
THE BIG GREEN SPACE

A BROOKSIDE EXPLORATION THROUGH WELL-HEELED SOUTHWEST LONDON,
ON A REMARKABLY GREEN JOURNEY NORTHWARDS TO THE THAMES.

Walk along the modestly sized Beverley Brook and you can hardly fail to be impressed by the sheer size of southwest London's urban commons – vital green lungs in some very select suburbs and the longest joined-up parkland in London. That they join up to make one contiguous swathe means you can really stretch your legs and pace out in this quasi-country walk, which takes in an eerie Victorian graveyard, stalked by a devilish imp in the 1830s. If you want to extend it, there are almost infinite possibilities, with a vast network of official and unofficial paths over Wimbledon Common, where the

DISTANCE/DIFFICULTY 7 miles. Easy.

DROP-OUT POINT After 4, 6 miles and 6½ miles

TIME 3½hrs

MAP OS Explorer map 161; a *Guide to the Beverley Brook Walk* with a map can be downloaded from 🖰 www.merton.gov.uk/visiting/attractions/beverleybrookwalk.html

START New Malden railway station ❋ TQ214687

FINISH Putney Bridge ❋ TQ242756

TAKING A BREAK Halfway House, Duke's Head, Star & Garter, The Eight Bells

GETTING THERE 🚃 To New Malden from Waterloo (22mins; 5–8 an hour, 4 on Sun)

DIRECTIONS TO START Turn right out of the station into Coombe Road windmill makes a useful objective, or into the breezy, rather wild expanse of Richmond Park with its lakes, herds of deer and splendid azaleas within the Isabella Plantation. Near Barnes Common, the centre of Barnes still evokes village origins, and soon after the brook you've been following all these miles finally discharges into the Thames. Francophiles will be able to collect a meat-like fungus still eaten by the French, and play that country's game of boules.

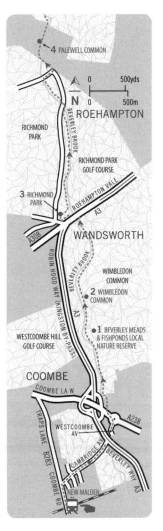

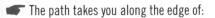 After turning right into Coombe Road, take the second turning on the right (Cambridge Avenue) and keep going to a woodland path ahead through a golf course. Continue through a subway under the A3, then left and left again on to the bank of the Beverley Brook. Continue along Westcombe Avenue, then turn left into Coombe Lane and right into Beverley Avenue. At the end turn left into a path, then right by some playing fields. Follow the brook on your left through woodlands and past the:

1 BEVERLEY MEADS & FISHPONDS LOCAL NATURE RESERVE

Kingfishers and mandarin ducks are often to be seen here.

The path takes you along the edge of:

2 WIMBLEDON COMMON

A huge expanse of woodland as well as heathy areas with heather and gorse, this is one of London's largest open spaces. It is designated a Site of Special Scientific Interest and is a habitat for many woodland birds and insects. Local inhabitants in the 16th century were obliged by law to practise archery regularly here, and the common was used for duels in the 19th century. The most famous was on 16 September 1809 between future prime minister George Canning (1770–1827) and future foreign minister Lord Castlereagh (1769–1822). Canning had tried to get Castlereagh sacked for sending troops to Holland to open a front against Napoleon which had proved disastrous. Castlereagh shot and wounded Canning in the leg.

☞ The path is part of the Capital Ring for a short way. Just before reaching a sports pavilion turn left across a bridge over the brook, and then across a footbridge over the A3 to Kingston Vale Road and turn right.

✋ The 85 bus to Putney can be caught in Kingston Vale Road.

☞ To continue the walk take the first left into the Robin Hood Gate leading into:

3 RICHMOND PARK

This huge area of rough pasture, woodland and ponds remains one of London's largest untamed expanses. Its appearance can have changed little since Charles I enclosed it within a ten-mile boundary wall as a hunting park. Some 300 red and 350 fallow deer graze; the rutting season is in the autumn and the young are born in June. The park is a noted site for ancient trees, including a number of oaks planted before 1637. These in turn attract over 1,300 species of beetle such as the rare cardinal click beetle and the spectacularly outsized and increasingly scarce stag beetle (known by some Londoners as a 'horny bug') – Britain's biggest beetle. Over a hundred species of birds can be seen in the park, including skylarks, kestrels and tawny owls. Beefsteak fungus (a fruit that looks like raw meat, which used to be cooked and eaten as a substitute for it and still is in France) grows here.

☞ Inside the park take the path to the right, and then bear right at a fork after a short distance. This takes you back to the brook where you turn left and follow it. Cross a wooden bridge over the brook and turn left over the road, going along the other bank through the park. Turn right at the next road bridge, to the Roehampton Gate exit. Turn left immediately following the park wall, back to the brook and over it, then turn right. This takes you through:

Peddling past deer in Richmond Park.

4 PALEWELL COMMON

This appears in 16th-century manorial records and was owned by the Spencer family. It was taken over by the council in 1921 following a petition from local residents, and has since been developed as a public play area including pitch and putt, boules (the French game), tennis, football and cricket.

☞ Bear right along the brook, past a pitch and putt course on the left and the brook on the right, then by some allotments to Hertford Avenue. Turn right and keep going to Upper Richmond Road where you turn right.

✋ There are stops in Upper Richmond Road for the 33, 337 and 493 buses to Putney, Richmond and Hammersmith.

☞ To continue the walk turn left off Upper Richmond Road into Priests Bridge. Here you will find beside the brook:

5 HALFWAY HOUSE

24 Priests Bridge, Barnes SW14 8TA

Dating back to 1863 it was renovated in 1938, serves Fuller's real ale and has a dartboard. Well-behaved dogs are welcome. Hot food includes a homemade curry of the day.

☞ Continue along Priests Bridge, turning left at the end back into the main road. Take the second left into Vine Road.

✋ Take a woodland path off to the right from Vine Road to Barnes railway station, less than a quarter of a mile away, for frequent trains to Waterloo.

☞ Otherwise follow Vine Road over two railway crossings close to each other, then turn left into Scarth Road and immediately right, parallel with Vine Road, to the junction with Station Road. Cross over and follow the path ahead which bears left through:

6 BARNES COMMON

This designated nature reserve is an excellent place to see birds such as green woodpeckers and flowers such as the white-flowered Burnet rose (which blooms from May to July). It is also a feeding ground for the speckled wood butterfly. It was owned by the church in medieval times but is now managed by Richmond upon Thames council.

☞ Cross over Mill Hill Road, and continue ahead until you return to the brook with a bridge over it. Don't cross the bridge but turn right before it, along the brook a short distance then follow the path to the right through the common. Take the first path that forks off to the left and keep going until you reach Rocks Lane, cross it and follow the grassy path ahead.

When you reach a small car park turn left between some floodlit football pitches and tennis courts on the left. On the right is:

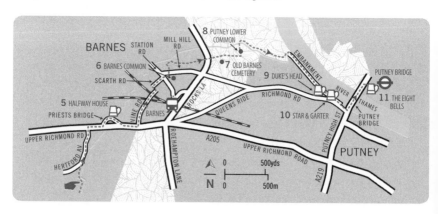

Old Barnes cemetery is said to be haunted.

7 OLD BARNES CEMETERY

Ghostly tales abound about this derelict and overgrown cemetery which was used from 1855 until the 1950s. A hovering nun is said to float over one of the graves, and Spring Heeled Jack (a devilish imp with pointed ears and piercing eyes) carried out a series of attacks on people in Victorian times. He was able to jump extraordinarily high, and was first seen in this area in 1837. Witnesses described him as devilish, terrifying and frightful in appearance, with a diabolical face, clawed hands plus sharp metallic claws, eyes like red balls of fire and an ability to breathe out blue and white flames. He was never caught.

☞ The path takes you through:

8 PUTNEY LOWER COMMON

The chiffchaff (a small olive-brown warbler which flits through trees and shrubs with its tail wagging) is among the birds that can be seen here in the summer. There are now hawthorn bushes where in Roman times it was open pasture and farmland.

☞ The path continues by some playing fields and through woodlands, and to the left across a footbridge over the brook. Then turn right and follow the brook all the way to the Thames (almost opposite Fulham football ground). Turn right along the Thames to Putney Bridge which is half a mile away. Overlooking the river are two pubs:

9 DUKE'S HEAD

8 Lower Richmond Rd, Putney SW15 1JN

A Victorian pub which is nearly 150 years old and serves Young's real ale and hot food.

10 STAR & GARTER

4 Lower Richmond Rd, Putney SW15 1JN

A hundred different wines and gins are available here, plus Old Speckled Hen and Greene King IPA real ales. It is close to the start of the annual Oxford and Cambridge University Boat Race, which has taken place between the rival universities on this stretch of the river since 1845. The pub's ballroom upstairs gives a good view of it. It was built in 1787 as a hotel for the boating and sailing community which thrived in those days.

☞ When you reach Putney Bridge cross it over the Thames, take the steps down to the left, go under the bridge and follow the road past another pub:

11 THE EIGHT BELLS

89 Fulham High Street, SW6 3JS

Food and real ale (including Fuller's London Pride and Hog's Back) is served.

☞ A few steps further is Putney Bridge tube station (on the District Line).

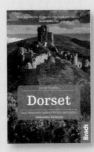
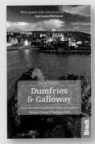
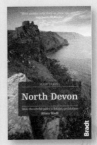

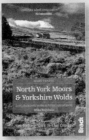
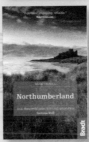
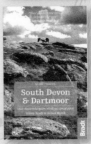

COLNE RIVERSIDE RAMBLE

NATURE IN A WATERY LANDSCAPE ON THE BANKS OF THE COLNE.

In the right season you might want to bring some fruit-picking equipment for this route along the River Colne. There may well be apples, sloes and blackberries. On our visit, the stinging nettles were particularly clean and young on this walk in the autumn which makes them very edible for soup (boiled) or wine (see *Food for Free* and others in *Useful publications*, page 11), though obviously you'll need rubber gloves and some scissors.

Otters and kingfishers frequent the Colne on its journey through the lakes, though in this nature reserve you're more likely to see moorhens, dragonflies, coots and ducks on and around the water. Irises, orchids, wild roses and water lilies

DISTANCE/DIFFICULTY 2½ miles. Easy.

TIME 1hr

MAP OS Explorer map 182

START Willowside, London Colney ❄ TL183036

TAKING A BREAK Green Dragon, The Bull

GETTING THERE ⊖ To High Barnet (Northern Line). Leave by station exit on left, follow the short slip road to Barnet Hill, turn left downhill to Bus Stop W on the right, get 84 bus to London Colney, Willowside stop (about 35mins, partly through pleasant countryside). Or 🚃 to Watford High Street (London Overground), go up the High Street to Bus Stop F for the 602 or 632 to London Colney, Willowside stop (about 50mins).

DIRECTIONS TO START See above

proliferate. In the lakes (which is private fishing) there are roach, perch and pike, while in the river (which is public fishing) there are chubb and pike.

It's only a short stroll, but you can make it a full day out by stopping for a pub lunch and visiting the child-oriented Willows Farm Village.

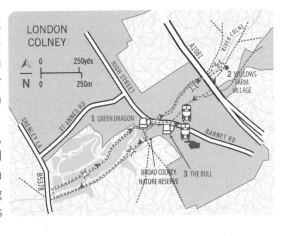

After getting off at the Willowside stop, continue in the same direction as the bus for a few yards past The Bull pub, and then across a bridge over the River Colne. On the other side turn left (following a signpost for 'Watling Chase Timberland Trail') down to the village green, past the Green Dragon pub, to the lakeside and turn right. Follow the river to a footbridge on the left, cross over it and then turn right (again signposted 'Watling Chase Timberland Trail').

Go past a sign saying 'Welcome to Broad Colney Nature Reserve', over another small bridge, turn right and at a crossing of paths continue ahead (signposted 'Watery Lane to Shenley Lane'). When you come to a fork bear right, sticking to the side of the lake.

River Colne leading to the road bridge built by Thomas Telford in 1775.

Just after a wooden bench (an ideal spot to sit and take in the view), turn right over a bridge (signposted 'Permissive off road bridleway link to Shenley Lane'), and then right again along the lakeside. At a wooden footbridge fork right.

When you come to the end of the lake, follow its edge round to the right, to the other side, until you reach a ford over the River Colne (very narrow at this point), take the path to the left, and follow the river on your right back to the village green. Here you are back at the:

1 GREEN DRAGON
 Waterside, London Colney AL2 1RB

An early 17th-century coaching inn with a beer garden overlooking the green and the lake. It has a sign proclaiming: 'Hot beer, lousy food, bad service', but we found the Fuller's London Pride, Abbot and Sharp's Doom Bar just the right warmth for our taste (there is an old joke that German visitors to the UK tell each other to drink their beer before it gets cold). The service was also warm, but we did not sample the food. Dogs (hot or otherwise) are allowed.

Go back over the bridge to the bus stop you came from and on the other side of the road is a stop for buses back to Barnet or Watford.

Tongue-in-cheek notice at the Green Dragon.

☛ Otherwise, continue along the river under the road bridge (built by Telford in 1775 and restored in 1998), then over a road and back to the lakeside through a wooded area. When you come to a wooden footbridge over the river to the right, don't cross it but keep ahead instead on the left bank. Go under the bypass and follow the route signposted 'Public footpath to Colney Heath, 2 miles'.

Turn right at the next concrete bridge, where a noticeboard reminds you this is the River Colne and advises you to have a close look for a few minutes as there are often fish swimming beneath the tree there. You may also be lucky enough to see dragonflies, moorhens or kingfishers.

On the other side is:

2 WILLOWS FARM VILLAGE
Coursers Rd, London Colney AL4 0PF ☎ 08701 299718
🖥 www.willowsfarmvillage.com ☉ daily 10.00–17.30 (last entry 16.30) ££

Farmyard animals such as sheep, goats, ponies and donkeys, as well as crops, are on display here, targeted at children with parents or grandparents. There are also funfair rides, children's shows, falconry displays and tractor rides.

☛ Turn right along the other riverbank back round the perimeter of the Farm Village. Turn right at the end into a road and under a flyover. After about 100 yards turn right through a black and yellow gate to a path which goes over a moat and then immediately left to the side of the lake. Go over a small footbridge to the left and round the lake (going quite close to a row of cottages on the left), through the woods and on to a road, where you turn right and ahead is:

3 THE BULL
🍺 Barnet Rd, London Colney AL2 1QU

Dating back to 1726, this inn has low timbered ceilings, a dartboard and pool table, a beer garden and a children's play area, and serves home-cooked food and real ales.

☛ Opposite the pub on the other side of the road is the stop for buses back to Barnet or Watford.

ANIMAL WORLD

WHITE HORSES, PEREGRINE FALCONS, BADGERS AND RARE BEETLES AWAIT IN THE SURREY FRINGES.

Chessington is a name most associated with its theme park and zoo, but this walk introduces you to some less celebrated gems. After a memorable mini-summit giving an unexpectedly wide view and passing within earshot of the children enjoying Chessington World of Adventures, you reach Ashtead Common. This is the largest of seven city commons in south London and a National Nature Reserve, with Sussex cattle grazing and giving it a noticeably countrified character. These cattle help keep the scrub grassland in sufficient trim for invertebrates and flora to thrive; the common is a noted site for nesting birds and birds of prey.

☛ Follow Garrison Lane to the junction with Leatherhead Road. Cross over diagonally to the left into Barwell Lane ahead. Go down this lane past some playing fields on the left, and then meadows on the right. Just after Chessington Recycling Station, the road bends to the right, and there is a kissing gate on the

---

DISTANCE/DIFFICULTY 5 miles. Easy with a few gradual climbs.

TIME 2–3hrs

MAP OS Explorer map 161

START Chessington South station ❄ TQ179633

TAKING A BREAK Barwell Café

GETTING THERE 🚊 To Chessington South station from London Waterloo (35mins; daily, 2 an hour) and Clapham Junction (25mins; daily, 2 an hour).

DIRECTIONS TO START Turn right out of station into Garrison Lane.

left with a sign stating: 'Warning, Animal behaviour is unpredictable, please do not feed them.' Go through this kissing gate into the path marked with the green and yellow 'Chessington Countryside Walk' arrows.

This path takes you through woods (including some fine cedar trees) up Winey Hill. Bear left near the top of the wood into a meadow and go straight through the middle of it slightly uphill. Near the top of the hill is a:

1 BRICK STAND VIEWPOINT

This shows you the distances and directions of places, including the BT Tower (14 miles away), that you can see from this excellent viewpoint, 246 feet above sea level. A bit further on by the very top is a pond which bizarrely has a fence going through the middle of it: we sincerely hope that any fish in it do not attempt to swim through to the forbidden side.

Continue ahead past the pond, down the hill to some more trees, including huge oaks, where you will hear the joyous screams of children in the Chessington World of Adventure to the left (when it is open). Go through another kissing gate, past

a meadow (where we saw three white horses galloping together), along a path with an electric fence on the right and a barbed wire one to the left. Just before you reach another fine oak tree, turn left over a stile, into the public footpath signposted 'Leatherhead Road, ⅓ mile.' This takes you to a track to the left (along the barbed wire fence of the Chessington World of Adventures) with signs 'Explorer Gate Park Entrance', and then on the left is the entrance to:

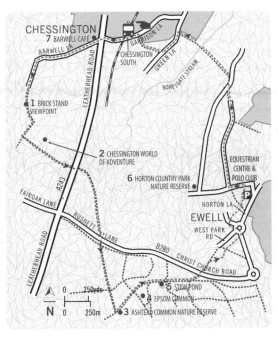

2 CHESSINGTON WORLD OF ADVENTURES & ZOO & SEA LIFE CENTRE

Leatherhead Rd, Chessington KT9 2NE ☎ 0871 663 4477
🖱 www.chessington.com 🕐 end Mar until early Nov, 10.00–17.00 or 18.00;
zoo also open w/ends in winter, 10.00–15.00 £££

A theme park with various rides as well as the long-established zoo, which first opened in 1931, and Sea Life Centre.

☛ Continue down the public footpath to the bottom, then cross over a stile ahead (signposted 'Public Footpath') through some woods.

When you go over another stile and reach a road (Leatherhead Road) with a sign pointing back to 'Claygate Common 1¼m', cross over it and go ahead on the bridleway signposted 'Ashtead Common 1 mile' through more woods, where butterflies and wild roses abound and there is an oak wood on the right.

Cross a small wooden bridge over a stream into the open.

Ashtead Common Nature Reserve.

AND THEY'RE OFF!

Dog-racing is not as well known as horse-racing at Epsom (walk 10), but can be seen on the surrounding downs. The whole area, including the famous race track where the Derby is run, is open to the public. Stop by to watch racehorses training on the sand gallops before popping in for a pint at the Tattenham Corner pub overlooking the race track.

WALKING THROUGH HISTORY

Some of the more colourful episodes of the country's rich history feature on these walks. These include the burial place of King Harold (killed at the Battle of Hastings), the murder of Thomas Becket, the struggle to keep Epping Forest open to the public and much more besides.

1 Lesnes Abbey was built in the 12th century in penance for the murder of Thomas Becket, **walk 9**. **2** This boundary post in Ashtead Common Nature Reserve marks the site where coal tax was levied as early as the Middle Ages right up until 1890, **walk 22**.

3 Lopping in Epping Forest in the 19th century depicted at Lopping Hall, Loughton, **walk 7**. 4 A mosaic outside Waltham Abbey where King Harold is buried, **walk 15**. 5 Detail from the *Golden Hinde II* replica galleon – Sir Francis Drake sailed the original around the world, **walk 23**. 6 Queen Elizabeth's Hunting Lodge in Epping Forest was built by Henry VIII in 1542, **walk 7**. 7 Famous horses and riders depicted on the gate to the enclosures at Epsom, **walk 10**. 8 The Old Operating Theatre (now a museum) where Keats watched operations including amputations, **walk 23**. 9 Corn-grinding stone by the River Wandle, **walk 13**.

40 Years of Pioneering Publishing

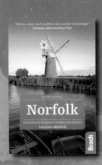

In 1974, Hilary Bradt took a road less travelled and published her first travel guide, written whilst floating down the Amazon.

40 years on and a string of awards later, Bradt has a list of 200 titles, including travel literature, Slow Travel guides and wildlife guides. And our pioneering spirit remains as strong as ever – we're happy to say there are still plenty of roads less travelled to explore!

Bradt ...take the road less travelled

When you come to a road (Rushett Lane) turn left then, after a few yards, turn right through a kissing gate on to a public bridleway, signposted 'Ashtead Common ½ mile'. This takes you ahead through the middle of an arable field, to the other side where there is a gap in the hedge, through which the bridleway goes slightly uphill (past a sign pointing to 'Leatherhead Road ½ mile' to the right and 'Ashford Common ¼ m' ahead) to some woods, which you enter through a kissing gate and a stile. This is part of:

3 ASHTEAD COMMON NATURE RESERVE

This ancient wooded common, owned by the Corporation of London, has a good number of pollarded oaks whose branches are cut on a rotational basis. Bats nest in the trees, while rotting wood houses fungi and rare invertebrates, and nectar from the flowers in the spring supports hoverflies, rare beetles, bees and butterflies. Two scheduled monuments are on the site: a Roman villa and a triangular earthwork. These are owned by the Corporation of London. From medieval times up to 1890, the Corporation had the power to tax coal coming into the city and marked the boundary with white iron posts, some of which are nearby, indicating the points where the tax became due.

Turn left along the bridleway (No. 29) signposted 'Epsom Common ½ mile' past one of these white iron posts. Keep on the bridleway past another sign 'Epsom Common ¼ mile', to a crossing of paths (with a sign 'Rushett Lane ½m' to the left) where you continue ahead following the bridleway to another crossroads signposted 'Christchurch Road, ⅓ mile.' This takes you through woods and then into the open. This is:

4 EPSOM COMMON

Up until World War II this was used for grazing, but then it was ploughed up to grow crops during the food shortage. Now, as a Site of Special Scientific Interest, grazing has been reintroduced in part of the common to conserve woodland and flora.

☛ After a while you will see on the right:

5 STEW POND
Christ Church Rd, Epsom

'Stew' means 'fish', and the pond was constructed by the Abbot of Chertsey in the 12th century evidently for that very purpose. It is stocked with a variety of carp and coarse species (for day fishing tickets ☎ 020 8777 9489).

☛ Follow the 'Chessington Countryside Walk' arrow ahead through woods to a track. When it reaches a wooden gate, fork to the left, following the 'Chessington Country Walk' and 'Thames Down Link' arrows, to a road (Christ Church Road), which you cross and follow the bridleway ahead signposted 'Horton Lane ¼ mile'. This takes you through a tree-lined

avenue, over another road, to West Park Road on the left, which leads to West Park Hospital (where peregrine falcons have been seen on its cooling towers). Just past West Park Road and a 'Noble Park' sign is a narrow public footpath marked 'Chalky Lane ½ mile' to the left, which you take. Follow this through a gate and turn right into:

6 HORTON COUNTRY PARK
One of the distinctive but less celebrated features of the Surrey landscape is the scattering of sanatoria and hospitals; this used to be an area of farmland providing food and work for patients from the nearby psychiatric institutions. In 1973, about 400 acres of it were purchased by Epsom and Ewell Borough Council to establish the country park and nature reserve, with fields, hedgerows, woods and ponds that provide habitats for a range of fauna, such as green woodpeckers, badgers, blue damselflies and butterflies. It makes notable blackberrying terrain in late summer.

☛ Cross over a narrow lane and continue ahead through woods, and then right into a fenced track round a paddock. Just after it bends to the left, turn right through a gate, and then turn sharp left around a car park. Then look on the left for a path with an easily missed 'Chessington Countryside Walk' sign. It is near a sign to the Information Centre to the right, where boards give information about Horton Country Park and the Thames Down Link (a 15-mile walk from the Thames at Kingston to Westhumble on the North Downs) which can be joined nearby.

Having made sure you have found the signposted path to the left, follow it as it goes right, near a cottage, and ahead past an Equestrian Centre and Polo Club, and on to a track beside more horse fields. When you come to a fork in the tracks take the one to the left (arrowed), and when you reach a junction of tracks take a footpath ahead through more trees, to a kissing gate and stile into another arable field, where you will see houses ahead. Turn right following the edge of the field, to another field where you continue ahead to the other side, where there is a footbridge over a stream (Bonesgate Stream). Cross the bridge and go ahead through a tree-lined path between fields, with signs of badgers and ladybirds, which eventually goes by back gardens of houses to a road (Green Lane). Turn left, signposted 'Chalky Lane ⅔ mile', along a path by Green Lane Farm Boarding Kennels and Cattery (birds and small pets also taken) through trees, and then rejoin the road, where after a few yards turn right up some steps into the public footpath signposted 'Garrison Lane ¼ mile'. This takes you past a golf course on the left, and back to a road (Garrison Lane) where you turn left and see Chessington South station on the other side of the road.

7 BARWELL CAFÉ

202 Leatherhead Rd, Chessington KT9 2HU

The only refreshment available near Chessington South station is this traditional good-value café, just past the station.

SEND US YOUR SNAPS!

We'd love to follow your adventures using our *Freedom Pass London* guide – why not send us your photos and stories via Twitter (@BradtGuides) and Instagram (@bradtguides) using the hashtag #freedompass. Or you can email your photos to info@bradtguides.com with the subject line 'Freedom Pass pics' and we'll tweet and instagram our favourites.

23 | DISTANCE 4½ MILES
DIFFICULTY EASY
TIME 3HRS | LONDON BRIDGE TO BLOOMSBURY

LITERARY LONDON

A BIBLIOPHILE'S PILGRIMAGE THROUGH THE CAPITAL'S HEART.

This walk visits the homes and workplaces of world-famous writers over six centuries from Geoffrey Chaucer and William Shakespeare to T S Eliot and Dorothy L Sayers, with the chance to go inside the homes of Charles Dickens and Dr Johnson, and to imbibe at the latter's drinking-hole, the classically unchanged Ye Olde Cheshire Cheese. You'll also see the places connected with some infamous and lesser-known figures such as the dissolute poet Algernon Charles Swinburne, who scandalised society, and the great wit Sydney Smith.

The route takes in a memorable cross-section of urban scenery and non-literary attractions, past Borough Market and the admirably preserved George Inn, along the South Bank past the Clink Museum and over the Millennium Bridge from the Tate Modern to St Paul's, before continuing on over Fleet Street and through Clerkenwell into Bloomsbury.

DISTANCE/DIFFICULTY 4½ miles. Easy.

DROP-OUT POINT Frequent, from bus stops or tube stations.

TIME 3hrs

MAP Any A–Z

START London Bridge ✵ TQ329801

FINISH Russell Square ✵ TQ302822

TAKING A BREAK The George Inn, Cockpit Tavern, Ye Olde Cheshire Cheese, A Friend at Hand

GETTING THERE 🚆 or ⊖ to London Bridge station

DIRECTIONS TO START Leave station by the main railway exit, by the taxi rank and bus station, to London Bridge Street opposite

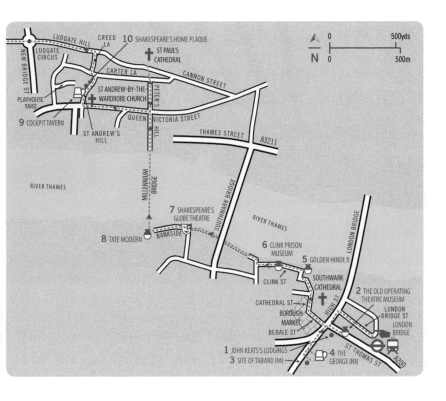

☞ Continue down London Bridge Street to the junction with Borough High Street, and turn left. At the first junction with St Thomas Street turn left. A few doors down on the right is:

1 JOHN KEATS'S LODGINGS

8 St Thomas St, SE1 9RS

The poet Keats (1795–1821) lodged here from 1815 to 1816 when a student at nearby Guy's and St Thomas's Hospitals, as a plaque informs us. After being an apprentice apothecary-surgeon he became a surgeon's pupil at Guy's on 1 October 1815. Four weeks later he was appointed as a dresser to Mr Lucas, a surgeon at St Thomas's, which was then in St Thomas Street. Mr Lucas had a reputation for being rather bungling during operations. Keats was then trained by Sir Astley Cooper, the great surgeon of Guy's who had been trained at St Thomas's. Keats became licensed to practise as an apothecary on 25 July 1816, but never got his surgeon's certificate and abandoned surgical

Millennium Bridge with St Paul's Cathedral in the background.

practice altogether in 1817. 'My last operation was the opening of a man's temporal artery,' he recalled. 'I did it with the utmost nicety, but reflecting on what passed through my mind at the time, my dexterity seemed a miracle, and I never took up the lancet again.'

He became a poet instead and his poem *O Solitude* was published in 1816, but the following year he was savagely attacked by the critic John Lockhart for being of the 'low-born Cockney school of poetry' (his father was an ostler and tavern keeper). This depressed Keats and he was soon beset with financial problems, in 1819 becoming very ill with tuberculosis. By then he was living in Hampstead (see page 51).

☞ Almost opposite is:

2 THE OLD OPERATING THEATRE, MUSEUM & HERB GARRET

9a St Thomas St, SE1 9RY ☎ 020 7188 2679 🖱 www.thegarret.org.uk
🕐 daily 10.30–17.00 ££ 🪙

Entry to the museum is up 32 steepish spiral steps leading into the garret of St Thomas's Church, which was used as a place to store and dry herbs used for medicinal purposes. Beyond is an intact early operating theatre: Keats would have watched operations being performed here when it was part of the original St Thomas's Hospital (which moved to its present site at Lambeth in 1862 to make way for the railways). They were mainly amputations which had to be completed in a minute or less in those days before modern anaesthetics were invented. It has many fascinating exhibits including some fearsome-looking surgical instruments (including a long steel hooked instrument called a 'male urethral sound', which was passed down the urethra to locate bladder stones) and bleeding (in the medical sense) apparatus.

☛ Retrace your steps to the junction with Borough High Street and turn left. Walk a short distance until you come to Talbot Yard on the left. Three doors down on the left is a plaque commemorating:

3 GEOFFREY CHAUCER & THE TABARD INN

This is the site of the Tabard Inn, established in 1307 and demolished in 1873. The pilgrims set off from here in April 1386 in *Canterbury Tales* as described by poet Geoffrey Chaucer (1342–1400), the son of a vintner. Chaucer wrote this around 1387, describing how 29 pilgrims of various professions met in the inn where the host (Harry Bailey) suggested they each should tell four stories on the road, two on the way to Canterbury and two on the way back. He offered a free supper on their return to the teller of the best story.

Every schoolboy's favourite is perhaps 'The Summoner's Tale', about a hypocritical friar who claims to live a life of poverty but seeks money for the church from a dying man. The man says he will let him have all he has if he solemnly swears to share it equally among all the other friars, which he does. He tells him it is hidden beneath his buttocks, and when the friar gropes there the man unleashes a fart louder than any horse's. The friar is very angry at this 'odious mischief' but feels bound by his oath. He therefore suffers the indignity of breaking wind over a cartwheel, around which 12 friars are gathered with their noses next to the spokes, so that 'every man have his part, the sound and odor of a fart'.

☛ Retrace your steps to the junction with Borough High Street and turn right. The next turning on the right is George Inn Yard, where you will find on the right:

4 THE GEORGE INN

George Inn Yard, 77 Borough High St, SE1 1NH

Both William Shakespeare (see pages 201–2 and 203) and Charles Dickens (pages 209 and 211–12) drank in this pub, which has existed since the late 1500s. It was rebuilt in 1677 and is the only remaining galleried coaching inn in London. Dickens featured it in his novel *Little Dorrit* (first serialised from 1855 to 1857). It is now owned by the National Trust and serves Greene King real ales. An excellent place for a pub meal inside or out in the courtyard.

☛ Retrace your steps to the junction with Borough High Street and turn right, past Borough Market on the left, and turn left into Bedale Street. Follow this under a railway bridge, along the other side of Borough Market, into Cathedral Street ahead (with Southwark Cathedral on the right) and then bear left at the fork, and right into Clink Street.

On the right in St Saviour's Dock by the Thames is the:

5 GOLDEN HINDE II

St Saviour's Dock, SE1; ticket office is round the corner at 1 Pickfords Wharf, Clink Street, SE1 9DG ☎ 020 7403 0123 🖱 www.goldenhinde.com ◷ daily 10.00–17.30 ££ 🪙

This is a full-size replica of the galleon in which Sir Francis Drake sailed around the world from 1577 to 1580. It offers a 'living history experience' and 'pirate fun days' for families.

☛ Continue along Clink Street, turning left by the Old Thameside Inn, through Pickfords Wharf, which is still in Clink Street. Just before a railway arch, on the left is:

6 THE CLINK PRISON MUSEUM

1 Clink St, SE1 9DG ☎ 020 7403 0900 🖱 www.clink.co.uk ◷ daily from 10.00, closes 21.00 Jul–Sep, 18.00 Oct–Jun weekdays, 19.30 w/ends ££ 🪙

The museum is built on the site of what it describes as England's 'most notorious medieval prison' which was there from 1144 to 1780. Those incarcerated included heretics, drunkards, harlots and religious zealots. Visitors are invited to 'handle torture devices and to view and hear all about the tales of torment and many misfortunes of the inmates of the infamous Clink Prison'.

☞ Continue along Clink Street to the end. Turn right by The Anchor pub into Bank End, and then left into Bankside along the Thames. Follow this under Southwark Bridge, and after a short distance on the left, on the corner of New Globe Walk, is:

7 SHAKESPEARE'S GLOBE THEATRE

21 New Globe Walk, SE1 9DT ☎ 020 7902 1400 for information, 020 7401 9919 for tickets. 🖥 www.shakespearesglobe.com ⊙ See website for information about tours and exhibition.

William Shakespeare (1564–1616) and his partners built the original open-air theatre a few hundred yards from this site in 1599 and staged his plays there; many of his plays were first performed at The Rose, the first theatre on Bankside close by – the archaeological site is being excavated and it is hoped it will become a visitor attraction.

The son of an ale taster (a legal quality controller) who could not read or write, Shakespeare shared neither his father's respect for the law nor his illiteracy, becoming first a deer poacher and then a playwright. He travelled to London in 1592 to take up acting and often performed on beer barrels at inns. One anecdote has it that he was appearing in a play with fellow actor Richard Burbage, whom he overheard making an assignation with a woman who lived nearby. She told him to announce himself as Richard III to keep his real identity a secret. Shakespeare left before the end of the play, announced himself as Richard III and went to bed with her. Burbage turned up only to receive a message: 'William the Conqueror came before Richard III.' The playwright died of a fever following a drinking bout, according to John Ward, the Vicar of Stratford. Famously Shakespeare's will bequeathed his widow Anne Hathaway his 'second best bed' and furniture.

As well as the reconstructed open-air theatre here, there is now a newly opened indoor candlelit playhouse in honour of Sam Wanamaker (1919–93). He was so moved by the theme of a play in which he was acting in Washington DC in 1943 that he joined the American Communist Party. After serving in the US Army from 1943 to 1946 he left the party and went to Hollywood. He was blacklisted there in 1952 during the McCarthy anti-communist witch-hunt. So he moved to England where he became director of the New Shakespeare Theatre in Liverpool in 1957, then joined the Shakespeare Memorial Theatre at Stratford-upon-Avon as an actor. He founded the Shakespeare Globe Trust in 1970 and raised over $10 million to reconstruct the theatre in its original form. His daughter, the actress Zoe Wanamaker, appeared in the BBC television programme *Who Do You Think You Are?* in 2009, which revealed his activities were monitored in this country by MI5.

☞ Continue along the bank to the:

8 TATE MODERN

Bankside, SE1 9TG ☎ 020 7887 8888 ﹝ www.tate.org.uk ◷ daily 10.00–18.00

This free-to-enter gallery within the former Bankside Power Station houses the country's leading collection of modern and contemporary art, from 1900 to the present day.

☞ Just opposite the gallery is the Millennium Footbridge, which you cross over the Thames. On the other side go ahead up Peter's Hill to Queen Victoria Street. If you wish to visit St Paul's Cathedral (**£££** 🪙) continue ahead up the path and steps to it.

Otherwise turn left into Queen Victoria Street. Just past the strangely named St Andrew-by-the-Wardrobe church, turn right into St Andrew's Hill. A short way up on the left is the:

9 COCKPIT TAVERN

7 St Andrew's Hill, EC4V 5BY

A pub has been on this site since the 16th century. It was a major venue for gambling on cock fights, and retains a gallery from where the gamblers would have watched the fights. Nowadays it is a small friendly pub serving real ales such as Old Speckled Hen, Pedigree and Adnams.

ON 10TH MARCH 1613
WILLIAM SHAKESPEARE
PURCHASED LODGINGS
IN THE BLACKFRIARS
GATEHOUSE
LOCATED NEAR
THIS SITE

☞ On the opposite corner to the pub is:

10 SHAKESPEARE'S HOME
Ireland Yard

A plaque confirms: 'On 10 March 1613 William Shakespeare purchased lodgings in the Blackfriars Gatehouse located near this site.' This is where he lived after purchasing the Blackfriars Theatre in 1613 with fellow actors as an additional venue to the Globe for their plays. This was also the main entrance to the theatre, which was in the vicinity of Playhouse Yard at the end of this alley.

☞ Continue up St Andrew's Hill, left into Carter Lane, then immediately right into Creed Lane, up to Ludgate Hill. Turn left, past Hardy's Original Sweetshop on the corner of Pilgrim Street, down to Ludgate Circus with Fleet Street ahead.
   On the right-hand corner of Fleet Street is a:

11 BUST OF EDGAR WALLACE

This prolific novelist (1875–1932) first sold newspapers at Ludgate Circus at the age of 11 when playing truant from school. A year later he left school and got a job round the corner in Farringdon Street as a lowly print-reader's boy. A decade or so later, after being a Grimsby trawler cook, milkman, building labourer and soldier, he was back in Fleet Street as the war correspondent of the *Daily Mail* (during the Boer War) and editor of the *Evening News*. The *Mail* sent him to the Congo to disprove stories of Belgian atrocities in 1907, but he found them to be true and reported his findings: these were suppressed, and when he refused to write the original lies he was sacked. So he used his Congo experiences to write the *Sanders of the River* novels which proved best-sellers and launched his career as an author.

The imagination he used in his fiction could also be used in reporting real events, as demonstrated by his report of George V's coronation for the *Evening Times*, which he wrote the day before it actually happened. He also wrote about a 'confession' by Crippen (who in fact went to the gallows protesting his innocence of the murder of his wife) for this same paper which led to it being closed down.

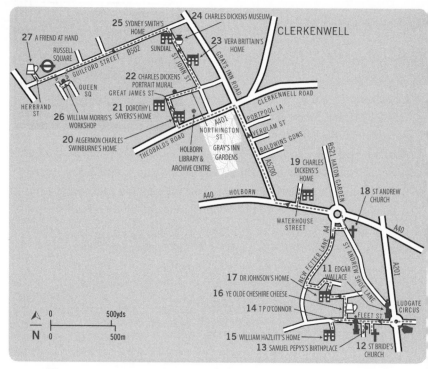

His career as a novelist took off with 46 novels being published in ten years and selling millions. He also wrote plays, having 17 produced in the last six years of his life, including three in the West End at the same time, which earned him another £100,000. One of these plays he wrote in four days, and one of his novels over a weekend, and on top of this he became a Hollywood screenwriter. Considering he had been abandoned at birth by his actress mother, raised by a Billingsgate fish market porter and risen to such fame and fortune, he could well have written a film about his own life.

☞ Go up Fleet Street, and take the second turning on the left, a small passage called St Bride's Avenue. This takes you to the entrance of:

12 ST BRIDE'S CHURCH
St Bride's Av, Fleet St, EC4Y 8AU

The journalists' church, where among those commemorated with memorial plaques are:

Allen Hutt (1901–73), who wrote for Communist Party journals just after the General Strike of 1926 and then joined the party's newspaper, the *Daily Worker*, from its first issue in 1930. He was then involved in its successor, the *Morning Star*, until 1971 and in this role won several awards for newspaper design. His son Sam is a gynaecologist who also performs country and western music as Hank Wangford.

Bert Hardy (1913–95), a press photographer known for his work in *Picture Post* magazine in the 1940s and 1950s. A working-class lad from nearby Blackfriars in a family of seven, he left school at 14 and worked processing photos in a chemist. He bought a very basic camera and signed for an agency, then went freelance. He made his name with photos of firefighters working through the Blitz in 1941. Later in the war he worked for the army, photographing the D-Day landings, the liberation of Paris, the crossing of the Rhine, and the liberation of Belsen concentration camp. He always maintained you did not need expensive cameras and he demonstrated this by using a simple box camera to produce an iconic picture of two women sitting on the breezy Blackpool promenade in 1951.

☛ Return to Fleet Street, turn left, and then first left into Salisbury Court. A few yards on the left is:

13 SAMUEL PEPYS'S BIRTHPLACE

Salisbury Court, EC4Y 8AA

A plaque confirms this is the birthplace of diarist Samuel Pepys, although it wrongly gives the date of his birth as 1632. In fact he was born here when it was a tailor's shop on 23 February 1633. The date of his death is given correctly as 1703.

At the age of 15 he witnessed the beheading of Charles I, and remarked: 'The memory of the wicked shall rot.' He got a job as a government clerk for £50 a year and liked to stroll around London mixing with all classes. For breakfast in a nearby pub called the Harp and Ball he had a draught of ale and pickled onions, which he often vomited up after heavy drinking the night before. After a short time working in his office, he returned to the tavern at lunch to drink more and sing bawdy songs before visiting prostitutes in St James's Park, and a few more hours in the office.

His sexual encounters in pubs were recorded in his diaries from 1660 to 1669 and included Betty Martin in the Trumpet Tavern, Mary in the Harp and Ball, Mrs Martin in the Swan Tavern, Betty Lane (whom he 'towzed' in an unnamed pub), and Deborah Willet (whose breasts he fondled in another alehouse).

His wealth increased considerably after he became responsible for ordering supplies of victuals for the navy in 1665, and he benefited from 'rewards' for contracts. He also used money which should have been paid to seamen in the navy to pay the crew of his own private vessel to plunder Dutch ships, and then kept the booty instead of handing a share to the crown. He was consequently charged with piracy and committed to the Tower in 1679, but the charges were dropped nine months later. Pepys became Secretary of the Navy in 1685, and when it was defeated three years later by William of Orange of Holland when invading and taking the crown, Pepys's position became vulnerable. He was charged with treason and detained, but again was released after a few months.

☞ Return to Fleet Street, turn left, and on the left is:

14 T P O'CONNOR BUST
78 Fleet St, EC4Y 1HY

The pen of this journalist and parliamentarian (1848–1929), states the caption of the bust, 'could lay bare the bones of a book or the soul of a statesman in a few vivid lines'. Born in Athlone, Ireland, he entered the UK parliament for Galway in 1880 and had the longest unbroken period of service in the House of Commons. He was also the first president of the British Board of Film Censors.

☞ Continue further up Fleet Street and turn left into Bouverie Street. A few yards on the right (just past the corner of Pleydell Street) is:

15 WILLIAM HAZLITT'S HOME

6 Bouverie St, EC4Y 8AX

William Hazlitt (1778–1830), the great essayist, lived here in 1829 as confirmed by a plaque. By then he had been socially ostracised for the publication in 1823 of *Liber Amoris*, an agonising account of his insane infatuation for his landlady's daughter, a simple girl called Sarah Walker. It contained many intimate details and 'lacked nothing in frankness'. It led Robert Louis Stevenson to abandon writing a biography of him. Hazlitt was twice divorced and he earned many enemies for his support of the French Revolution, and for his writings in favour of the poor and against those who exploited them. But on his deathbed his last words were: 'Well, I have had a happy life.'

He also lived in Mitre Court, off Fleet Street opposite Fetter Lane.

☛ Return to Fleet Street, turn right and a few yards on the left (just past Hind Court) turn left into a narrow passage under an arch called Wine Office Court. On the right is:

16 YE OLDE CHESHIRE CHEESE

Wine Office Court, 145 Fleet St, EC4A 2BU

This ancient tavern, which was rebuilt in 1667 after the Great Fire of London, was the local tavern for Samuel Johnson who lived nearby (see next entry). His chair and an original copy of his dictionary are on display here. Other literary figures to have drunk here include Alexander Pope, Charles Dickens, Oliver Goldsmith, Voltaire, Mark Twain, Alfred Tennyson, Arthur Conan Doyle and G K Chesterton. Samuel Smith real ales are served, as well as hot food.

☛ Continue up Wine Office Court and bear left into Gough Square, turn right then left and in the far left corner is:

17 DR JOHNSON'S HOUSE

17 Gough Square, EC4A 3DE ☎ 020 7353 3745 🖱 www.drjohnsonshouse.org
🕒 Mon–Sat, 11.00–17.30 (closes 17.00 Oct–Apr) £; half price for National Trust members 🍪

Samuel Johnson (1709–84) lived here in the early 1750s when compiling his famous dictionary (published in 1755). Now the house displays on its entrance one of his most famous quotations: 'When a man is tired of London he is tired of life.' But earlier, in his poem of 1738 called *London*, he expressed his disgust at how the poor were oppressed in the capital, having experienced it himself. Early on he lived on bread and water alone in the Marylebone Fields area where highway robbers operated and he became very shabby, and was later incarcerated in the nearby Fleet Prison for debt. A visiting clergyman there saw him gobbling his food 'so fast that the veins stood out on his forehead', which he considered to be worse than the eating manners of 'Eskimos and Hottentotts'; perhaps this contributed to his notorious flatulence. When he had money he was always very generous to the poor and homeless.

His sense of humour came over when he defined 'lexicographer' in his own dictionary as 'a writer of dictionaries, a harmless drudge'. When his wife died in 1752 he was grief-stricken and observed: 'Marriage has many pains, but celibacy has no pleasures.' He did not remarry, however, having famously observed that this showed 'the triumph of hope over experience'. And he did not use prostitutes, as he disapproved strongly of the trade that dealt 'with women like a dealer in any other commodity... as an ironmonger sells ironmongery'.

In this house are various exhibits including a 19th-century stained-glass window of Johnson. From 1776 he lived the rest of his life nearby at 8 Bolt Lane, off Fleet Street.

☛ After visiting this, turn left out of the house into Pemberton Row and then left into West Harding Street to Fetter Lane, where you turn right. Follow this into New Fetter Lane and up to Holborn Circus. To the right on the corner of St Andrew Street is:

18 ST ANDREW CHURCH
5 St Andrew St, EC4A 3AB

Bill Sykes, in *Chapter 21* of *Oliver Twist* by Charles Dickens, looks up to the clock tower of this church, and notices it is seven o'clock and urges young Oliver: 'You must step out! Come, don't lag behind already, Lazy-legs!'

Iris Murdoch (1919–99) in her 1954 novel *Under the Net* also has a character looking at the church tower.

The first written record of the church is in AD951, but Roman pottery, discovered in its crypt, indicate it was here for much longer. In 1666 it survived the Great Fire of London but was in such a bad state of repair that it was rebuilt by Christopher Wren anyway.

Turn left up Holborn to the Prudential building at numbers 138–142 on the right. Go through the arch and into Waterhouse Square. On the right above eye level is a brown plaque to:

19 CHARLES DICKENS'S HOME
Waterhouse Sq, 138–142 Holborn, EC1N 2ST
The novelist rented rooms here from 1833 to 1837, when it was part of Furnival Inn. While here he wrote *Sketches by Boz* and most of the *Pickwick Papers*.

Retrace your steps to Holborn, turn right and continue to Grays Inn Road, where you turn right. When you reach the crossroads with the Yorkshire Grey pub on the corner, turn left into Theobalds Road. Just past Holborn Library and Archive Centre (where there are many illuminating exhibitions) turn right into Great James Street. A couple of doors on the right is:

20 ALGERNON CHARLES SWINBURNE'S HOME
3 Great James St, WC1N 3DB
The dissolute poet (1837–1909) lived here from 1873 to 1879, during which time he became deaf. He boasted of some truly bestial acts, one involving a pig which earned him the pejorative epithet 'Swine Born' from *Punch* magazine. The author Thomas Carlyle described him as 'standing up to his neck in a cesspool, and adding to its contents'. Swinburne's poems about sadism, masochism, flagellation (which he had learned at Eton) and rejection of Christianity caused public outrage, so his publishers disowned him. He befriended another scandalous writer, Marie Louise de la Ramée, who wrote salacious novels under the name of Ouida. While visiting her in the Langham Hotel he collapsed drunk on the floor, where he was picked up by yet another notorious writer, Oscar Wilde, who dumped him on a chaise longue. During his life Swinburne moved from being a Roman Catholic to a nihilist, and a Tory to a republican.

☞ Further up the street on the other side (just before the Rugby Tavern) by the junction with Northington Street is:

21 DOROTHY L SAYERS'S HOME
24 Great James St, WC1N 3ES

A plaque confirms detective story writer Dorothy L Sayers (1893–1957) lived here from 1921 to 1929. Her 1930 novel *Strong Poison*, featuring the amateur detective Lord Peter Wimsey, is set in this immediate area. Wimsey first appeared in the 1923 novel *Whose Body* and then 13 other stories. The author became the leading crime writer of her day and became president of the Detection Club. She later turned to writing plays covering serious historical and theological subjects. An Anglican, she became churchwarden in 1952 at the London parish of St Thomas-cum-St Anne's. Her philosophy was 'The only Christian work is good work, well done.'

☞ Turn into Northington Street and a few yards on the left opposite Cockpit Yard is:

22 CHARLES DICKENS PORTRAIT MURAL
16 Northington St (corner of Kirk St), WC1N 2NW

This is marked as 'Dickens Inn' on Google Maps, and he may well have drunk here when living round the corner in Doughty Street. This would explain the somewhat frayed portrait near the top of the building. In his day the pub was called the White Lion and the street was called Little James Street. It remained as a pub until at least 1985.

☞ Continue along Northington Street to the Lady Ottoline pub where you turn left into John Street. This leads into Doughty Street. On the right (just past Roger Street) is:

23 VERA BRITTAIN & WINIFRED HOLTBY'S HOME
58 Doughty St, WC1N 2JT

Vera Brittain (1893–1970) was a writer, feminist and pacifist, who published poetry, fiction and essays. She was deeply influenced by the book *Women and Labour* by Olive Schreiner. In World War I she volunteered to nurse wounded soldiers, which she found traumatic and convinced her of the wickedness of war. This was reinforced when her fiancé, Roland Leighton, was killed in 1915. After the war, despite the objections of her father, she went to Oxford University where she met Winifred Holtby and graduated with her in 1921. She described her close liaison with her in *Testament of Youth* in 1933, and *Testament of Friendship* in 1940. When Vera married George Catlin they were joined in the household by Winifred. George knew that the two women's relationship was not a lesbian one, but its closeness still rankled with him. Vera became a pacifist in 1934 and was a leader of the Peace Pledge Union during World War II. After the war she strongly opposed nuclear weapons and formed the Campaign for Nuclear Disarmament in 1957.

Vera was the mother of politician Shirley Williams (born in 1930), a Labour Party minister (now Baroness Williams of Crosby), who formed the Social Democratic Party. Winifred Holtby (1898–1935) had several novels published, the most famous of which was *South Riding*, set in Yorkshire and published just after her death. Variously a journalist, socialist, feminist and pacifist, she was active in the Independent Labour Party in the late 1920s and became a director of the feminist journal *Time and Tide* in 1926. A keen supporter of equal rights, she criticised the pre-apartheid racist legislation introduced by General Smuts in South Africa. High blood pressure led to her early death.

☛ Ten doors further along on the same side is:

24 CHARLES DICKENS MUSEUM
48 Doughty St, WC1N 2LX ☎ 020 7405 2127 🖱 www.dickensmuseum.com
🕐 Mon–Sat, 10.00–17.00 ££ 🪙

Charles Dickens (1812–70) lived here from 1837 to 1839 when he was writing *Oliver Twist*, which was serialised over two years in a magazine. He also wrote *Nicholas Nickleby* while living here.

As a 15-year-old, Dickens had worked as a clerk for Ellis and Blackmore solicitors at nearby Holborn Court, Gray's Inn. He impressed his employers with his eagerness and intelligence, and entertained his fellow clerks by mimicking 'the low population of the streets of London in all their varieties', as well as popular singers and actors. He stayed there for a year and a half before moving to the firm of Charles Molloy at 8 New Square, Lincoln's Inn. The work here he found dull so he left after a few months. Then he learned shorthand and became a court and parliamentary reporter. This was a great improvement on having to work in a hated blacking (shoe polish) factory for a pittance at the age of 12 while his father was in jail for debt.

He had a pet raven called Grip and was able to perform conjuring tricks such as pouring ingredients into a hat and turning them into a plum pudding, and turning bran into a guinea pig. He also liked to roam the 'more dreadful streets of London' at night, including those in Limehouse with its opium dens, and to stare into the dark waters of the Thames.

The Museum has over 100,000 items relating to Dickens, including original manuscripts, rare editions, personal items and paintings.

☞ A few doors up on the other side is:

25 SYDNEY SMITH'S HOME
14 Doughty St, WC1N 2PL

The author and wit Sydney Smith (1771–1845) lived here, as confirmed by a plaque, in fact from 1803 to 1806. He wished to become a barrister but was pressurised by his father into becoming a clergyman. He became a popular preacher and lecturer as well as a writer. Radical for his times, he supported education for women, the abolition of slavery and Catholic emancipation. In 1831 he became a resident canon at St Paul's Cathedral.

Among his quotations are:

He had occasional flashes of silence that made his conversation perfectly delightful (about Macaulay).

You must not think me necessarily foolish because I am facetious, nor will I consider you necessarily wise because you are grave.

Never try to reason the prejudice out of a man. It was not reasoned into him, and cannot be reasoned out.

☛ Continue to the junction with Guilford Street and turn left.

If you want to know the time but have no watch and it is a sunny day, take the first left into Doughty Mews, to number 19 on the right, and look upwards at the sundial.

Otherwise continue along Guilford Street, and turn left down a small passage called Queen Anne's Walk. This takes you into Queen's Square. Turn right and first on the right is:

26 WILLIAM MORRIS'S WORKSHOP
Queen Court, 26 Queen Sq, WC1N 3BB

Writer and designer William Morris had a workshop here from 1865 to 1881 and lectured in the Working Men's College nearby. He kept an owl in his room and imitated an eagle by jumping off a chair with a heavy flop. See more details about him on pages 91–2, 118 and 120.

☛ Continue a few yards to the corner of the square and then right through another small passage, the unmarked Queen Square Place, back into Guilford Street. Turn left and then take the first turning on the right, Herbrand Street, where on the right just past the Horse Hospital on the corner of Colonnade is:

27 A FRIEND AT HAND
2–4 Herbrand St, WC1N 1HX

A Taylor Walker pub which was first established in 1797 as the Hansom Carriage. The writer Thomas Stearns Eliot (1888–1965) described the pub in his collection of poems *Old Possum's Book of Practical Cats*, which later inspired Andrew Lloyd Webber's musical *Cats*. Today its customers include the surrealist comedian Noel Fielding. It serves real ales including Fuller's London Pride and Sharp's Doom Bar.

☛ After refreshing yourself turn right out of the pub and walk a few yards to Bernard Street, then turn right to Russell Square tube station (Piccadilly Line) just round the corner.

FEISTY FEMALES PUB CRAWL

DRINK A TOAST TO SEVEN CONTRASTING WOMEN
WHO HAVE MADE THEIR MARK, EACH IN HER OWN INIMITABLE WAY.

A pub crawl with a difference: this transport-assisted Freedom Pass exploration of four separate walks within one grand tour takes in a septet of drinking holes and stories of the women after which they are named or, in the instance of one pub, a statue stands outside. Beginning in the West End, it recalls Charles II's mistress, pays homage to a great World War I nurse and raises a glass to the 'fair maid of the inn'. Then a bus ride to Bloomsbury is the prelude to literary society host Lady Ottoline Morrell, before moving on to make the acquaintances of The Witch Queen of Kentish Town and a famous suffragette. It ends theatrically in West Brompton, at a pub named after one of the greatest actresses of her time.

DISTANCE/DIFFICULTY 2½ miles. Easy walking between bus and tube journeys.

TIME 1½hrs walking, plus plenty of time for the pub visits

MAP Any A–Z

START Charing Cross station ✳ TQ302804

FINISH West Brompton station ✳ TQ255785

TAKING A BREAK The Nell Gwynne Tavern, The Chandos, Molly Moggs, The Lady Ottoline, Mother Red Cap, Charlotte Despard, Little Langtry

GETTING THERE 🚌/🚇 To Charing Cross station

DIRECTIONS TO START Turn right out of the main railway station entrance into the Strand

After turning right into the Strand go to Bull Inn Court, a small alleyway tucked away a short distance on the left beside the Adelphi Theatre. Here you will find:

1 THE NELL GWYNNE TAVERN
2 Bull Inn Court, WC2R 0NP

A pub on this site (the Old Bull Inn) is where diarist Samuel Pepys met 'the mighty pretty Nell Gwynne' (1650–87) in 1667. She was then aged 17 and was involved in a troilistic relationship with two poets, the dissolute Charles Sedley and the foul-mouthed Charles Buckhurst. She became the mistress of Charles II (whom she referred to as her Charles III because of these other two lovers called Charles). She gave birth to two sons of the king. The first called Charles was in 1670 when she was living in the Cock and Pie pub (where she served the king pigeon pie in bed), on the site of Bush House. The second, James, was born the following year when the king had moved her into Pall Mall. James died at the age of eight in Paris 'of a sore leg'.

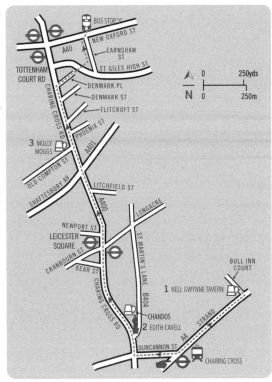

Nell had earlier been pressed into being a child prostitute in Macklin Street off Drury Lane. When she famously became the mistress of the king at the age of 17, she had no qualms about being a 'kept woman'. When her coachman got in a fight and she asked him why, he said it was because the other man had described her as a 'whore'. When she laughed and said 'but I am a whore', he said he resented being called 'a whore's coachman'. Later, when being booed in her coach by a crowd who mistook her for another of Charles's mistresses, the French catholic Louise de Keroualle, Nell stuck her head out of the window and declared: 'Pray, good people, be civil! I am the Protestant whore!' This so delighted the crowd that they stopped booing and cheered her heartily.

She was also popular for not using her position with the King to curry political favour, unlike his other mistresses. This was expressed in a poem at the time:

Hard by Pall Mall lives a wench call'd Nell.
King Charles the Second he kept her.
She hath got a trick to handle his prick,
But never lays hands on his sceptre.

When she died she was buried at nearby St Martin's Church. In her will she gave money to get poor debtors out of prison.

This pub is also where actor William Terris was stabbed to death in 1897 by Richard Prince, a stage hand at the Adelphi theatre, the Gallery Entrance of which is next to the pub. Prince was sent to Broadmoor criminal asylum.

The barmaid of this cosy little bolt-hole was most welcoming when inviting us to scale the scaffolding outside, amusingly advertised as an 'adult climbing frame'. We were served a decent pint of Umber Ale from the Growler brewery in Essex and Fuller's London Pride.

☛ Return to the Strand, turn right, walk to Trafalgar Square, turn right into St Martin's Place, where you will see:

2 EDITH CAVELL'S STATUE

St Martin's Place (opposite the Chandos pub, 29 St Martin's Lane, WC2N 4ER)
This British nurse (1865–1915) was executed by a German firing squad in Brussels for helping British soldiers escape to neutral Holland in World War I. She is described on the monument as 'Nurse, Patriot and Martyr'. Yet on the eve of her death she said she did not wish to be considered as a martyr, but just 'a nurse who tried to do her duty.' Neither did she wish to be described as a patriot, stating: 'I realise that patriotism

is not enough. I must have no hatred or bitterness towards anyone.' This was originally omitted from the engraving on her monument but is now included. Slogans on the sides praise Devotion, Fortitude, Sacrifice and Humanity, along with 'Faithful until Death' and 'For King and Country'.

Cavell became an assistant nurse at Tooting in 1895 and the following year was accepted for training at London Hospital in Bow Road. She was then night superintendent at St Pancras Infirmary in 1901 and then assistant matron at Shoreditch Infirmary in 1903. Then in 1907 she became matron at a training school for nurses in Brussels, and saw it grow from four trainees to 60.

When the Germans occupied Brussels in 1914 they allowed her to continue working in the hospital. When hundreds of British soldiers were left stranded after the defeat in the Battle of Mons just 30 miles away, the resistance movement took two of the wounded to Edith. After treating them she took them to the border. This became an established escape route, used by over 600 soldiers in eight months. A German police raid led to the arrest of her and 34 others in August 1915. One of the charges was 'conducting soldiers to the enemy' to which she replied at her trial: 'My preoccupation has not been to aid the enemy but to help the men who applied to me to reach the frontier; once across the frontier they were free.' She was one of the five sentenced to death and was shot by firing squad at dawn on the day after the sentence was delivered.

When this statue of her was unveiled, the artist Whistler did not think it resembled her very accurately, so he quipped, 'My God, they've shot the wrong woman.'

The Chandos is a Samuel Smith's pub so its prices are cheaper than others in the area but they are gradually catching up.

☞ Continue up Charing Cross Road, past Leicester Square and Shaftesbury Avenue, to Old Compton Street on the left, where on the corner is:

3 MOLLY MOGGS
2 Old Compton St, W1D 4TA

The writer John Gay wrote a song about Molly (1699–1766) in 1726 entitled *Molly Mogg, Fair Maid of the Inn.* This was when she was keeper of the Rose Inn in Wokingham (now demolished). Some of the song's lyrics go:

> When she smiles on each guest, like her liquor
> Then jealousy sets me agog
> To be sure there's a bit for the Vicar,
> And so I shall love Molly Mogg.

Despite her beauty she remained unmarried after the death of her lover in 1730, but was constantly 'the toast of the gay sparks of her day'. This pub is also small and cosy and it boasts of 'entertaining Soho since 1731'. There is a free drag-queen cabaret show every night and over the small stage are life-size golden figures of showgirls, rescued from a skip 15 years ago after being thrown out by a nearby theatre. There is also a singing competition every six weeks with prizes of £250, £150 and £100.

We were served a good pint of Greene King London Glory.

Turn left and continue up Charing Cross Road to the top, bending right into Denmark Place, round Centre Point to New Oxford Street. On the opposite side of the road just to the right is Bus Stop Y. Here you can take any bus (19, 38 or 55, all of which are frequent) for a nine-minute journey to the Grays Inn Road stop. When you get off, go back a few yards, turn right into John Street, and on the first corner on the right is:

4 THE LADY OTTOLINE

11a Northington St, Bloomsbury WC1N 2JF

An elegantly furnished and decorated pub where you can have mulled wine (or real ales such as Sharp's Doom Bar, Dark Star and Sambrook's Junction) round a real log fire. On the ground floor there is a picture of Lady Ottoline Morrell (1873–1938) in Bedford Square in 1909; there are more pictures of her upstairs. It was at 44 Bedford Square that she lived and hosted literary parties from 1906 until 1910, when she moved round the corner to 10 Gower Street.

Born Ottoline Violet Anne Cavendish-Bentinck, she was the niece of the eccentric and reclusive fifth Duke of Portland, and descended from the Hapsburgs. She married the Liberal MP Philip Morrell and had many lovers (including artists Augustus John and Henry Lamb), but was always discreet to avoid embarrassing her husband.

Among those to be helped at her literary gatherings were writers such as T S Eliot, Aldous Huxley (who portrayed her in his novel *Crome Yellow*), D H Lawrence (who based *Lady Chatterley* and a character in *Women in Love* on her) and Walter de la Mare. The Russian ballet dancer Vaslav Nijinsky attended one of her lunches and likened her to a giraffe, adding hastily a 'graceful' not a 'gangling' one. She was six feet tall and accepted the compliment.

But her biggest admirer was the philosopher Bertrand Russell, the third Earl Russell, who danced the hornpipe at one of her parties. They became lovers and he wrote over a thousand letters to her in under a year between March 1913 and January 1914. She complained of his bad breath and insisted he shave off his large moustache and cremate it in the fireplace. He said her face was long and thin like a horse and she used too much scent and powder. She did indeed wear flamboyant make-up as well as feathers, huge hats and garish fashions.

Lady Ottoline was also frank and outspoken, qualities which Russell admired, and had a robust sense of fun, revelling in the vulgarity of music hall comedy.

☛ Take the Northington Street exit, turn right, and when you reach Grays Inn Road turn right and a couple of yards away is Bus Stop CB. Here you catch the 17 bus for the 25-minute journey to Holloway (every 8–15 minutes). Get off at the last stop, and walk a few yards up Holloway Road where on the corner of Witley Road is the:

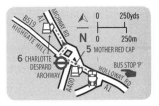

5 MOTHER RED CAP

665 Holloway Rd, N19 5SE

Mother Red Cap was the nickname of Jinney Bingham (1600–80), also known as 'Mother Damnable' and 'The Witch Queen of Kentish Town'. Several of her husbands died in strange circumstances.

The MOTHER BLACKCAP in 1776

This painting of Mother Red Cap can be found in the nearby Black Cap pub.

The first, 'Gypsy' George Coulter, was hanged for stealing sheep in nearby Holloway. The second, called Darby, beat her when drunk and disappeared after Jinney told her parents about his violence. Her parents were later hanged for using witchcraft to kill a woman. The third husband, named Pitcher, was burned to death in Jinney's oven. She was tried for his murder but acquitted after a neighbour gave evidence that Pitcher 'often got into the oven to hide himself from her tongue'. Jinney was also accused of poisoning a lodger but the inquest failed to establish this. Her cottage stood where the World's End pub now is at 174 Camden High Street (it was called the Mother Red Cap until 1986 and still has a bar named after her). She helped shelter highway robber Moll Cutpurse (who had a pub named after her in Tottenham which has recently been renamed the Crow Bar).

Jinney was suspected of being a witch because she wore a cape with bats on it, a red hat and always had a large black cat. Crowds therefore taunted her outside her house but she just screamed profanities back at them. She was described in 1870 by Samuel Palmer in his *History of St Pancras* as having 'a large broad nose, heavy shaggy eyebrows, sunken eyes and lank and leathery cheeks; her forehead wrinkled, her mouth wide and her looks sullen and unmoved. On her shoulders was thrown a dark grey frieze, with black patches, which looked at a distance like flying bats.'

A rhyme about her concluded:

Her features were shrivelled and brown as a mummy's hide,
And she passed for a witch, whose amusement was homicide.

This pub once had a picture of her with a pot of ale in one hand and cakes in the other with another rhyme:

Old Mother Red Cap, according to her tale,
Lived twenty and a hundred years by drinking this good ale;
It was her meat, it was her drink and medicine beside,
And if she still had drunk this ale she never would have died.

Samuel Pepys dropped into the pub with his wife and laughed at the likeness between the picture and the barmaid serving him.

The pub now has a pool table, but (despite the sign outside) no dartboard any more. Three different sports channels on televisions can be viewed simultaneously (football, horse-racing and rugby or Gaelic football). It is a down-to-earth drinking pub but has no real ale (just gassy Whitbread).

The pub's hanging sign is completely unrelated to Mother Red Cap (and does not even bear her name), so we have a picture of her from the Black Cap in Camden High Street.

☛ Go up Holloway road to Archway station, then up Archway Road (off Tollhouse Way) to the corner of Despard Road where on the left is:

6 CHARLOTTE DESPARD

🍺 17–19 Archway, N19 3TX

Imprisoned twice in nearby Holloway prison for her suffragette activities, Charlotte Despard (1844–1939) later moved to Ireland to be jailed twice more and become a member of Sinn Fein and then the Communist Party of Ireland. She also wrote poetry and novels.

Born into a wealthy Irish family, she was reared by relatives in London from the age of 15 after her father died and her mother was committed to a lunatic asylum. At the age of 26 she married banker Maximilian Despard (after whom Despard Road next to the pub is named). When he died 20 years later, she threw herself into social work after being appalled at the poverty she witnessed in London. She joined the marxist Social Democratic Federation and then the Independent Labour Party in 1901. Five years later, she joined the suffragettes and was imprisoned twice for her activities, before meeting Gandhi in 1909 who impressed her with his tactics of passive resistance. In the same year she visited Dublin, when the employers locked out all workers who remained in a trade union and starved them into submission. She finally moved to Ireland in 1921 and took up its struggle for independence, and was often raided by police and attacked by mobs. When she moved to Belfast in 1934, her house was burned down by another mob, so she moved to Whitehead on the coast where she was declared bankrupt.

Charlotte Despard Avenue is named in her honour in Battersea, where she was a Labour candidate in 1918 but defeated because of her pacifist and anti-war views. She had also been a Poor Law guardian in Lambeth from 1894 and campaigned vigorously for its reform.

This modern furnished pub serves bottled craft ales, porters, stouts, ciders and wines.

☛ Return to Archway station, get a Northern Line tube train to Embankment. Change to the District Line (Wimbledon Branch) and get off at West Brompton. Turn left out of the station into Old Brompton Road which becomes Lillie Road, and just past the corner of Seagrave Road is the:

7 LILLIE LANGTRY
19 Lillie Rd, West Brompton SW6 1UE

Actress Lillie Langtry (1853–1929) became famous as the mistress of Edward VII when he was Prince of Wales. He was impressed with her reckless style even in the presence of Queen Victoria, and lavished gifts on her. When he remarked 'I've spent enough on you to buy a battleship,' she retorted in a flash: 'And you've spent enough in me to float one!' Her addresses within a mile or so of this pub were in Eaton Place, 8 Wilton Place and 21 Pond Street.

She was born in Jersey, where she married Edward Langtry when he docked there in his 60-ton yacht. 'I met the owner and fell in love with the yacht,' she admitted.

They moved to London where she saw and met Prince Edward riding in Hyde Park. 'He is a very large man, but appeared to ride well for one of his bulk,' she commented. When she was presented to Queen Victoria, the young Lillie wore three large ostrich feathers in her hair, lampooning the prince's crest. Her Majesty was not amused, but Lillie was unperturbed.

When Edward ended the affair she started one with his nephew, Prince Louis Alexander of Battenberg, and bore his daughter Leanne-Marie. This led her friend Oscar Wilde to suggest she become an actress to support the child. He got a friend to coach her and her stage career took off. He also wrote *Lady Windermere's Fan* about society's hypocritical attitude to her and her illegitimate daughter.

After her husband left her she lived with a jockey who drank himself to death. She also became a racehorse owner, and in 1897 was the first woman to have a winner of the Cesarewitch, with Merman which ran shoeless. As well as the £39,000 prize she won a bet of £10,000 at 8–1.

The artist Millais, who was also born in Jersey, advised her to become a writer, which she finally did with the novel *All At Sea* when in her sixties.

When asked how her beauty had affected her she replied: 'Life has taught me that beauty can have its tragic side. It is like a great wealth in that respect. It promotes insincerity, and it breeds enemies. A really beautiful woman, like a very rich man, can be the loneliest person in the world. She is lucky if she knows her friends.'

The pub is a large, modern and friendly, but has no real ale.

☛ Retrace your steps the short distance back to West Brompton station.

DISTANCE 4 MILES
DIFFICULTY EASY
TIME 2HRS

LEICESTER SQUARE TO HIGHGATE

KARL'S TRAIL, ON YOUR MARX

WALK AND BUS ROUTE FROM THE HEART OF THE WEST END IN THE FOOTSTEPS OF A REVOLUTIONARY THINKER.

Find out in this amble through Soho, Fitzrovia and Bloomsbury where 'the founder of modern communism', Karl Marx (1818–83), fenced with a murderer, smashed street gas lamps on a drunken pub crawl and narrowly avoided arrest, prescribed himself opium for his carbuncles, was summonsed for non-payment of rates and wrestled. By total contrast, you'll also see some of the places where he wrote and lectured on some of his most classic works on political economy, and learn about the sad fate of his daughter Eleanor.

DISTANCE/DIFFICULTY 4 miles. Easy (apart from one short moderate climb), plus bus rides.

DROP-OUT POINT After 2½ miles.

TIME 2hrs (sections of walking interspersed with 40mins on various buses)

MAP Any A–Z

START Leicester Square tube station ✳ TQ299808

FINISH Highgate Cemetery ✳ TQ288869

TAKING A BREAK The Wheatsheaf, The King & Queen, The Rising Sun, Jack Horner, British Museum café, Sir Robert Peel, Whittington Stone

GETTING THERE ⊖ To Leicester Square (Northern and Piccadilly lines)

DIRECTIONS TO START Leave station by Exit 2 (Leicester Square and China Town) then turn left up Charing Cross Road

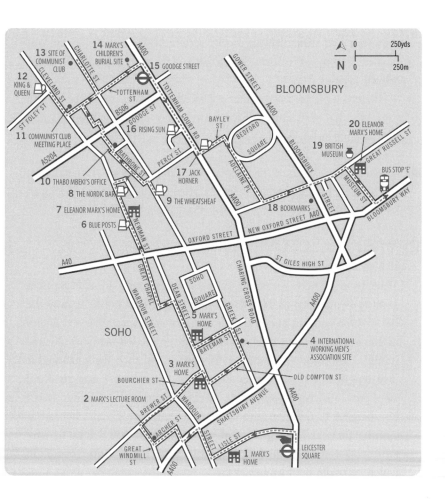

☞ After leaving the station and going up Charing Cross Road, take the first left into Little Newport Street. Go past Leicester Court, where the road becomes Lisle Street ahead, then past Leicester Place, and on the next corner on the left is:

1 THE FORMER GERMAN HOTEL FOR REFUGEES

1 Leicester St, WC2H 7BL

Now Moules restaurant, this was the German Hotel (a transit camp for refugees) in early 1850 when Marx and his family stayed here after being evicted from 4 Anderson Street, Chelsea. The rent for two small rooms in the German Hotel was high. When they therefore had difficulty paying it, recalled Marx's wife Jenny, 'our host refused to serve us our breakfast and we were forced to look for other lodgings'.

There is a plaque on the site, not to Marx but to composer Johann Strauss (1804–49), 'father of the waltz', who lodged here on his first visit to England in April 1838.

☛ Continue along Lisle Street (the heart of China Town) to the end, then turn right into Wardour Street, then first left into Shaftesbury Avenue, first right into Rupert Street, first left into Archer Street, and on the first corner on the right is:

2 MARX'S LECTURE ROOM
20 Great Windmill St, W1D 7LQ

Marx lectured here on a political economics course from November 1849 to September 1850 when this was the Red Lion (it is now the Be At One cocktail bar). His fellow German revolutionary Wilhelm Liebknecht at these lectures noted: 'Marx proceeded methodically. He stated a proposition, the shorter the better, and then demonstrated it in a lengthier explanation, endeavouring with utmost care to avoid all expressions incomprehensible to the labourers. Then he requested his audience to question him. If this was not done he commenced to examine them and he did this with such pedagogic skill that no flaw, no misunderstanding escaped him. He also made use of a blackboard, on which he wrote the formulas – among them those familiar to all of us from the beginning of *Capital*.'

The course was run by the Deutsche Arbeiter Bildungs Verein (the German Workers' Education Society), of which Marx was a member.

Marx's close comrade, collaborator and benefactor, Friedrich Engels (1820–95), also gave lectures here. One visitor described how they went from the ground floor 'grog shop' up a flight of stairs to a hall-like room which could hold around 200 people at tables with benches. They ate a simple evening meal and 'smoked out of one of the honour pipes lying on all the tables, their jugs of grog before them'. He continued: 'At one end of the hall stood a grand piano, which in unmusical London was the best proof to us that we had found the right room.' They were able to buy a glass of porter and a 'penny packet of tobacco' as well as communist tracts from the association's library.

Now you can get seven different vodkas, 21 vodka cocktails (including Undercover Squirrel, Moscow Mule and Screaming Orgasm), a Russian punch containing more vodka and a Cuban Pussy rum.

☞ Turn right into Great Windmill Street, then first right into Brewer Street. When you reach Wardour Street, go ahead through a passageway called Bourchier Street. At the end on the right-hand corner with Dean Street is:

3 MARX'S FIRST DEAN STREET HOME
64 Dean St, W1D 4QQ

This is where Marx and his family lived from 8 May to 2 December 1850. Referring to this stay, Jenny Marx said: 'We found two rooms in the house of a Jewish lace dealer and spent a miserable summer there with the four children.' Their son Henrich Guido (nicknamed 'Fawkesy'), who had been born on 5 November 1849 in Chelsea, died here under a year old.

☞ Continue to the right, down Dean Street and almost immediately left into Old Compton Street. Then take the second left into Greek Street. A short distance on the right is:

4 INTERNATIONAL WORKING MEN'S ASSOCIATION SITE
18 Greek St, W1D 4DS

Here the International Working Men's Association (the First International), of which Marx was a leading member, met from 1864 to 1866. Again there is a plaque, but again not to Marx. It is a green one telling us this is where comedian Peter Cook set up the ironically named Establishment Club which lasted from 1961 to 1964. In recognition of this it is now a bar called Zebrano at the Establishment.

☛ Continue up Greek Street and turn left into Bateman Street. Continue over Frith Street (with Ronnie Scott's Jazz Club to the left), past the Chinese Mutual Aid Workers' Club on the left (No. 12), to Dean Street. Turn right and a few yards on the right (on the corner of Royalty Mews) is:

5 MARX'S SECOND DEAN STREET HOME
28 Dean St, W1D 3RA

A blue plaque at the Quo Vadis restaurant records inaccurately that Marx lived here from 1851 to 1856 (when his landlord was an Italian cook called John Marengo). In fact he lived there from December 1850. During this time the family lived in great poverty and two more of the children died: first Franziska (who was born here in 1851) in 1852, and then Henry Edgar (known as Moosh or Mouche) in 1855 from consumption and an inherited disorder at the age of eight.

The overcrowded living conditions in their two rooms here (one being used as a study by Marx) were described by a Prussian police agent who visited Marx to spy on him. The furniture was all broken, he said, and 'the smoke and tobacco fumes make your eyes water so much that for a moment you seem to be groping about in a cavern'. Marx smoked cigars

Now a restaurant, this building was Marx's home between 1851 and 1856.

a lot. The agent continued: 'Everything is dirty and covered with dust, so that to sit down becomes a thoroughly dangerous business.' Most of the chairs were broken, except one, which was offered to visitors, but it was also the one on which the children had been 'playing at cooking' and it still had mess on it so 'if you sit down, you risk a pair of trousers'. Marx, he added, led a gypsy existence, often being dirty and drunk, staying up all night and sleeping fully clothed during the day.

Twice Marx had to pawn his overcoat in 1853 while living here. In the 1851 census he is recorded living here as 'Charles Mark, Doctor (Philosophical Author)'.

☞ Continue up Dean Street and turn second left into St Anne's Court, where you can have various flavours of vodka and other drinks in the Russian-themed Revolution Bar (where there were 30 different flavours of Russian vodka when we visited and enjoyed the fruit salad one).

Retrace your steps to Dean Street, turn left, take the next left into Carlisle Street (with the Nellie Dean pub on the corner), and then right at the end into Great Chapel Street (past the Star bar). Follow this to Oxford Street and over it to Newman Street ahead. Follow this to the first corner on the left with Eastcastle Street where you will find:

6 THE BLUE POSTS
81 Newman St, W1T 3ET

Here Marx attended meetings of the Communist Club from 1874 to 1877.

☞ Opposite is:

7 ELEANOR MARX'S HOME
13 Newman St, W1T 1PN

Marx's daughter Eleanor (1855–98) lived at this address in 1883 with Edward Aveling (1849–98) even though he was married to another woman, so defying the conventions of the time. The house was knocked down to make way for a Royal Mail sorting office which has recently been abandoned. But number 14, the house next door, is still standing and gives you an idea of what it looked like.

☞ Continue up Newman Street, to on the right:

8 THE NORDIC BAR
25 Newman St, W1T 1PN

In offices above here Marxist Ronnie Kasrils, head of intelligence of the banned African National Congress in exile from South Africa, trained people to assemble 'letter bombs' to be exploded during the struggle against apartheid in the 1960s. The light explosives were at the bottom of a bucket containing anti-government leaflets which were shot up into the air and spread widely. This attracted huge publicity and assured the black population that the ANC was still active even though driven underground.

☞ A couple of doors further on, turn right into Newman Passage (an old cobbled alley through which Marx may have fled from chasing police after smashing street lamps in Tottenham Court Road, see later) and go through to the corner of Rathbone Street and the Newman Arms (on which George Orwell based the Proles' Pub in his novel *Nineteen Eighty-Four*).

Turn right and walk a few yards into Rathbone Place and the corner of Percy Mews to:

9 THE WHEATSHEAF
25 Rathbone Pl, W1T 1DG

This pub dates back to at least 1800 and is much the same as it was in Marx's day, when he attended meetings of the First International in the same street in the 1860s, and fenced in a salon with a revolutionary who was later hanged for murder.

The latter was Emanuel Barthelemy, a Frenchman who had fought on the barricades of the Paris Commune in 1848 and been condemned to death but was saved by an amnesty and transported for life instead. One day in December 1854, he set off from the salon in Rathbone Place to assassinate Napoleon III. On the way he decided to collect some unpaid wages for work done for a soda manufacturer at 73 Warren Street, and shot him dead when he refused to pay. For this he was hanged in the following month.

According to German revolutionary Wilhelm Liebknecht, who observed Marx and Barthelemy fencing, Marx 'lustily gave battle to the Frenchman... what Marx lacked in science he tried to make up in aggressiveness... unless you were cool he could really startle you'. Barthelemy was critical of Marx because he 'would not conspire and disturb the peace'.

The anarchists set up the International Club in Stephen Mews, behind The Wheatsheaf, in 1883.

☞ Go back up Rathbone Street, past the Newman Arms to the Duke of York on the corner of another alley, Charlotte Place. Opposite this is:

10 THABO MBEKI'S OFFICE
49–51 Rathbone St, W1T 1NW
This is where the African National Congress met in exile from South Africa. Thabo Mbeki, a Marxist who later succeeded Nelson Mandela as president of South Africa, worked here from 1967 to 1970.

☞ Go through Charlotte Place to Goodge Street, and continue ahead into Goodge Place opposite (another cobbled passageway). At the other end you will reach Tottenham Street. On the corner on the right is the Fitzrovia Neighbourhood Centre with a mural showing Olaudah Equiano (top left), a radical former slave whose autobiography of 1789, describing the cruelty of slavery, helped bring about its abolition, and the Venezuelan revolutionaries Simon Bolivar (middle) and Francisco de Miranda (bottom right), all of whom lived nearby. Turn left and on the next corner is:

11 COMMUNIST CLUB MEETING PLACE
49 Tottenham St, W1T 4RZ
The Communist Club met here in the basement spasmodically from 1878 to 1882 and then permanently until 1902. Marx and Lenin both visited here. The club had its own choir, billiards table, and food and drink. It was also where William Townshend, a shoemaker who attended meetings of the First International, lived in 1895.

☞ Turn right and a few yards further up Cleveland Street on the left-hand corner with Foley Street is:

The King & Queen pub: a former Chartist meeting place.

12 THE KING & QUEEN

1 Foley St, W1W 6DL

This was the nearest pub to the Communist Club. In 1848 it had been used as a meeting place for the Washington Brigade of the Chartists. It was also the house of call for the West End branch of the Alliance of Cabinet Makers (who kept a library here) and by shoemakers. It had 20 flavours of vodka on our visit, including a very palatable Stolichnaya vanilla.

☞ Retrace your steps and turn left into Tottenham Street, then follow it to the crossroads with Charlotte Street. Turn left, and about a dozen doors along on the left (just past Chitty Street on the other side) is the:

13 COMMUNIST CLUB SITE

107 Charlotte St, W1T 4QB (now part of Astor College)

This is where the Communist Club moved in 1903. Lenin was present for the opening of the club, being here for the congress of the Russian Social Democratic Party in the Anglers Club Hall of the English Club, also in Charlotte Street. It was at this meeting that the party split into the Mensheviks and Bolsheviks. Lenin revisited the club in 1911. It was closed by a police raid in 1918.

☞ Continue along Tottenham Street to Tottenham Court Road. On the left hand corner is the:

14 BURIAL GROUND OF THREE OF MARX'S CHILDREN
Whitfield Gardens, 79 Tottenham Court Rd, W1T 4TB

Marx buried his eight-year-old son Henry Edgar here in 1855, after death from consumption and an inherited intestinal disorder. Marx was so distressed that he had to be restrained from hurling himself into the grave. Two of Marx's other children were already buried there, Henrich Guido in 1850 and Franziska in 1852, both about a year old. It was then the graveyard of George Whitefield's Tabernacle at 79 Tottenham Court Road (now the American Church). The coffins and remains were all disinterred in 1898 and reinterred in Chingford Mount Cemetery. One gravestone survives, that of John Procter of 94 Tottenham Court Road who died in 1834, aged 74, and his wife Mary who died in 1840, aged 77.

On the glass panels showing characters of the area, Marx and Darwin feature facing each other (it was temporarily removed for restoration at the time of writing). Darwin, whose great discoveries of evolution of the species opened this book, lived nearby in what is now the Darwin Building at 110 Gower Street. And Marx, whose theory of the evolution of social systems closes the book, also lived nearby as we have learned.

☞ Turn right into Tottenham Court Road and a few doors down on the same side is:

15 GOODGE STREET TUBE STATION
73 Tottenham Court Rd, W1T 2HG

Marx's daughter Eleanor entertained here when it was the Athenaeum Hall in 1887 and 1890. With her partner Edward Aveling she gave music and poetry recitals. In February 1898 she was lodging at nearby 135 Gower Street to be near Aveling while he was having an operation in University College Hospital. A month later Eleanor died in a house in Sydenham after swallowing prussic acid which Aveling had provided her. The inquest concluded she had committed suicide while 'labouring under mental derangement'. Many suspected Aveling had tricked her into a double suicide pact and then pulled out himself.

☞ Continue down Tottenham Court Road to the corner of Windmill Street on the right, where you will find:

16 THE RISING SUN
46 Tottenham Court Rd, W1T 2ED

One of just six pubs surviving from Marx's pub crawl in the 1850s of the 18 pubs that existed then in Tottenham Court Road. He was with his German revolutionary friends Wilhelm Liebknecht and Edgar Bauer. In the last pub, when well oiled, they encountered a group of 'Odd Fellows' and compared German and English culture with them, predictably ending in a fight. The outnumbered Germans fled, stumbled over some paving stones and, at 2 o'clock in the morning, used them to smash four or five street gas lamps before a policeman arrived. Marx knew the back alleys well and managed to escape through them (probably Percy Passage and Newman Passage visited earlier on this walk) to his home in Dean Street.

The Rising Sun is on the corner of Windmill Street where Chartist pork that had been produced on co-operative farms was sold in 1848, and where the Autonomie anarchist club at number 6 was raided in 1892. At another pub 'just off Tottenham Court Road' the last English meeting of the First International took place in September 1871, five years before finally being disbanded in America.

☞ Continue down Tottenham Court Road, to the corner of Bayley Street, on the left, where you will find the:

17 JACK HORNER
234–236 Tottenham Court Rd, W1T 7QJ

This Fuller's pub was called The Italian in the 1850s when Marx drank there on his pub crawl (and was renamed the Bedford Head by 1872).

☞ Turn left into Bayley Street, to Bedford Square, and turn right (past blue plaques to Thomas Wakeley and Thomas Hodgin), and at the end turn left into Great Russell Street, go past the Trades Union Congress headquarters on the right (with a large sculpture of one worker helping another to his feet), to Bloomsbury Street. Turn right and a few yards on the same side is:

18 BOOKMARKS

1 Bloomsbury St, Bloomsbury WC1B 3QE

This is a Marxist bookshop, which we think should spell its name Bookmarx. It promised to stock this book if it was published, so pop in and check.

☛ Return to Great Russell Street and turn right. A few yards on the left is:

19 THE BRITISH MUSEUM

Great Russell St, WC1B 3DG ☎ 020 7323 1234 🖱 www.britishmuseum.org
🕙 daily 10.00–17.30; Fri 10.00–20.30

Marx used the Reading Room here to research many of his great works including *Das Kapital*. He got his reader's ticket in June 1850, and spent the first three months reading back issues of the *Economist*. This was before the new reading room was completed in 1857. In the old reading room he worked on *Address of the Central Committee of the Communist League*, *The Class Struggles of France* and *Eighteenth Brumaire of Louis Bonaparte*. The Keeper of Printed Books was an Italian revolutionary, Antonio Panizzi, who planned the new library, which was built under a glass dome that accommodated thousands of books.

Marx sat in seat number 07 in the new library and drew on reports of official commissions of enquiry designed to strengthen capitalism by controlling its worst social consequences.

Because he suffered from carbuncles he also read up medical books and prescribed himself opium, arsenic and creosote.

The Reading Room is still there (the large circular structure in the middle straight ahead from the main entrance, within the glazed-over Great Court, which has a stylish café), but has been closed to the public for some years except for special temporary exhibitions. There are plans however to reopen it and possibly highlight where Marx sat.

See also pages 64–5.

☞ As you leave, directly opposite the museum's main entrance/exit is:

20 ELEANOR MARX'S HOME
55 Great Russell St, WC1B 3BA

Marx's daughter lived here from 1884 to 1886 with her partner Edward Aveling. To celebrate her 31st birthday in 1886, she staged an amateur performance of Ibsen's *A Doll's House* here. Among the cast with her and Aveling were playwright Bernard Shaw, and May Morris (daughter of William Morris). It is now part of Helen Graham House, numbers 52–57.

☞ A few yards to the right is the Museum Tavern on the corner of Museum Street, which you go down to the end, then turn left into Bloomsbury Way.

✋ On the same side of the road, next to St George's Church Bloomsbury, is Bus Stop E. Here you can take several buses to Holborn tube station (or Tottenham Court Road in the opposite direction) if you wish to drop out.

☞ To continue take the 55 bus from Stop E for a ten-minute journey to the St John Street stop (a request stop straight after Hatton Garden). Go back a short distance from the stop and take the first right into Clerkenwell Green. On the opposite side of the green is the:

21 MARX MEMORIAL LIBRARY
37a Clerkenwell Green, EC1R 0DU ☎ 020 7253 1485 📱 www.marx-memorial-library.org 🕐 13.00–14.00, Mon–Thu by appointment

Marx's daughter Eleanor spoke here on 'Bloody Sunday' (13 November 1887) and later in support of the dockers' strike on 20 October 1889 and at other rallies. Lenin had an office here in exile from 1901 to 1902 when he edited the Russian Social Democratic newspaper *Iskra*, issues 22 to 38. While here you can purchase *Marx in London* by Asa Briggs and John Callow, from which much of the information for this walk was obtained.

☞ Turn left out of the library and on the next corner is The Crown Tavern. It is worth going upstairs to the Apollo Room which was a concert hall in Marx's time.
  Return to Clerkenwell Road.

From here you can get buses to Holborn, Waterloo or Oxford Circus. Or you can go down Turnmill Street, almost opposite, to Farringdon tube station on the right.

To continue the walk turn right, then second left into Farringdon Road, and on the right is:

22 DAILY WORKER/MORNING STAR OFFICE SITE
75 Farringdon Rd, EC1M 3HQ

The communist daily newspaper, the *Daily Worker* (which was renamed the *Morning Star* in 1966), was published here from 1945 until the mid-1980s.

Return to Clerkenwell Road, turn right and, just past Turnmill Street, on the same side and opposite Clerkenwell Green, you will find Bus Stop K. Take the 55 bus from here for a 15-minute journey to Tottenham Court Road station. Continue ahead a short distance and turn right into Tottenham Court Road.

A short distance on the left is Bus Stop C. From here take the 24 bus for a 21-minute journey to the Queens Crescent stop in Kentish Town. Follow the direction of the bus up Malden Road, and take the third on the left into Grafton Terrace. A short distance on the right is:

23 MARX'S GRAFTON TERRACE HOME
46 Grafton Terrace, Kentish Town NW5 4HY

Marx and his family lived at this address from October 1856 to March 1864 (when it was 9 Grafton Terrace, Fitzroy Road, having been built in 1849 by open fields). While residing here Marx wrote *A Contribution to the Critique of Political Economy* and *The Theory of Surplus Value*. And it was also here that his wife Jenny contracted smallpox, from which she never fully recovered.

Just past this house (and opposite number 54) is a path to the left behind a block of flats signposted to '109–134 Maitland Park Road'. Turn into this, go down some steps under an arch, and into a crescent to the left. A few yards along this crescent on the left is:

24 MARX'S MAITLAND PARK ROAD HOME

101–108 Maitland Park Rd, Kentish Town NW3 2HE

There is a plaque on the second floor of the building informing us that Marx lived here from 1875 for the rest of his life (when it was number 41). Just before this he had lived at nearby 1 Maitland Park Road (when it was called 1 Modena Villas), which has since been demolished and replaced by a block of flats called The Grange. It was in the study there that Marx completed the first volume of *Das Kapital*. For the first time the children had a room each, but the extra space meant extra rent and Marx, who said he was 'as hard up as a church mouse', was summonsed for non-payment of rates. He was nonetheless asked to serve as a constable for the parish for one year in 1868, which he rejected. This was used against him when he applied for British citizenship six years later, and had it refused on the grounds of a police report describing him as a 'notorious German agitator who had not been loyal to his own king and country'.

☞ Return to Grafton Terrace and then to Malden Road and Bus Stop KZ (from which you came). Almost opposite the bus stop is the:

25 SIR ROBERT PEEL

108 Malden Rd,
Kentish Town NW5 4DA
A friendly community pub with a dartboard and pool table.

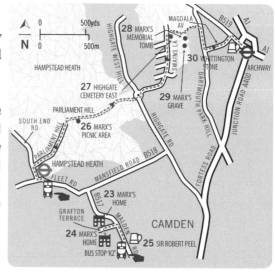

☞ From Bus Stop KZ take the 24 bus to Hampstead for a four-minute journey to the last stop (Royal Free Hospital/Hampstead Heath Station). Follow the road ahead to South End Road, past the Garden Gate pub, and right into

South Hill Park, past Hampstead Heath railway station. Continue uphill and take the right fork into the road Parliament Hill. At the top is:

26 MARX'S PICNIC AREA ON HAMPSTEAD HEATH

Marx loved to take his family to picnic on the heath on Sundays, even when living in Soho rather than the closer Kentish Town. His friend and fellow German revolutionary, Wilhelm Liebknecht, who often joined them, recalled: 'A Sunday on Hampstead Heath was the highest pleasure for us. The children spoke of it all week and grown people too anticipated it with joy. The trip itself was a feast. From Dean Street, where Marx lived, it was at least an hour and a quarter, and as a rule, a start was made at 11AM... some time was always consumed in getting everything in readiness, the chicken cared for and the basket packed. That basket... it was our commissary department, and when a man has a healthy strong stomach... then the question of provisions plays a very large role. And good Lenchen [the family's housekeeper] knew this and had for often half-starved and, therefore, hungry guests a sympathising heart. A mighty roast veal was the centrepiece hallowed by tradition for the Sunday in Hampstead Heath.'

After their walk to the heath, he continued, 'we would first choose a place where we could spread our tents at the same time having due regard to the possibility of obtaining tea and beer. But after drinking and eating their fill, as Homer has it, the male and female comrades looked for the most comfortable place of repose or seat; and when this had been found he or she – provided they did not prefer a little nap – produced the Sunday papers they had bought on the road, and now began the reading and discussing of politics – while the children, who rapidly found comrades, played hide and seek behind the heather bushes. But this easy life had to be seasoned by a little diversion, and so we ran races, sometimes we also had wrestling matches, or putting the shot (stones) or some other sport.'

They were often joined by Engels who lived nearer in Primrose Hill (see page 56).

☞ When you enter the heath, take the path going straight ahead. Take the first path to the right after a short distance which goes up to Kite Hill. This is 322 feet above sea level and has an outstanding view across to south London. Follow the main path down the other side, ignore a path off to the right, and when another path crosses over take the left fork (with ponds down to the left). At the bottom, go ahead through a staggered crossroads and then a short distance to a road (Swains Lane). Follow Swains Lane for about ten minutes with a moderate climb towards the end until you come on the right to:

27 HIGHGATE CEMETERY EAST

Swain's Lane, N6 6PJ ☎ 020 8240 1834 🖱 www.highgate-cemetery.org £

As you pay the entry fee you will receive a map of the cemetery showing the locations of Marx's Memorial Tomb (C2) and the original grave where he is actually buried (C3), as well as graves of other Marxists including Yusuf Dadoo (1909–83), the South African communist and anti-apartheid campaigner, Paul Foot (1937–2004), the investigative journalist, political campaigner and author, and Claudia Jones (1915–64), the Trinidadian communist and founder of the Notting Hill carnival. If you manage to sneak in without paying and have no map, follow the path ahead and bear left at the first fork. On the right where the path bends to the right, is:

28 MARX'S MEMORIAL TOMB

This massive bronze bust of Marx on a huge granite plinth is inscribed with his famous appeal from *The Communist Manifesto*: 'Workers of all lands, unite'. At the base is engraved his other famous quotation: 'The philosophers have only interpreted the world in various ways. The point however is to change it.' Sculpted by Lawrence Bradshaw, it was erected in 1954 and unveiled by Harry Pollitt (1890–1960), the general secretary of the Communist Party of Great Britain.

WORKERS OF ALL LANDS
UNITE

KARL MARX

☞ Follow the path another 100 steps or so to a single grave to Nora Joyce on the left. Turn right here by Arthur Joseph Lockett's grave. Another 50 or 60 paces on the right (between the graves of Thomas Copp and William Collis) is:

29 MARX'S GRAVE

This flat gravestone with no upright headstone is where Marx was buried on 17 March 1883, with about 20 people present. Engels gave the main address. Describing Marx's outstanding achievement, he declared: 'Just as Darwin discovered the law of development or organic nature, so Marx discovered the law of development of human history.'

So just as this book started with Darwin it ends with his contemporary, Marx.

☞ For the nearest tube station (about a 12-minute walk) return to the entrance, turn right, then immediately right again through Waterlow Park. Keep to the edge of the park on the right with the cemetery fencing, forking right four times, through to Dartmouth Park Hill at the other end. Then turn right downhill, then left into Magdala Avenue. At the junction at the end turn right into Highgate Hill. A short way down on the same side (if you need refreshing) is:

30 WHITTINGTON STONE

54 Highgate Hill, Archway N19 5NE

A modern pub with a pool table and dartboard. There is also hot food and outside seating.

A stone nearby marks where Dick Whittington, when leaving London, heard Bow Bells which he took as a good sign, and so 'turned again' and returned to the capital and became its Lord Mayor.

☞ A short distance further down is Archway tube station (Northern Line).

INDEX

PAGE NUMBERS IN *ITALIC* REFER TO IN-TEXT PHOTOGRAPHS.

A

African National Congress (ANC) 230, 231
Aldenham Country Park 144–5, 148–9, *150*
Aldenham Reservoir 147, 150, *150*
Aldenham Sailing Club 150
All Saints, Carshalton 129
All Saints, Kings Langley 41–2
Amersham Cricket Club 161
Amersham Museum 160
Anne Boleyn's Well 128
Ashtead Common Nature Reserve 190, *192*, 193

B

Baird, John Logie 26
Ball, John 33–4, 41
Banstead Woods 44–7, *45*, *46*
Barnes Common 182
Barthelemy, Emanuel 230–1
Batchworth Lock Canal Centre 85
Bates, Dr Benjamin 162
Beatles 59
Becket, Thomas 92, 93, 119
Beddington Park 129
beefsteak fungus 180
Beverley Brook 178, 179
Beverley Meads & Fishponds Local Nature Reserve 179
Bingham, Jinney (Mother Redcap) 219–21
Blitz Firemen Memorial 63
Bookmarks 235
books, recommended 10–11
Box Hill 24–30
Brecht, Bertolt 61
Brick Stand Viewpoint 191
Bridges, Wayne and Sarah 172–3, *173*
British Museum 64–5, 235
Brittain, Vera 210–11
Broad Colney Nature Reserve 186–8
Brooklands Lakes 175
Buckle, Matthew 47
Burne-Jones, Edward 85, 92, 141
Burney, Fanny 30

Burton, Richard 146–7
Bus Bombing Memorial (7 July 2005) 62–3

C

cabman's shelter 64
Camden Lock Market 57
Camley Street Natural Park 58–9
Camlet Moat 154–5, *154*
Carshalton Ponds 125
Cassiobury Park & Nature Reserve 38–9
Cavell, Edith 216–17
Chaplin, Charlie 153
Charles Dickens Museum 211–12
Chartists 84, 232, 234
Chaucer, Geoffrey 199
Chertsey Bridge 134
Chessington 190–5
Chessington World of Adventures & Zoo & Sea Life Centre 192
Chipstead Downs 44
Christmas Tree Farm & Tea Garden 21
Christofi, Styllou 52
churches 15–16, 19, *19*, 30, 33–4, 41–2, 59, 70–1, 84–5, 103–4, *104*, 129, 141–2, 145–7, 159–60, 164–5, 167, 204–5, 208–9
Churchill, Winston 153
Clare, John 74
Clink Prison Museum 200–1
Coalhouse Fort 109, 114–15
Cold War 105
Collins, Wilkie 62
Colne Valley Linear Park 88–9
commons, downs and heaths 50–1, 94, 96–9, 100, 101–2, 178–80, 181, 182, 183, 190, 193
Communist Club 231, 232–3
Connaught Water 75
Cornmill Meadows Dragonfly Sanctuary 142
Cox, Christopher 42
grave *42*
Cranmer, Thomas 142
cricket 34, 151, 161

Crompton, Richmal 23
Croxley Common Moor Nature Reserve 87

D

Dadd, Richard 62
Dahl, Roald 159, 164, 167, 168
Daily Worker/Morning Star 205, 237
Dartford Railway Station 177
Darwin, Charles 14–17, 20, 23, 233, 241
Deen City Farm 120
Denbies Winery & Vineyard 28, *28*
Derby race 29, 96, 98
Despard, Charlotte 221–2
Dickens, Charles 59, 61–2, 68, 171–2, 200, 208, 209, 210, 211–12
mural *22*, 23
Dodd, Revd William 68
Down House 16–17, *16*
Downe 14–23
Downe Bank 20
Downe Church (St Mary's) 15–16

E

East Tilbury marshes 113, *113*
Ebborn, Eliza 146
Ebury Way 80, 86–7, *86*
Eliot, T S 213, 219
Ellis, Ruth 52
Elstree 144–7, 151
Elstree Cricket Club 151
Elstree Studios 151
Empire Windrush 109–10
Engels, Friedrich 56, 226–7, 239
Epping Forest 72–9, *77*
Epsom Common 193
Epsom Downs 96–9
Establishment Club 227

F

farm visits 21, 120, 148–9, 189
Farningham 171
Farthing Downs 100, 101–2, *103*, *106*
film and TV locations 39, 151, 158–9, 164

fishing 80–1, 109, 128, *128*, 133, 140, 147, 175, 187, 194
The Folly 102
Folly Bridge 172
foraging 11, 81, 134, 186, 194
fossil bed 93
Fox, Charles James 65
Freedom Pass 11, 12

G

Gandhi, Mahatma 63, 222
gardens 121, 152, 155
German Hotel for Refugees 225–6
ghosts 128, 154–5, 183
Go Ape Tree Top Adventure Obstacle Course 157
Godwin, William 59
Golden Hinde II 200
Gorky, Maxim 61
Government Row 139
Grand Union Canal 36–43, *38*, 80, 85–6, *85*, 147
Great Missenden 159, 167–9
Grove Park 125
gunpowder mills 141
Gwynne, Nell 215–16

H

Hamilton, Emma 119
Hampermill Lake 88
Hampstead Bathing Pools 51
Hampstead Green 54
Hampstead Heath 48, 50–1, 239
Hangrove Wood 20
Happy Valley 100, 105–6
Hardy, Bert 205
Hardy, Thomas 60
Harold, King 141–2
Harry's Bench 114, *114*
Hazlitt, William 207
Heartwood Forest 32–5, *35*
Hell Fire Club 145, 162
Henry VIII 69, 73, 75, 111, 114, 119, 142, 159
Heronsgate 84
Hess, Rudolf 153
Highgate Cemetery 240
Highgate Ponds 50
highwaymen 76
Holtby, Winifred 211

Honeywood Museum 126
horse riding 98–9, 120
Horton Country Park 194
hot-air ballooning 169
Hughes, Ted 56
Hunterian Museum 67–8
Hutt, Allen 205
Huxley, Aldous 219

I

International Working Men's
Association 227, *227*

J

Jacobites 111
Jagger, Mick 175, 177
Japanese Water Garden
152, 155
Johnson, Samuel 68, 207–8

K

Keats, John 27, 51, 197–8
Keats's House & Museum 51
Kite Hill 240
Knox, John 159

L

Labelliere, Major Peter 25–6
Ladies Who Bus 12–13, *13*
Lairage Land Local Nature
Reserve 88
lakes and ponds 88, 125,
130–1, 162, 175, 194
Laleham Park 134
Langtry, Lillie 222–3, *223*
Lawrence, D H 100, 101, 219
Lenin, Vladimir 53, 231, 232,
233, 236
Lesnes Abbey ruins 90, 92–3
Lesnes Abbey Wood 90–4, 95
Liebknecht, Wilhelm 226,
230–1, 234, 239
Lincoln's Inn Fields 66
Little Missenden 162–5, *163*
Litvinoff, Maxim 53
Lollards 159
Lopping Hall 78–9
Lucan family 134
Luci, Richard de 92–3

M

MacDonald, Margaret 67
MacDonald, Ramsay 54, 67
manure, free 17, 96, 99
maps 10
marshes 88, 108, 113, 140

Marx, Eleanor 229, 233–4, 236
Marx, Karl 56, 65, 224,
225–41, *228*, *232*, *240*
Marx Memorial Library 236
Mbeki, Thabo 231
Merton Abbey Mills Market
119–20, *119*
Mick Jagger Centre 175
Midsomer Murders 158–9,
163, 164
Millennium Bridge *198*, 202
Missenden Abbey Parkland
166–7
Moll Cutpurse 71, 220
Molly Moggs 217–18
Moon, Keith 135
Morden Hall Park 120–1, *121*
More, Thomas 68–9
Morrell, Lady Ottoline 218–19
Morris, William 91–2, 118,
119, 120, 213
grave *92*
murals 22, 23, 151, 210
museums and galleries 51,
64–5, 66, 67–8, 81–4,
126, 141, 160, 168, 198–9,
200–1, 202, 211–12, 235

N

nature reserves 38–9, 46, 87,
88, 124–5, 142, 149, 179,
186–8, 190, 193
Nelson, Horatio 27, 119
Nijinsky, Vaslav 219
Norbury Park 29
Nordic Bar 230
North Downs 100

O

Obelisk 154
O'Casey, Sean 61
O'Connor, Feargus 84
O'Connor, P 206, *206*
Old Barnes Cemetery 183,
183
The Old Curiosity Shop 68
Old Fort 25
The Old Operating Theatre,
Museum & Herb Garret
198–9
open air swimming 50, 51
Orwell, George 53, *53*
Oxhey Park 88–9

P

Palewell Common 181

Paradise Merton 119
parakeets 134
parks 29, 38–9, 58–9, 88–9,
120–1, 125, 129, 134, 144–5,
153–4, 166–7, 180, 194
Parliament Hill 51
Peasants' Revolt 33–4, 41,
142, 176
Penn, William 81–4
Penton Hook Island 133–4
Pepys, Samuel 110–11,
205–6, 221
Perrotts Wood Nature Reserve
46
Piggott, Lester 98
Plath, Sylvia 56
Primrose Hill 55, *55*
Proctor, Ian 150
pubs and inns
Abbey Arms, Abbey Wood 95
The Black Friar, Blackfriars
71
Black Horse, Great
Missenden 169
Blacksmith's Arms,
Cudham 18
The Bridges, South Darenth
172–3
The Bull, London Colney 189
Burford Bridge Hotel 27
Charlotte Despard,
Archway 221–2
The Chequers, Darenth 174
The Chequers, Farningham
171
Coach & Horses,
Rickmansworth 84
Cock & Dragon,
Cockfosters 157
Cockpit Tavern, City of
London 202
The Constitution, Camden 58
Crown Inn, Little
Missenden 163
The Crown, Waltham
Abbey 143
Duke's Head, Putney 184
The Eagle, Amersham 160
The Eight Bells, Putney
Bridge 184
The Engineer, Primrose
Hill 57
The Fishery, Elstree 149
The Flask, Hampstead 50
The Fox, Coulsdon Common
105

pubs and inns *cont...*
A Friend at Hand,
Bloomsbury 213
Full Moon, Little Kingshill 166
George & Dragon, Downe 21
George Inn, Borough 200
George Inn, Great Missenden
167
Green Dragon, London
Colney 188, *188*
The Green Man, Sandridge 35
The Greyhound, Carshalton
128
The Greyhound, Enfield 139
Halfway House, Barnes 181
Hare & Hounds, Croydon 131
Harry's Bar, Hunton Bridge 40
The Hufflers Arms, Dartford
177
Jack Horner, Fitzrovia 234
The King & Queen, Fitzrovia
232, *232*
Kingfisher, Chertsey 135
King's Head, Hunton
Bridge 40
King's Oak, High Beach 75
The Lady Ottoline,
Bloomsbury 218–19
Lillie Langtry, West
Brompton 222–3
The Lion Hotel, Farningham
171–2
Lord Palmerston, Carshalton
125
Magdala, Hampstead 52
Molly Moggs, Soho 217–18
Mother Red Cap, Archway
219–21, *220*
The Navigation Harvester
Inn, Ponders End 139
Nell Gwynne Tavern, Covent
Garden 215–16
The Paper Moon, Dartford
175–6
The Pembroke, Coulsdon 107
The Pennsylvanian,
Rickmansworth 81, *81*
Queen's Head, Downe 21
Queen's Head, Sandridge 35
Ramblers Rest, Coulsdon
46–7
Red Lion, Little Missenden
163–4
Richmal Crompton, Bromley
23
The Rising Sun, Fitzrovia 234

pubs and inns *cont...*
  Robin Hood, Loughton 75
  The Roebuck, Hampstead 54
  Rose & Crown, Kings Langley 43
  Running Horses, Mickleham 29
  Saracen's Head, Kings Langley 43
  Seven Stars, Holborn 69
  The Ship, East Tilbury 115
  The Ship, Holborn 66
  Sir Robert Peel, Kentish Town 238
  Star & Garter, Putney 184
  Stepping Stones, Westhumble 28
  Surrey Arms, Mitcham 123
  Tattenham Corner, Epsom Downs 99
  The Victoria, Bushey 89
  Victoria Tavern, Loughton 77–8
  Wat Tyler, Dartford 176
  The Wheatsheaf, Fitzrovia 230–1
  The Wicked Lady, Wheathampstead 34
  The William Morris, Merton Abbey Mill 120
  The Worlds End, Tilbury 110–11, *110*
  Ye Olde Cheshire Cheese, Fleet Street 70, 207
  Ye Olde Leather Bottle, Belvedere 95
Putney Lower Common 183

Q
Queen Elizabeth's Hunting Lodge 73–4, *74*

R
Ramney Marsh 140
Rann, John 76
Rare Breeds Farm 148–9
Ray, Martha 145
Red House 91–2
Regent's Canal 57–8, *57*
Relph, Harry (Little Titch) 18
reservoirs 137, 147, 150, *150*
Richard II 41, 142, 176
Richards, Keith 175, 177
Richmond Park 179, 180, *181*
River Chess 85, 86

River Colne 86–7, 88–9, 186–9, *187*
River Darent 170–1, 172, 174–5, 177
River Fleet 48, 50–1, 59, 61, 71
River Gade 36, 39, 86–7
River Lee 136–9, *138, 140*
River Misbourne 158, 160–1, 164, 169
River Mole 27, *27*
River Thames 132–5, 183–4
River Wandle 116, 119, 123, 128, *128*, 129–30, *130*
Riverside Park playground 88–9, *88*
Roald Dahl Museum & Story Centre 168
Roberts, Harry 73, 76
Robeson, Paul 61
Rolling Stones 171, 175, 177
Roman villa 193
Roosevelt, Theodore 70
Rose Garden 121
The Rose Theatre 201
Royal Gunpowder Mills 141
Royal Small Arms factory 139
Russell, Bertrand 219
Russell Square 64

S
sailing 150, *150*
St Andrew, Holborn 208–9
St Bride's, Fleet Street 204–5
St John the Baptist, Little Missenden 164–5
St Leonard's, Sandridge 33–4
St Mary the Virgin, Old Amersham 159–60
St Mary the Virgin, Rickmansworth 84–5
St Michael & All Angels, Mickleham 30
St Nicholas, Elstree 145–7
St Pancras Old Church 59, *60*
St Paul's Cathedral *198*
St Peter & St Paul's, Chaldon 103–4, *104*
St Peter & St Paul's, Cudham 19, *19*
St Peter & St Paul's, Great Missenden 167
salmon ladder 133
Sartre, Jean-Paul 61
Sassoon, Sir Philip 152, 153, 155

Sayers, Dorothy L 210
seals 108
Shakespeare, William 200, 201, 203
Shakespeare's Globe Theatre 201–2
Shardeloes Lake 162
Shardeloes Manor House 162
Shaw, George Bernard 236
Shelly, Percy Bysshe 51, 60
Sir John Soane's Museum 66
Sites of Special Scientific Interest 29, 44, 72, 87, 105–6, 115, 142, 179–80, 193
Smith, Henry 'Dog' 47
Smith, Sydney 212
Snuff Mill 121
Soane, Sir John 59, 60, 66
Solomon's Memorial & Viewpoint 26
South Bay Wildlife Refuge 149
South Bucks Way 161, 162, 165
South Hill Park 52–3
Spanish Armada 112
Spenser, Edmund 172
Spring Heeled Jack 183
Stanshall, Viv 135
Stew Pond 194
Stopes, Marie 29
Strauss, Johann 226
Swinburne, Algernon Charles 92, 209

T
Tabard Inn 199
Tate Modern 202
Terris, William 216
Thomas, Dylan 135
Three Rivers Museum 81–4
Tilbury 108–15, *113*
Tilbury Fort 108–9, 111–12, *111*
Tilbury Riverside Terminal 109–10
Trent Country Park 152, 153–4
Turpin, Dick 73, 76, 155
Tyler, Wat 41, 176

U
Unity Theatre site 61, *61*

V
Vaughan Williams, Ralph 28
Victoria, Queen 75, 223

The View Visitors' Centre 74
Viewpoint Sundial 102, *103*
vineyard 28

W
Waddon Ponds 130–1
Wallace, Edgar 203–4
Waltham Abbey 141–2, *142*
Wanamaker, Sam 201–2
Water Tower 127
watercress 158, 172
Waterside Centre 137
Weare, William 146
Webb, Philip 92
Wheathampstead Cricket Club 34
Whippendell Woods 39
Whittington Stone 241
Wilde, Oscar 209, 223
Wilderness Island 124–5
wildlife habitats 25, 54, 113, 133, 141, 147
  see also commons, downs and heaths; marshes; nature reserves; parks; Sites of Special Scientific Interest; woods
wildlife hospital 156
Wilkes, John 69, *69*
Willingdale, Thomas 73, 74, 78, 79
Willows Farm Village 189
Wimbledon Common 178–80
Winnie the Pooh's 100 Aker Wood 147, 148, *148*
Wollstonecraft, Mary 59
wood sculptor's workshop 156
woods 20, 32–5, 39, 44–7, 72–9, 90–4, 105–6
Woolf, Virginia 63–4, *63*
Workers' Memorial 39
World War I 42, 111–12, 216–17
World War II 42, 63, 102, 115, 141, 153
The Worlds End, Tilbury 110–11, *110*
WRAS Wildlife Hospital & Animal Centre 156
Wren, Sir Christopher 70, 209

Y
Ye Olde Cheshire Cheese, Fleet Street 70, 207
Ye Olde Loppers Cottage 78
Yeats, W B 56